Commercial and Economic Law
in the European Union

Commercial and Economic Law in the European Union

Second Edition

Jules Stuyck

This book was originally published as a monograph in the International
Encyclopaedia of Laws/Commercial and Economic Law.

General Editor: Roger Blanpain & Frank Hendrickx
Volume Editors: Jules Stuyck & Evelyne Terryn

Published by:
Kluwer Law International B.V.
PO Box 316
2400 AH Alphen aan den Rijn
The Netherlands
E-mail: international-sales@wolterskluwer.com
Website: lrus.wolterskluwer.com

Sold and distributed in North, Central and South America by:
Wolters Kluwer Legal & Regulatory U.S.
7201 McKinney Circle
Frederick, MD 21704
United States of America
Email: customer.service@wolterskluwer.com

Sold and distributed in all other countries by:
Air Business Subscriptions
Rockwood House
Haywards Heath
West Sussex
RH16 3DH
United Kingdom
Email: international-customerservice@wolterskluwer.com

DISCLAIMER: The material in this volume is in the nature of general comment only. It is not offered as advice on any particular matter and should not be taken as such. The editor and the contributing authors expressly disclaim all liability to any person with regard to anything done or omitted to be done, and with respect to the consequences of anything done or omitted to be done wholly or partly in reliance upon the whole or any part of the contents of this volume. No reader should act or refrain from acting on the basis of any matter contained in this volume without first obtaining professional advice regarding the particular facts and circumstances at issue. Any and all opinions expressed herein are those of the particular author and are not necessarily those of the editor or publisher of this volume.

Printed on acid-free paper

ISBN 978-94-035-1333-1

e-Book: ISBN 978-94-035-1380-5
web-PDF: ISBN 978-94-035-1403-1

This title is available on www.kluwerlawonline.com

Printed in the United Kingdom by CPI Group (UK) Ltd, Croydon, CR0 4YY.

The Authors

Jules Stuyck graduated from KU Leuven in 1970 and obtained his PhD degree from the same University in 1975. Until September 2013, Jules taught Substantive Law of the European Union (EU) at the University of Leuven (KU Leuven) and at the Radboud Universiteit Nijmegen, the Netherlands. He is now emeritus professor at both Universities. In recent years, he has been teaching European Law at the Université Panthéon-Assas Paris 2, France and still teaches European Consumer Law at that University. From 2000 until 2015, he taught European Competition Law at the Central European University in Budapest, Hungary. He is the author of about 450 publications in various fields, including a leading handbook on commercial practices law. He is a member of the editorial board of several Belgian and European legal journals. As an attorney (Brussels bar, since 1984), Jules Stuyck has long experience in EU law and consumer law. He regularly assists private clients as well as the European institutions (Commission and Council), agencies and bodies before the European Courts. In the last twenty years, he has pleaded numerous cases in various fields, including competition, State aid, the customs union (CU), free movement, public procurement, trade mark and trade practices law, media law and environmental law. He is also an experienced litigator in the Belgian courts, specializing in market practices, competition law and intellectual property (IP). Jules Stuyck has been with Crowell & Moring since 2017, as senior counsel.

Pierre M. Sabbadini is a lawyer at Liedekerke Wolters Waelbroeck Kirkpatrick. He was admitted to the Brussels bar in 2012. His practice focuses on European and Belgian competition law as well as on State aid law. Pierre is a member of the board of the Belgian Chapter of the International League of Competition Law. He holds a Master's in Business Law (2009) and a Master's in European Competition and IP Law from the University of Liège (2010). Pierre assisted in the drafting of parts of the chapter on competition law (Part II Chapter 1).

Ellen Van Nieuwenhuyze graduated from Ghent University in 2010 and obtained an LLM from King's College London in 2011. In 2015, she obtained a PhD in EU Food Law, focusing on the regulation of nutrition and health claims. She joined the Brussels Bar later that year and is currently working as a legal assistant at the Court of

3

The Authors

Justice of the European Union (CJEU) (General Court (GC)). Ellen has authored various publications on EU law in general and EU food law. She is the member of the editorial committee of *Journal de droit européen* (J.D.E.) and *Revue européenne de droit de la consommation/European Journal of Consumer Law* (R.E.D.C.). Ellen assisted in the drafting of Parts I ((Introductory Part) and II (The Internal Market).

Table of Contents

Table of Contents

6

Chapter 3. Freedom of Establishment and Freedom to Provide Services

Table of Contents

Table of Contents

Table of Contents

Table of Contents

14

List of Abbreviations

AAC	Average Avoidable Costs
CAP	Common Agricultural Policy
CCT	Common Customs Tariff
CU	Customs Union
CCP	Common Commercial Policy
CFP	Common Fisheries Policy
CJEU	Court of Justice of the European Union
DG COMP	Directorate General for Competition (European Commission)
EAEC	European Atomic Energy Community
EC	European Community/European Communities/Treaty on European Community
ECB	European Central Bank
ECN	European Competition Network
ECSC	European Coal and Steel Community
EEA	European Economic Area
EEC	European Economic Community
EMU	Economic and Monetary Union
EP	European Parliament
EU	European Union
GC	General Court of the European Union
EUMR	European Union Merger regulation
IP	Intellectual Property
IPR	Intellectual Property Rights
MEOP	Market Economy Operator Principle
MEIP	Market Economy Investor Principle
NCAs	National Competition Authorities
NGOs	Non-governmental organizations
OECD	Organisation for Economic Co-operation and Development
OEM	Original Equipment Manufacturer
R&D BER	Research & Development Block Exemption Regulation

List of Abbreviations

SEA	Single European Act
SPC	Supplementary Protection Certificates
TTBER	Technology Transfer Block Exemption Regulation
TEU	Treaty on European Union
TFEU	Treaty on the Functioning of the European Union
UCI	*Union cycliste internationale*
UK	United Kingdom
US	United States
VABER	Vertical Agreements Block Exemption Regulation
VAT	Value Added Tax
WTO	World Trade Organization

Preface

This monograph is different from the national monographs in the IEL Commercial and Economic Law. Its scope is narrower, since a lot of rulemaking at EU level often takes place in the form of directives that have to be implemented in national law. These rules are discussed in the national monographs of the Member States of the EU. Accordingly, since there are numerous EU measures in the field of e.g., company law, securities, insurance law, commercial agency, copyright, trade mark law, designs and models, and late payments, the present monograph does not deal with 'commercial law' in the strict sense. The relevant rules are discussed in the national monographs of the Member States in the IEL on Company law, Insurance Law, Intellectual Property and Commercial and Economic Law. The EU regulations in the field of Intellectual Property Rights (IPR) and insolvency are also disregarded here since they are basically ancillary to national provisions in the relevant area.

This monograph includes EU competition law which is part of 'economic law' within the meaning of the IEL. It is one of the basic policies of the Union. In contrast, EU consumer law is not included because it mainly consist of directives that have to be transposed (and generally were transposed) in national law.

Following the structure of the national monographs, this monograph contains a general introduction on the EU, its institutions and law making. The present monograph deals with provisions of the Treaties (the Treaty on the European Union (TEU) and the Treaty on the Functioning of the European Union (TFEU), secondary Union law – regulations and directives – and case law of the European Courts relating to the internal market and those that govern the action of the Union in certain fields: the so-called common policies (like competition policy or the common commercial policy (CCP) with regard to third countries, the common agricultural policy (CAP) and the common transport policy), where the EU has extensive competencies. 'Other policies' (like environmental or consumer policy), where the EU can supplement the actions of the Member States or give national policies in the relevant field an orientation are disregarded. This monograph is with the assistance, for the first edition, of Pierre M. Sabbadini and Ellen Van Nieuwenhuyze.

This second edition updates the law as it was on 31 January 2019.

Preface

General Introduction

Chapter 1. Introductory Remark

§1. Background

1. This monograph only deals with parts of the substantive law of the EU. Institutional and procedural questions are disregarded (except for some fundamental institutional aspects discussed in the present chapter).

The present chapter will be limited to some general figures and a brief history of the European Union (EU).

§2. Brief History

2. On 18 April 1950, in Paris, the Benelux States, the Federal Republic of Germany, France and Italy signed the Treaty establishing the European Coal and Steel Community (ECSC). The idea, coming from Jean Monnet, was that integrating the basic industries of in particular Germany and France who had just finished WWII would create peace and prosperity, which would eventually lead to the economic and even the political integration of participating European countries. The ECSC was created for a period of fifty years. After expiry of that period in 2002, coal and steel were integrated in the general EC Treaty (*see* hereafter).

3. On 25 March 1957, the six Member States of the ECSC signed in Rome the Treaty establishing the European Economic Community (EEC) and the Treaty establishing the European Atomic Energy Community (EAEC). Both treaties entered into force on 1 January 1958 for an indefinite period of time.

4. Originally, the three Communities had (at least formally) each their own institutions (e.g., the High Authority of the ECSC and a Commission for the EEC and a Commission for the EAEC).

5. Since the entry into force, in 1967, of the Treaty establishing a single Council and a single Commission of the European Communities (Merger Treaty) the EEC (later the EC), the ECSC and the EAEC, together the 'European Communities' or 'EC', share the same institutions.

6. In the 1970s and 1980s, six countries joined the EC: Denmark, Ireland and the United Kingdom (UK) (1973), Greece (1980), and Portugal and Spain (1986).

7. The year 1987 was the year of entry into force of the Single European Act (SEA), signed at Luxembourg on 17 February 1986 and at The Hague on 28 February 1986. The SEA brought important amendments to the EC treaties, in particular by providing for a cooperation procedure (now: the ordinary legislative procedure) of the European Parliament (EP) and the Council for the adoption of legislative acts and the introduction of qualified majority within the Council for the adoption of acts for the completion of the internal market.

8. On 1 November 1993, the Treaty on European Union (TEU), signed at Maastricht on 7 February 1992, entered into force. The EC formed the first pillar of a three-pillar system. The two new pillars were the 'Common Foreign and Security Policy' and 'Police and Judicial Cooperation in Criminal Matters'. In 2009, the Lisbon Treaty has integrated the provisions of the three pillars in a single building (the EU).

9. On 1 January 1994 the Treaty, establishing the European Economic Area (EEA), signed at Porto on 1 May 1992 (with Liechtenstein, Norway and Iceland), entered into force.

10. On 15 April 1994, the World Trade Organization (WTO) Agreement, to which the EU is a party, was signed in Marrakech.

11. Austria, Finland, Norway and Sweden joined the EU on 1 January 1995. The same day the WTO Agreement entered into force.

12. On 2 October 1997, the Treaty of Amsterdam was signed. This Treaty again amended the EC Treaty on some important points.

13. The date of 1 January 1999 saw the start of the third phase of Economic and Monetary Union (EMU) between eleven of the Member States as well as the introduction of the euro.

14. In December 2000, the Treaty of Nice, again amending the founding treaties, was signed. That Treaty entered into force on 1 January 2002.

15. In 2002, the European Steel and Coal Community (ESCS) expired. Coal and steel were integrated within the EC (now the EU).

16. On 1 May 2004, ten new Member States acceded: Estonia, Latvia, Lithuania, Poland, the Czech Republic, Slovakia, Hungary, Slovenia, Malta and Cyprus.

17. On 1 January 2007, Bulgaria and Romania acceded.

18. On 1 December 2009, the Lisbon Treaty entered into force. This Treaty merged the existing Communities (first pillar) with the two other pillars and created one legal person: the EU.

19. On 1 July 2013, Croatia joined as the EU's twenty-eighth Member State.

20. On 23 June 2016, a referendum in the UK resulted in a majority voting for a so-called Brexit (the UK leaving the EU). On 29 March 2017, the UK triggered Article 50 TEU: the formal decision to withdraw from the EU, a process of maximum two years (complete).

21. At the end of January 2019, the EU and the UK still had not reached an agreement on Brexit. The deadline for Brexit expires on 29 March 2019.

§3. SOME DATA ON THE EU

22. On 1 January 2015, the EU population was estimated at 511,522,671 million, an increase compared to two years before by 3.3 million. The EU covers over 4 million km^2, which is less than half the size of the United States (US). France has the biggest surface area and Malta is the smallest Member State.

Member State	Geographical Size	Population
Austria	83,879 km^2	88,772,865
Belgium	30,528 km^2	11,351,727
Bulgaria	111,002 km^2	7,101,859
Croatia	56,594 km^2	4,154,213
Cyprus	9,251 km^2	854,802
Czech Republic	78,867 km^2	10,578,820
Denmark	42,921 km^2	5,748,769
Estonia	45,227 km^2	1,315, 635
Finland	338,435 km^2	5,503,297
France	632,833.6 km^2	66,989,083
Germany	357,340 km^2	82,521,653
Greece	131,957 km^2	10,768,193
Hungary	93,024 km^2	9,797,561
Ireland	69,797 km^2	4,6784,3,83
Italy	302,073 km^2	60,589,445
Latvia	64,573 km^2	1,950,116
Lithuania	65,300 km^2	2,847,904
Luxembourg	2,586 km^2	590,667

Member State	Geographical Size	Population
Malta	316 km^2	460,297
The Netherlands	41,540 km^2	17,081,507
Poland	312,679 km^2	37,972,964
Portugal	92,225 km^2	10,309,573
Romania	238,391 km^2	19,664,350
Slovakia	49,035 km^2	5,435,343
Slovenia	20,273 km^2	2,065,895
Spain	505,970 km^2	46,528,966
Sweden	438,574 km^2	9,995,153
UK	248,528 km^2	65,808,573

The EU currently has twenty-four official languages.

Official Language	Since
Dutch, French, German, Italian	1958
Danish, English	1973
Greek	1981
Portuguese, Spanish	1986
Finnish, Swedish	1995
Czech, Estonian, Hungarian, Latvian, Lithuanian, Maltese, Polish, Slovak, Slovenian	2004
Bulgarian, Irish, Romanian	2007
Croatian	2013

Chapter 2. The Legal System of the EU

§1. THE EC BECAME EU

23. The Treaty on EU (Maastricht), which entered into force in 1994, amended the EEC, the ECSC and the EAEC Treaties, created a three-pillar system (the EC, the common foreign policy and judicial cooperation) which was abandoned in 2009 by the Treaty of Lisbon. Today, twenty-eight countries are members of the EU. After Brexit: twenty-seven. The EU is presently governed by two basic Treaties: TEU and TFEU (the Treaty on the Functioning of the European Union). The EAEC Treaty still exists separately.

§2. COMMON PROVISIONS

24. Title I of the TEU contains common provisions that relate to the foundations of the Union, its objectives, its relationship with its members, its powers and fundamental principles.

I. The Foundations of the Union

25. Article 2 TEU relates to the foundations of the EU, and states that 'the Union is founded on the values of respect for human dignity, freedom, democracy, equality, the rule of law and respect for human rights, including the rights of persons belonging to minorities. These values are common to the Member States in a society in which pluralism, non-discrimination, tolerance, justice, solidarity and equality between women and men prevail'.

II. Objectives of the Union

26. Article 3 TEU contains the Union's objectives.

1) The Union's aim is to promote peace, its values and the well-being of its peoples.
2) The Union shall offer its citizens an area of freedom, security and justice without internal frontiers, in which the free movement of persons is ensured in conjunction with appropriate measures with respect to external border controls, asylum, immigration and the prevention and combating of crime.
3) The Union shall establish an internal market. It shall work for the sustainable development of Europe based on balanced economic growth and price stability, a highly competitive social market economy, aiming at full employment and social progress, and a high level of protection and improvement of the quality of the environment. It shall promote scientific

and technological advance. It shall combat social exclusion and discrimination, and shall promote social justice and protection, equality between women and men, solidarity between generations and protection of the rights of the child.

It shall promote economic, social and territorial cohesion, and solidarity among Member States. It shall respect its rich cultural and linguistic diversity, and shall ensure that Europe's cultural heritage is safeguarded and enhanced.

4) The Union shall establish an economic and monetary union whose currency is the euro.

5) In its relations with the wider world, the Union shall uphold and promote its values and interests and contribute to the protection of its citizens. It shall contribute to peace, security, the sustainable development of the Earth, solidarity and mutual respect among peoples, free and fair trade, eradication of poverty and the protection of human rights, in particular the rights of the child, as well as to the strict observance and the development of international law, including respect for the principles of the United Nations Charter.

6) The Union shall pursue its objectives by appropriate means commensurate with the competences which are conferred upon it in the Treaties.

III. Relationship of the Union and Its Members

27. Article 4 TEU governs the relationship between the Union and the Member States.

1) In accordance with Article 5 [TEU], competences not conferred upon the Union in the Treaties remain with the Member States.

2) The Union shall respect the equality of Member States before the Treaties as well as their national identities, inherent in their fundamental structures, political and constitutional, inclusive of regional and local self-government. It shall respect their essential State functions, including ensuring the territorial integrity of the State, maintaining law and order and safeguarding national security. In particular, national security remains the sole responsibility of each Member State.

3) Pursuant to the principle of sincere cooperation, the Union and the Member States shall, in full mutual respect, assist each other in carrying out tasks which follow from the Treaties.

The Member States shall take any appropriate measure, general or particular, to ensure fulfilment of the obligations arising out of the Treaties or resulting from the acts of the institutions of the Union.

The Member States shall facilitate the achievement of the Union's tasks and refrain from any measure which could jeopardise the attainment of the Union's objectives.

IV. Fundamental Principles

28. Article 5 TEU contains the principles governing the Union's competences; including the principles of subsidiarity and proportionality.

1) The limits of Union competences are governed by the principle of conferral. The use of Union competences is governed by the principles of subsidiarity and proportionality.
2) Under the principle of conferral, the Union shall act only within the limits of the competences conferred upon it by the Member States in the Treaties to attain the objectives set out therein. Competences not conferred upon the Union in the Treaties remain with the Member States.
3) Under the principle of subsidiarity, in areas which do not fall within its exclusive competence, the Union shall act only if and in so far as the objectives of the proposed action cannot be sufficiently achieved by the Member States, either at central level or at regional and local level, but can rather, by reason of the scale or effects of the proposed action, be better achieved at Union level.

   The institutions of the Union shall apply the principle of subsidiarity as laid down in the Protocol on the application of the principles of subsidiarity and proportionality. National Parliaments ensure compliance with the principle of subsidiarity in accordance with the procedure set out in that Protocol.
4) Under the principle of proportionality, the content and form of Union action shall not exceed what is necessary to achieve the objectives of the Treaties.

   The institutions of the Union shall apply the principle of proportionality as laid down in the Protocol on the application of the principles of subsidiarity and proportionality.

29. Other important general principles are contained in the TFEU, in particular the principle of integration of the protection of the environment, consumers and animal welfare in other policies (Articles 11, 12, 13 TFEU); the recognition of the importance of services of general economic interest (Article 14 TFEU); transparency (Article 15 TFEU); the protection of personal data (Article 16 TFEU); the recognition of religions (Article 17 TFEU) and last but not least the principle of non-discrimination (Articles 18–25 TFEU). The latter principle has given rise to several directives prohibiting sex discrimination and discrimination on the basis of race, religious and similar factors, and age.

V. Fundamental Rights and Unwritten General Principles

30. The EU institutions, as well as the organs of the Member States when acting within the realm of Union law, have to respect general principles of good administration, such as legal certainty and the protection of legitimate expectations. Their conduct can also be examined in the light of the fundamental rights as enshrined in the EU Charter of Fundamental Rights. Notably the following rights play a complementary role in the appraisal of restrictions to the internal market freedoms: the freedom of expression (e.g., in relation to restrictions on advertising) and the freedom to conduct a business.[2]

---

2. *See* recently Judgment of 20 December 2017, *Global Starnet*, C-322/16, EU:C:2017:985.

Chapter 3. The Institutions and Bodies

§1. The Institutions

31. The EU has the following seven institutions (Article 13(1) TEU):

- an EP, with a maximum 786 MEPs (Members of the European Parliament), directly elected for five years. The last elections were held in 2014;
- a European Council, composed of a president, the heads of State or government of the Member States and the president of the Commission;
- a Council (of Ministers), with one representative of each Member State government, assisted by a Committee of Permanent Representatives (COREPER);
- a Commission (the European Commission), which is composed of the College of Commissioners of twenty-eight members, acting independently from the Member States;
- a Court of Justice of the European Union (CJEU), which currently consists of two courts: the Court of Justice and the General Court (GC);[3]
- a European Central Bank (ECB), which is the monetary authority for the eurozone Member States;
- a Court of Auditors.

32. Originally, the powers of the EP were rather limited. With regard to Community legislation, the EP had only an advisory power. Additionally, until 1979, the members of the EP were not elected directly. The SEA considerably extended the influence of the EP by giving it the right to co-decide with the Council on the adoption of legislation. An important change introduced by the Lisbon Treaty is that the co-decision procedure has become the ordinary legislative procedure, meaning that it has become the norm for the majority of policy areas. The ordinary legislative procedure is set out in Article 294 TFEU. A first step in the procedure is the submission of a proposal by the European Commission to the EP and the Council. Hereafter, the EP shall adopt its position at first reading and communicate it to the Council. If the latter approves this position, the act concerned will be adopted in the wording which corresponds to the position of the EP. However, if it does not approve this position, the Council shall adopt its position at first reading and communicate it to the EP.

If within three months of such communication, the EP:[4]

- approves the Council's position at first reading or has not taken a decision, the act concerned shall be deemed to have been adopted in the wording which corresponds to the position of the Council;
- rejects, by a majority of its component members, the Council's position at first reading, the proposed act shall be deemed not to have been adopted;

---

3. From 2005 until 1 September 2016, there was a Public Service Tribunal, the competences of which are henceforth exercised by an enlarged General Court.
4. Article 294(7) TFEU.

– proposes, by a majority of its component members, amendments to the Council's position at first reading, the text thus amended shall be forwarded to the Council and to the Commission, which shall deliver an opinion on those amendments.

If, within three months of receiving the EP's amendments, the Council, acting by a qualified majority:[5]

– approves all those amendments, the act in question shall be deemed to have been adopted;
– does not approve all the amendments, the President of the Council, in agreement with the President of the EP, shall within six weeks convene a meeting of the Conciliation Committee.

§2. OTHER BODIES

33. The EU has many other bodies, including funds (in the field of agriculture, social and regional policy), consultative committees (such as the Economic and Social Committee and the Committee of the Regions), and finally agencies created by separate regulations (such as the European Food and Safety Authority,[6] the Agency for Border Control Frontex,[7] the European Chemicals Agency,[8] the European Medicines Agency[9] and many others). Most of the agencies have no or only limited regulatory powers but carry out tasks of an advisory, technical, implementing or management nature.

---

5. Article 294(8) TFEU.
6. Created by Regulation (EC) No 178/2002 of the European Parliament and of the Council of 28 January 2002 laying down the general principles and requirements of food law, establishing the European Food Safety Authority and laying down procedures in matters of food safety, *OJ* L 31, 1.2.2002, p. 1.
7. Council Regulation (EC) No 2007/2004 of 26 October 2004 establishing a European Agency for the Management of Operational Cooperation at the External Borders of the Member States of the European Union, *OJ* L 349, 25.11.2004, p. 1.
8. Regulation (EC) No 1907/2006 of the European Parliament and of the Council of 18 December 2006 concerning the Registration, Evaluation, Authorisation and Restriction of Chemicals (REACH), *OJ* L 304, 22.11.2007, p. 1.
9. Regulation (EC) No 726/2004 of the European Parliament and of the Council of 31 March 2004 laying down Community procedures for the authorisation and supervision of medicinal products for human and veterinary use and establishing a European Medicines Agency, *OJ* L 136, 30.4.2004, p. 1.

Chapter 4. The Nature of Union Law

34. Many provisions of Union law have direct effect, which means that they can be invoked by individuals in national courts. Not all provisions of primary Union law are directly effective. The following conditions have to be fulfilled: (i) by its nature a provision must be able to confer rights on an individual; (ii) it must not leave the addressee of the obligation a discretionary latitude (an example is Article 107 TFEU, which confers a margin of discretion on the Commission to authorize State aid measures); (iii) it must contain a clear and unconditional obligation (a negative example is old Article 67 EEC, on free movement of capital, which was subject to liberalization of the free movement of persons).

Notable examples of directly effective Treaty provisions are the internal market freedoms (free movement of goods, persons, services and capital). Some provisions have horizontal direct effect, meaning that they can be invoked by individuals and private companies against other individuals and private companies (e.g., Articles 101 and 102 TFEU, on competition law, which are discussed in Part II, Chapter 1). The case law of the Court of Justice interpreting the Treaty provisions on the internal market is essentially the result of preliminary references by national courts who are called to apply directly effective Treaty provisions in disputes between individuals and national authorities.

35. In its seminal *Van Gend & Loos*[10] and *Costa v. Enel*[11] judgments, the CJEU established the important principle of primacy of Union law, namely that provisions of Union law have precedence over provisions of national law. If the latter are contrary to Union law, they have to be disregarded. Particularly relevant is the consideration of the Court in *Costa v. Enel* that 'the law stemming from the Treaty, an independent source of law, could not, because of its special and original nature, be overridden by domestic legal provisions, however framed, without being deprived of its character as Community law and without the legal basis of the Community itself being called into question'.

---

10. Judgment of 5 February 1963, *Van Gend & Loos*, 26/62, EU:C:1963:1.
11. Judgment of 15 July 1964, *Costa v. Enel*, 6/64, EU:C:1964:66.

Chapter 5. Sources of Union Law

36. Union law has primary sources which take precedence over secondary and supplementary sources.

37. Primary law includes the Treaties (TEU and TFEU), the amending EU Treaties, the protocols to the Treaties, the Treaties on new Member States' accession to the EU and the Charter of Fundamental Rights.

38. Secondary Union law consists in the first place of unilateral acts adopted by the institutions based on the Treaties. Article 288 TFEU distinguishes the following binding acts:

– regulations: they are directly applicable and have a general scope;
– directives: they are addressed to the Member States;
– decisions: individual acts that can be addressed to one or more Member States or one or more other person.

Recommendations and opinions are referred to as non-binding acts adopted by the institutions. Moreover, in practice, the Commission also issues notices, guidelines and communications.

Secondary Union law moreover comprises certain agreements, namely international agreements signed by the EU and a country or outside organization, agreements between Member States, and agreements between the EU institutions.

39. The case law of the CJEU, the general principles of Union law and international law qualifies are sources of Union law.

Chapter 6. Remedies Against Infringements of Union Law

§1. Infringement Procedure

40. Where a Member State infringes a provision of Union law, e.g., by restricting free movement in a way which is contrary to one of the internal market provisions of the Treaty or by failing to implement a directive timely or correctly, the Commission can bring an action against that Member Sate before the CJEU (Article 258 TFEU). Pursuant to Article 259 TFEU, Member States can initiate infringement proceedings if they consider that another Member State has failed to fulfil an obligation under the Treaty. If the action of the Commission or another Member State is successful, the Member State concerned has to take all the measures which are necessary to cease the infringement (Article 260(1) TFEU). Where the Member State fails to comply with the judgment of the CJEU, the Commission can bring a second action against the Member State and ask the Court to impose a financial penalty on the Member State (Article 260(2) TFEU).

§2. Claims for Damages

41. In its seminal judgment in *Francovich*,[12] the CJEU held that Member States are liable for damages vis-à-vis persons who have suffered a prejudice as a result of a violation of Union law. It indicated that in the event of non-transposition of a directive, there is a right to reparation if: (1) the result prescribed by the directive entails the granting of rights to individuals, (2) the contents of those rights are identified on the basis of the provisions of the directive concerned, and (3) there is a causal link between the breach of the State's obligation and the damage suffered by the affected parties. Later, the Court pointed out the requirement of a sufficiently serious breach of Union law, which is fulfilled where a Directive is not correctly implemented.[13]

In *Courage*,[14] the CJEU extended this ruling and held that undertakings (businesses) are liable vis-à-vis victims for the harm caused by infringements of Articles 101 and 102 TFEU (prohibition of restrictive agreements, respectively of abuse of a dominant position).

§3. Inapplicability of Technical Regulations

42. Directive 98/34/EC,[15] which replaces the old Directive 83/189/EEC,[16] contains an obligation for Member States to notify to the Commission all drafts of new

---

12. Judgment of 19 November 1991, *Francovich,* C-6/90, EU:C:1991:428.
13. Judgment of 8 October 1996, *Dillenkofer*, Joined cases C-178/94 et seq., EU:C:1996:375, para. 26.
14. Judgment of 20 September 2001, *Courage,* C-453/99, EU:C:2001:465 (*see* the further evolution in the subsequent case law in the chapter on competition law).
15. Directive 98/34/EC of the European Parliament and of the Council of 22 June 1998 laying down a procedure for the provision of information in the field of technical standards and regulations, *OJ* 1988, L 204/37.

technical rules. The Commission can then consult with the other Member States and, where appropriate, propose rules at the EU level. In a series of judgments starting with *CIA Security*,[17] the CJEU decided that where a Member State has failed to notify to the Commission a technical rule pursuant to the Directive this rule is not enforceable before the national judge.[18] The unenforceability of a technical rule that has not been notified to the Commission can also affect the validity of a contract concluded between private operators.[19]

---

16. Council Directive 83/189/EEC of 28 March 1983 laying down a procedure for the provision of information in the field of technical standards and regulations, *OJ* 1983, L 109/8.
17. Judgment of 30 April 1996, *CIA Security,* C-194/94, EU:C:1996:172.
18. *See*, e.g., Judgment of 13 June in *Lemmens*, C-226/97, EU:C:1998:296, para. 33; Judgment of 6 June 2002, *Sapod Audic*, C-159/00, EU:C:2002:343, para. 49; Judgment of 8 November 2007, *Schwibbert*, C-20/05, EU:C:2007:652, para. 33.
19. *Sapod Audic*.

Chapter 7. The Sphere of Action of the TFEU

§1. Overview

43. Most of the provisions of the TFEU and of the acts of the institutions adopted pursuant to that Treaty are economic in nature.

The Treaty contains rules on the functioning of the internal market, the so-called common policies (CAP, common transport policy, competition policy, CCP), the rules on the functioning of the EMU and some other policies (industry, consumers, health, environment, youth, education, etc.), as well as rules of a non-economic nature, such as those relating to an area of justice, freedom and security. The non-economic provisions of the TFEU will not be discussed in this monograph. Moreover, not all economic provisions will be discussed. Instead, the focus will be on the internal market and the common policies.

§2. Aims and Instruments of the EU

44. According to Article 3(1) TEU 'the Union's aim is to promote peace, its values and the well-being of its peoples'. Article 3(2) TEU provides that 'the Union shall offer its citizens an area of freedom, security and justice without internal frontiers, in which the free movement of persons is ensured in conjunction with appropriate measures with respect to external border controls, asylum, immigration and the prevention and combating of crime'.

The first part of Article 3(3) TEU is central for this monograph: 'The Union shall establish an internal market. It shall work for the sustainable development of Europe based on balanced economic growth and price stability, a highly competitive social market economy, aiming at full employment and social progress, and a high level of protection and improvement of the quality of the environment … .'

Pursuant to paragraph 4 of Article 3 TEU 'The Union shall establish an economic and monetary union whose currency is the euro.'

Part I. The Internal Market

Chapter 1. From a Customs Union via a Common Market/Internal Market to an EMU

§1. DIFFERENCE BETWEEN A CUSTOMS UNION AND A FREE TRADE AREA

45. The core of what is now the EU is a customs union (CU). CUs are arrangements among countries allowing the free movement of goods within that union, and characterized by a common customs tariff (CCT) regarding goods imported from third countries which have been put into free circulation in the CU. It is a stronger form of integration than a free trade area.

As in a CU, in a free trade area no customs duties are levied on goods originating in other Member States of the area. However, in contrast to what is the case in a CU, there is no common external customs tariff. Instead, each Member State applies its own customs tariff to goods originating in third countries.

An example of a free trade area is the EEA which was concluded in 1994 between the EU and three European Free Trade Association (EFTA) States (Iceland, Liechtenstein and Norway).

In a CU, like the EU, once a good is put into free circulation in a Member State – which includes the payment of the duty provided for by the CCT of the union – it will be assimilated to a good originating in that Member State and it can therefore freely circulate throughout the Union without any charges being imposed by the other Member State to which it is exported (*see* Article 29 TFEU).

46. The EU is based on a CU. It has a CCT for all goods originating in third countries, with some preferential regimes, e.g., for goods originating in developing countries. Goods that are cleared under the CCT can freely circulate in other Member States without further charges. They are assimilated to goods produced in a Member State.

§2. THE INTERNAL MARKET

47. The original EEC Treaty established a common market, a notion that has gradually been replaced by the notion of internal market. In the present Treaties, the notion of common market has disappeared. The terms 'internal market' and 'common market' are closely related, as they can be considered different stages in the integration process. The Court of Justice held indeed that the 'common market' is a stage in the integration process, which aims to remove all the barriers to intra-Community trade with a view to the merger of national markets into a single market giving rise to conditions as closely as possible to a genuine 'internal market'.[20]

The internal market comprises a CU, but it is more than just that. It includes the removal of obstacles to the free movement of goods other than tariff barriers (customs duties and charges having equivalent effect, *see* hereafter). In addition, it supposes the removal of obstacles to the free movement of persons, services, capital and payments and, finally, the putting in place of a CCP (external commercial relations) and a common competition policy.

The notion 'internal market' has been introduced in the EC Treaty by the SEA in 1987. Article 26 TFEU defines the internal market as an area without internal borders with free movement of goods, persons, services and capital. The internal market constitutes a further step in economic integration ('an area without internal frontiers').

According to the White Paper from the Commission (1985) on 'Completing the Internal Market',[21] the completion of the internal market requires the removal of physical, technical and fiscal barriers for the free movement of goods, persons, services and capital.

§3. The Economic and Monetary Union

48. In the 1990s, it was believed that the consolidation of the internal market creates the need for an EMU. The Maastricht Treaty inserted the necessary provisions to that effect in the EC Treaty. These provisions can now be found in Articles 119–144 TFEU. As will be seen hereafter, the EMU has not been entirely successful. Not all Member States qualified for the adoption of the euro, while others preferred to stay outside the eurozone. Greece was even threatened with expulsion of the zone, as illustrated by discussions on a possible 'Grexit' in mid-2015. The guiding principles of the EMU are an open market economy with free competition (Article 119 TFEU) and price stability (Article 127 TFEU).

§4. Union Policies

49. The EC Treaty already provided not only for the establishment of an internal market but also for common policies and other 'policies'. The field of action of the Union has progressively been expanded over the years by several amending treaties.

50. The common policies – where the Union enjoys important (legislative) powers – are the common agriculture and fisheries policy (Articles 38–44 TFEU), the common transport policy (Articles 90–100 TFEU), the CCP (Articles 206–207 TFEU) and competition policy, including State aid (Articles 101–108 TFEU).

---

20. Judgment of May 1982, *Schul Douane Expediteur*, 15/81, EU:C:1982:135, para. 33.
21. European Commission, White Paper on Completing the Internal Market, COM(85) 310 final.

51. The other policies, where the Union generally enjoys less important powers, are social policy, education, vocational training and youth (Articles 151–166 TFEU), culture (Article 167 TFEU), public health (Article 168 TFEU), consumer protection (Article 169 TFEU), trans-European networks (Articles 170–172 TFEU), industry (Article 173 TFEU), economic and social cohesion (Articles 174–178 TFEU), research and technological development (Articles 179–190 TFEU), environment (Articles 191–193 TFEU), energy (Article 194 TFEU), tourism (Article 195 TFEU), civil protection (Article 196 TFEU), and administrative cooperation (Article 197 TFEU).

The Union also has competences in non-economic fields, such as border checks, asylum and immigration,[22] inserted by the Treaty of Amsterdam, and police and judicial cooperation in civil and criminal matters[23] (the former third pillar of the Maastricht Treaty) (now: 'area of freedom, security and justice'[24]).

§5. Free Movement and the Completion of the Internal Market

I. Positive and Negative Integration

52. The achievement of the European internal market (one single market for the whole of the Union) implies the removal of existing obstacles for the free movement of goods, persons, services and capital.[25] This is achieved in two complementary ways. First, there are directly effective Treaty articles (i.e., provisions that can be relied upon by individuals in national courts) prohibiting obstacles to these freedoms. Integration through the application of the directly effective basic Treaty freedoms is sometimes called 'negative integration'. However, not all obstacles to free movement are prohibited by these articles. This is because the CJEU accepts obstacles, resulting from disparities between national rules that are justified in the general interest. These disparities can only be removed by harmonization measures adopted by the Union legislature, a second type of integration referred to as 'positive integration'.

II. Negative Integration

53. As already said, negative integration is the fruit of the application of the directly effective Treaty provisions on free movement of goods, persons, services and capital.

Free movement of goods relates to the removal of both tariff barriers (Articles 30 and 110 TFEU) and non-tariff barriers (Articles 34–37 TFEU).

With regard to the free movement of persons, the Treaty makes a distinction between the free movement of workers (employed people) (Articles 45–48 TFEU),

---

22. Articles 77–80 TFEU.
23. Articles 81–89 TFEU.
24. Articles 67–89 TFEU.
25. Article 26(2) TFEU.

and the free movement of self-employed persons and legal persons (such as companies). The latter freedom is called right of establishment (Articles 49–55 TFEU). For self-employed persons and companies, the Treaty also provides for the freedom to provide services, which applies where the service provider has no permanent link with the Member State in which the service is provided) (Articles 56–62 TFEU).

Finally, there is the free movement of capital and payments (Articles 63–66 TFEU).

III. Positive Integration

54. Positive integration refers to the introduction of common standards believed to be reasonable across the Union. The original Treaty provided for a transitional period of twelve years (1 January 1958–31 December 1969) for the establishment of the common market. However, at the expiry of that period many obstacles remained, *inter alia* due to the fact that the adoption of harmonization directives required unanimity in the Council (Article 100 EEC).

55. Articles 114–118 TFEU are the general provisions on harmonization, of which Article 114 is undoubtedly the most important one.

Specific harmonization provisions exist, e.g., with regard to the freedom of establishment (Article 53 TFEU), the free provision of services (Article 59 TFEU) and taxes (Article 113 TFEU).

These provisions will be discussed in Chapter 2 of Part I.

Chapter 2. Free Movement of Goods

§1. Overview of Treaty Provisions

56. Article 30 TFEU prohibits custom duties and charges having an equivalent effect between Member States. In addition, Article 110 TFEU prohibits discriminatory and protective internal taxation with regard to goods.

57. Articles 34–37 TFEU deal with non-tariff barriers to the free movement of goods. While Article 34 TFEU prohibits all quantitative import restrictions and measures having equivalent effect, Article 35 TFEU lays down a ban on quantitative export restrictions and measures having equivalent effect. Article 36 TFEU contains an exhaustive list of grounds of justification for import and export restrictions (public order, public health, industrial property etc.). Finally, Article 37 TFEU provides that Member States have to adjust commercial monopolies such as to eliminate discrimination.

§2. Tariff Barriers: Customs Duties and Charges Having Equivalent Effect – Internal Taxation

I. The Customs Union

58. Article 28 TFEU proclaims that the Member States form a CU. The Union has one CCT for all goods entering from third countries. There are no customs due for goods originating in other Member States.

59. Article 29 TFEU contains the principle that goods which are put into free circulation in the Union are assimilated to goods originating in one of the Member States. Goods are put into free circulation where they enter the Union (in either of the Member States) are cleared by the customs (i.e., the relevant custom duties are paid according to the Common Custom's Tariff (CCT) and all formalities have been complied with) and for which no refund on custom duties has taken place. Such goods are assimilated to goods originating in a Member State.

II. Elimination of Customs Duties Between Member States

60. Article 30 TFEU prohibits all customs duties between Member States. On 1 July 1968, the CCT was established, but this does not mean that from that date on tariff restrictions between Member States have completely disappeared (*see* next section on charges having equivalent effect). Indeed, a transitional period was foreseen for the abolition of customs duties between the Member States and the application of common customs duties.

III. Prohibition of Charges Having Equivalent Effect

61. Article 30 TFEU contains a ban on charges having an effect equivalent to custom duties.

A. The Prohibition

62. The prohibition of customs duties could easily be circumvented by the Member States if the Treaty allowed them to impose other types of charges on goods entering their territory from or leaving their territory to another Member State. Therefore, the Treaty also prohibits charges which are not custom duties in the proper sense but have the same effect.

63. In Case 24/68 *Commission v. Italy,*[26] the CJEU has given the following definition to a charge having equivalent effect:

> any pecuniary charge, however small and whatever its designation and mode of application, which is imposed unilaterally on domestic or foreign goods by reason of the fact that they cross a frontier, and which is not a customs duty in the strict sense … even if it is not imposed for the benefit of the state, it is not discriminatory or protective in effect and if the product on which the charge is imposed is not in competition with any domestic product.

64. The notion encompasses all charges imposed by reason of the fact that goods cross the border, irrespective of their nature, whether there is a discriminatory effect or not. Pursuant to Article 28(2) TFEU, the prohibition of Article 30 TFEU applies to goods originating in another Member State or in a third country and being put into free circulation in another Member State.

65. The original Treaty provisions contained a standstill provision, providing that no new charges on imports or exports could be introduced between Member States, as well as a proviso for the progressive abolition, during the transitional period, of all existing charges. These now redundant provisions have been repealed by the Treaty of Amsterdam.

66. Article 30 TFEU also applies if the charge has to be paid to a body distinct from the State, where it is imposed by the State.[27]

67. Moreover, the provision applies if the charge is likewise applied to imports from or exports to another part of the Member State in issue.[28]

---

26. Judgment of 1 July 1969, *Commission v. Italy*, 24/68, EU:C:1969:29.
27. Judgment of 1 July 1969, *Sociaal Fonds Diamantarbeiders*, 2/69 and 3/69, EU:C:1969:30; Judgment of 7 July 1994, *Lemaire v. NDALTP,* C-130/93, EU:C:1994 (concerning a charge to exports).
28. Judgment of 14 September 1995, *Maria Simitzi v. Dimos Kos*, C- 485/93 and C-486/93, EU:C:1995:281; Judgment of 9 September 2004, *Carbonati Apuani*, C-72/03, EU:C:2004:506.

B. 'Exceptions'

68. The Treaty does not contain any exceptions to the prohibition of Article 30 TFEU. In its case law, the CJEU has however identified three situations in which the prohibition does not apply. These are not really exceptions, but rather situations where the charge imposed on imported or exported goods cannot really be considered as a charge that is imposed unilaterally by a Member State on goods imported from elsewhere in the Union or on goods exported from that Member State to other Member States.

First, Article 30 TFEU does not apply to a charge which constitutes the remuneration of a service rendered to the importer or exporter.[29] This exception is strictly interpreted. If a charge is in essence the remuneration of a real service provided (to the importer or exporter) but (obviously) exceeds the actual value of the service, the amount in excess of the value will be qualified as a charge having equivalent effect.

Second, Article 30 TFEU does not oppose to charges related to inspections required by Union law, provided that they do not exceed the actual cost of the inspection for which they were charged.[30] These charges are not 'unilaterally' imposed by Member States, but rather the consequence of an obligation imposed by Union law. Such inspections are common in the veterinary field, e.g., a duty to inspect animals before they are exported.

Third, charges falling within the scope of internal taxation (*see* hereinafter) do not fall within the scope of Article 30 TFEU, but Article 110 TFEU, which prohibits discriminatory or protective measures, fully applies. Both provisions are mutually exclusive. However, if the tax on domestic products is fully compensated or if it is intended exclusively to support activities which specifically benefit the taxed domestic products it is nevertheless considered a charge having equivalent effect to a customs duty.[31]

IV. Internal Taxation

69. Included in a totally different chapter (on tax provisions), Article 110 TFEU is closely linked to Article 30 TFEU. It reads:

'No Member State shall impose, directly or indirectly, on the products of other Member States any internal taxation of any kind in excess of that imposed directly or indirectly on similar domestic products' (Article 110, (1)).

Moreover, 'no Member State shall impose on the products of other Member States any internal taxation of such a nature as to afford indirect protection to other products' (Article 110, (2)).

---

29. *See*, e.g., Judgment of 12 January 1983, *Donner*, 39/82, EU:C:1983:3 (charge for dealing with VAT for imported books by Post Office).
30. Judgment of 25 January 1977, *Bauhuis*, Case 46/76, EU:C:1977:6.
31. Judgment of 19 June 1973, *Capolongo v. Maya*, Case 77/72, EU:C:1973:65.

70. As with regard to Article 30 TFEU, it should be observed that this article also applies to goods that do not originate in another Member State, but which have been put into free circulation there.[32]

71. Although Article 110 TFEU only refers to imports, the CJEU held that it also applies to exports.[33]

72. Article 110 TFEU only applies to indirect taxes, such as value added tax (VAT) and excise duties. 'Internal taxation' in this article means any 'charge falling within a general system applying systematically to domestic and imported products according to the same criteria'.[34]

73. The first paragraph of Article 110 TFEU prohibits discriminatory internal taxation, and the second paragraph provides that internal taxation cannot give indirect protection to domestic goods. In *Commission v. France*,[35] the CJEU explained the relationship between the two paragraphs. Article 110(1) TFEU is based on a comparison of the tax burdens imposed on domestic products and on imported products which may be classified as 'similar', whilst the function of Article 110(2) TFEU is to cover, in addition, all forms of indirect tax protection in the case of products which, without being similar within the meaning of the first paragraph, are nevertheless in, even partial, indirect or potential, competition with certain products of the importing country.[36] It is sufficient to determine whether Article 110 TFEU, taken as a whole, may apply, i.e., whether the application of a given national tax system is discriminatory or, as the case may be, protective, in other words, whether there is a difference in the rate or the detailed rules for levying the tax and whether that difference is likely to favour a given domestic production. The case related to differential taxation (excise duties) for mainly domestically produced spirits obtained from wine and fruit on the one hand and, mainly imported, other types of spirits, such as whisky, on the other.

74. Taxes on goods that are generally higher for imported goods than for goods that are generally produced domestically can however be justified where the differentiation is based on objective criteria, such as the conditions of production and the raw materials used, or if they constitute a legitimate choice of economic policy to which effect is given by fiscal means.[37]

---

32. Judgment of 7 May 1987, *Cooperativa Co-Frutta*, 193/85, EU:C:1987:210.
33. Judgment of 29 June 1978, *Statens Kontrol v. Larsen*, 142/77, EU:C:1978:144; Judgment of 23 April 2002, *Niels Nygard v. Svineafgiftsfonden*, C-234/99, EU:C:2002:244.
34. Judgment of 19 June 1973, *Capolongo v. Maya*, 77/72, EU:C:1973:65.
35. Judgment of 27 February 1980, *Commission v. France*, 168/78, EU:C:1980:51.
36. *Ibid.*, para. 6.
37. Judgment of 14 January 1981, *Vinal v. Orbat*, 46/80, EU:C:1981:4, para. 12.

75. Article 110 TFEU does not apply if there is no similar or competing domestic production. However, if the tax does not fall under the definition of internal taxation, it may constitute a charge having equivalent effect within the meaning of Article 30 TFEU.[38] The two provisions are mutually exclusive; they cannot be applied together to the same measure.[39]

V. Reimbursement

76. Where economic operators have paid duties, charges or taxes that are found (by the Court of Justice) to violate the above-mentioned Treaty provisions, they can, under certain conditions, claim the reimbursement of the amounts unduly paid. There is a whole line of case law to that effect. In its recent Judgment in *Petrotel-Lukoil*[40] the Court of Justice summarizes this case law as follows:

> A Member State is in principle required to repay taxes levied in breach of EU law, in accordance with national procedural rules in accordance with the principles of equivalence (i.e. rules that are not less advantageous for the claimant than for breaches of national law) and effectiveness (i.e. rules that guarantee an effective reimbursement). However by way of exception to the principle of reimbursement of taxes incompatible with European Union law, repayment of a tax wrongly paid can be refused where it would entail unjust enrichment of the persons concerned. The protection of the rights so guaranteed by the legal order of the European Union does not require repayment of taxes, of charges and of duties levied in breach of European Union law where it is established that the person required to pay such charges has actually passed them on to other persons., In such circumstances, the burden of the charge levied but not due has been borne not by the trader, but by the purchaser to whom the cost has been passed on. Therefore, to repay the trader the amount of the charge already received from the purchaser would be tantamount to paying him twice over, which may be described as unjust enrichment, whilst in no way remedying the consequences for the purchaser of the illegality of the charge (see, to that effect, judgment of 14 January 1997, Comateb and Others, C-192/95 to C-218/95, EU:C:1997:12, paragraph 22, and of 6 September 2011, Lady & Kid and Others, C-398/09, EU:C:2011:540, paragraph 19).
> Where he charge provided for in that article is discriminatory internal taxation contrary to Article 110 TFEU that right to reimbursement covers the difference between the burden of the charge borne by the products placed on the EU market and the burden of the charge borne by domestic products, the latter charge taking due account of the advantage which those products would have received on an exclusive basis.

---

38. Judgment of 17 June 2003, *De Danske Bilimportører*, C-383/01, EU:C:2003:352.
39. *Ibid.*
40. Judgment of 1 March 2018, *Petrotel-Lukoil*, C-76/17, EU:C:2018:139.

§3. NON-TARIFF BARRIERS: QUANTITATIVE RESTRICTIONS ON IMPORTS AND EXPORTS AND MEASURES HAVING EQUIVALENT EFFECT: GENERAL REMARKS

I. Introduction

77. Whereas Article 30 TFEU deals with tariff barriers by banning customs duties between Member States and charges having equivalent effect, Articles 34–37 TFEU deal with non-tariff barriers. Article 34 TFEU prohibits quantitative import restrictions and measures having equivalent effect; Article 35 TFEU prohibits quantitative export restriction and measures having equivalent effect; Article 36 TFEU contains a common exhaustive list of grounds of justification for quantitative import, export and transit restrictions and measures having equivalent effect. Finally, Article 37 TFEU instructs Member States to adjust the existing commercial monopolies so as to eliminate discrimination.

These prohibitions have direct effect since the end of the transitional period, that is, 1 January 1970 for the original Member States.[41]

II. Quantitative Restrictions

78. With the entry into force of the EEC Treaty in 1958, quota had already largely been abolished within the framework of the Organisation for Economic Co-operation and Development (OECD). For industrial products, the last quantitative restrictions within the EEC were abolished on 31 December 1961.[42]

III. Measures Having Equivalent Effect

79. As will be shown hereafter, the prohibitions in Articles 34 and 35 TFEU, although worded exactly the same way, have been interpreted quite differently by the CJEU. They will therefore be discussed separately (§§ 4 and 5 hereafter). A last paragraph (§6) will be devoted to Article 37 TFEU, which deals with State monopolies.

---

41. For Art. 34 TFEU, *see* Judgment of 22 March 1977, in *Ianelli & Volpi*, 74/76, EU:C:1977:51; for Art. 35 TFEU, Judgment of 29 November 1978, *Pigs Marketing Board v. Redmond*, 83/78, EU:C:1978:214; and of 9 January 1992, *Delhaize Le Lion v. Promalvin*, C-47/90, EU:C:1992:250; for Art. 37 TFEU, *see* Judgment of 3 February 1976, in *Pubblico Ministero v. Manghera et al.*, 59/75, EU:C:1976:14.
42. Council Decision of 12 May 1960, *OJ* L 60, 12.9.1960, p. 1217.

§4. Measures Having an Effect Equivalent to Quantitative Import Restrictions (Articles 34 and 36 TFEU)

I. The Notion

80. At the end of the transitional period, the Commission issued directives on the implementation of what are now Articles 34 and 35 TFEU. A directive which was particularly relevant is Directive 70/50.[43] In short, this Directive stated that while provisions and administrative practices which do not specifically affect imports (or exports) do not in principle amount to measures having equivalent effect, they may nevertheless be caught by these provisions. The Directive gives examples of 'equally applicable' measures that may nevertheless be considered contrary to the Treaty because they make imports either more difficult or expensive than the sale of domestic products.[44]

Today the significance of the Directive – and especially of the examples of equally applicable measures it gives – is merely historical, but the case law of the CJEU has endorsed the view expressed in the Directive that equally applicable measures – i.e., measures applying in the same manner to imported goods and domestic goods – may nevertheless be incompatible with Article 34 TFEU.

81. In its *Dassonville*[45] landmark judgment on Article 34 TFEU (then Article 30 EEC), the Court of Justice gave a particularly wide definition of 'measures having equivalent effect', mentioned in Article 34 TFEU. It ruled that 'all trading rules enacted by Member States which are capable of hindering, actually or potentially, directly or indirectly, intra-Community trade, are to be considered as measures having an effect equivalent to quantitative restrictions'.[46]

82. While in *Dassonville* the Court did not define the concept of 'trading rules', it appears from later judgments that the concept is very broad indeed, encompassing not only rules relating to the composition, characteristics and presentation of products, but also requirements in the field of marketing, sales methods and advertising. A good example is *GB-INNO-BM v. CCL*,[47] in which the Court found that a prohibition under Luxembourg law for retailers to announce price reductions by comparing the reduced price with the former price and mentioning the period of validity of the offer at reduced price was contrary to Article 34 TFEU. Another illustration is given in *Buet*,[48] where a French law prohibiting the sale of educational material at the doorstep was found to be, an albeit justified, measure having equivalent effect. Indeed, already in *Dassonville* the Court conceded that Member States

---

43. *OJ* English Special Edition 1970(I), p. 17.
44. For example measures which lay down less favourable prices for imported products than for domestic products; measures which lower the value of an imported product, in particular by causing a reduction in its intrinsic value, or increase its costs; measures which prohibit or limit publicity in respect of imported products only, or totally or partially confine publicity to domestic products only.
45. Judgment of 11 July 1974, *Dassonville*, 8/74, EU:C:1974:82.
46. *Dassonville*, para. 5.
47. Judgment of 7 March 1990, *GB-INNO-BM v. CCL*, 362/88, EU:C:1990:102.
48. Judgment of 16 May 1989, *Buet v. Ministère Public*, 382/87, EU:1989:198.

are allowed to impose reasonable measures that hinder intra-Union trade. In that judgment, the Court did not give any criteria to determine whether a measure is reasonable or not. These criteria were set in a judgment of 1979, known as '*Cassis de Dijon*'.[49] Moreover, in later judgments not only advertising rules and rules on sales methods were found to come under the scope of Article 34 TFEU, but also rules on the circumstances in which goods can be sold, e.g., rules on opening hours for shops (like Sunday trading rules), where they were capable to affect trade with imported goods,[50] although again these measures of equivalent effect were found to be justified. The seminal judgment in *Keck & Mithouard*[51] has put an end to the automatic applicability of Article 34 TFEU to national provisions on so-called selling arrangements (rules on advertising, sales promotions and other rules on the circumstances in which goods can be sold, rather than rules affecting the marketing of the good as such, such as rules on composition or labelling). Finally, in its judgment in *Mickelsson & Roos*[52] of 2009 the CJEU has recognized the existence of a residual category of measures (being neither product-related nor selling arrangements) that fall within the scope of Article 34 TFEU if they affect 'access to the market' of goods coming from other Member States.[53]

Cassis de Dijon, Keck & Mithouard and *Mickelsson & Roos* will be discussed in more detail hereafter (*see* section IV).

II. Article 34 TFEU Only Applies to State Measures (and Measures of the Union)

83. Whereas the CJEU has conferred horizontal direct effect on the provisions relating to free movement of persons – in particular the prohibition of discrimination on the basis of nationality in Article 45 TFEU (free movement of workers), which therefore also applies to private employers vis-à-vis employees – there is no suggestion in the case law that Article 34 TFEU would apply to the conduct of non-State bodies.[54]

84. However, Article 34 TFEU also applies to measures taken by private bodies entrusted by law with public authority, like the Royal Pharmaceutical Society in the UK, which fixes the rules of conduct which are binding on all the members of the profession.[55] The same holds true for standardization and certification activities of a private-law body, where the national legislation considers the products certified by that body to be compliant with national law and that has the effect of restricting

---

49. Judgment of 20 February 1979, *Rewe Bundesmonopolamt für Branntwein ('Cassis de Dijon'),* C-120/78, EU:C:1979:42.
50. *See,* e.g., Judgment of 16 December 1992, *Council of the City of Stoke-on-Trent, Norwich City Council v. B & Q Plc,* C-69/91, EU:C:1992:519.
51. Judgment of 24 November 1993, *Keck & Mithouard,* C-267/91 and C-268/91, EU:C:1993:905.
52. Judgment of 4 June 2009, *Mickelsson & Roos,* C-142/05, EU:C:2009:336.
53. *Ibid.,* para. 28.
54. There have, however, been calls for the direct applicability of Art. 34 TFEU. *See,* e.g., Opinion of A.G. Trstenjak in the Judgment in *Fra.bo SpA,* C-171/11, EU:C:2012:176.
55. Judgment of 18 May 1988, *Regina v. Royal Pharmaceutical Society,* 266/87, EU:1989:2005.

the marketing of products which are not certified by that body.[56] Likewise, Articles 34 and 36 TFEU apply to private parties who rely on IPR where such reliance is likely to affect imports.[57] IPR are indeed rights conferred on individuals by the State.

85. On the other hand, on the basis of the principle of sincere cooperation (Article 4(3) TEU) Member States shall prevent private persons from restricting the free movement of goods.[58] In *Schmidberger*,[59] concerning obstruction of an important motorway in Austria for several days by environmental non-governmental organizations (NGOs), the Court reiterated that principle but accepted the argument put forward by Austria that the obstacle was justified by imperative reasons of general interest (*see* the 'rule of reason' discussed hereafter), namely the freedom of expression. The Court found that the nuisance caused by the action of the environmentalists was not disproportionate to the objective of expressing their opposition against the heavy traffic in a vulnerable region.[60]

86. Finally, the CJEU has recognized that Article 34 TFEU does not only apply to measures of the Member States but also to measures adopted by Union institutions.[61]

III. The Limited List of Grounds of Justification in Article 36 TFEU

87. According to Article 36 TFEU quantitative import (and export) restrictions and measures having equivalent effect can be justified for reasons of public morality, public policy or public security; the protection of health and life of humans, animals or plants; the protection of national treasures possessing artistic, historic or archaeological value; or the protection of industrial and commercial property. Such prohibitions or restrictions shall not, however, constitute a means of arbitrary discrimination or a disguised restriction on trade between Member States.

---

56. Judgment of 12 July 2012, *Fra.bo*, C-171/11, EU:C:2012:453.
57. *See* case law discussed hereafter, paras 97 et seq.
58. Judgment of 9 December 1997, *Commission v. France*, C-265/95, EU:C:1997:595.
59. Judgment of 12 June 2003, *Schmidberger*, C-112/00, EU:C:2000:333.
60. *Schmidberger*, para. 93.
61. *See*, e.g., Judgment of 12 July 2005, *Alliance for Natural Health and Others*, C-154/04 and C-155/04, EU:C:2005:449.

A. *The Justifications Listed in Article 36 TFEU*

1. Public Morality

88. The public morality exception has been applied to State restrictions prohibiting pornography or sex aids or regulating its sale.[62] There are no recent cases on this ground.

2. Public Policy

89. Public policy plays an important role as a ground of justification for restrictions to the free movement of persons, but not with regard to the free movement of goods.

3. Public Security

90. The leading case is *Campus Oil,*[63] in which the CJEU ruled that a Member State (in this case Ireland) which is totally or almost totally dependent on imports for its supplies of petroleum products may rely on grounds of public security within the meaning of Article 36 of the EEC Treaty (now Article 36 TFEU) for the purpose of requiring importers to cover a certain proportion of their needs by purchases from a refinery situated in its territory at prices fixed by the competent minister on the basis of the costs incurred in the operation of that refinery, if the production of the refinery cannot be freely disposed of at competitive prices on the market concerned.[64]

91. The quantities of petroleum products covered by such a system must not exceed the minimum supply requirement without which the public security of the State concerned would be affected or the level of production necessary to keep the refinery's production capacity available in the event of a crisis and to enable it to continue to refine at all times the crude oil for the supply of which the State concerned has entered into long-term contracts.

92. In contrast, and more recently, the Court held in *Commission v. Greece*[65] that by establishing and maintaining a system for the compulsory maintenance of emergency stocks of petroleum products which directly links the facility for marketing companies to transfer their storage obligation to refineries established in Greece to

---

62. Judgment of 11 March 1986, *Conegate Ltd v. H.M. Customs and Excise*, 121/85, EU:C:1986:114 (the seizure of imported sex dolls in the UK was found to be discriminatory since domestic goods of the same nature were freely available).
63. Judgment of 10 July 1984, *Campus Oil et al. v. The Minister for Industry and Energy et al.*, 72/83, EU:C:1984:256.
64. *Ibid.*, para. 51.
65. Judgment of 25 October 2001, C-398/98, *Commission v. Greece,* C-398/98, EU:C:2001:565.

an obligation to obtain their supplies of those products from those refineries, the Hellenic Republic had failed to fulfil its obligations under Article 34 TFEU.[66] The Greek government had only put forward economic arguments to defend the measure. Hence, unlike in *Campus Oil* recourse to Article 36 TFEU was of no avail.

4. The Protection of Health and Life of Humans

93. The need to protect the health and life of humans has played a tremendous role in the area of foodstuffs, medicines and safety regulations. In these areas, the Union has progressively enacted legislation harmonizing national laws, rendering the case law accepting restrictions for the importation of these goods on the basis of Article 36 TFEU less relevant. It should be noted that the Court has consistently held that the discretion of the Member States to decide on the level of public health is particularly wide where it is shown that uncertainties continue to exist in the current state of scientific research.[67]

94. The public health exception of Article 36 TFEU has also been accepted with regard to distribution methods of medicines. In *Deutscher Apothekerverband*,[68] the Court held that Article 36 TFEU may be relied on to justify a national prohibition on the sale by mail order of medicinal products which may be sold only in pharmacies in the Member State concerned (Germany) insofar as the prohibition covers medicinal products subject to prescription.[69] However, that provision cannot be relied on to justify an absolute prohibition on the sale by mail order of medicinal products which are not subject to prescription in that Member State.[70] Important considerations are that it is not impossible that also in the context of sales by mail order adequate information and advice may be provided, and that internet buying may have certain advantages, such as having the time to think about the questions to ask the pharmacists.[71]

5. The Protection of Health and Life of Animals

95. With regard to the need to protect the health and life of animals, it should be noted that in the context of animals used for human consumption and test animals the Union has largely harmonized national rules which relate to animal health and well-being.[72] Hence in *Gunnar Nilsson*,[73] the CJEU held that it followed from the

---

66. *Ibid.*, para. 32.
67. Member States can invoke the precautionary principle, but the measures have to be proportionate, *see*, e.g., Judgment of 23 September 2003, *Commission v. Denmark*, C-192/01, EU:C:2003:492.
68. Judgment of 11 December 2003, *Deutscher Apothekerverband v. DocMorris,* C-322/01, EU:C:2013:664.
69. *Deutscher Apothekerverband*, para. 124.
70. *Ibid.*, paras 112–116.
71. *Ibid.*, para. 113.
72. *See*, e.g., Council Directive 87/328/EEC of 18 June 1987 on the acceptance for breeding purposes of pure-bred breeding animals of the bovine species, *OJ* L 167, 26.6.1987, p. 54.

full harmonization of the zoötechnical and pedigree conditions relating to intra-Union trade in bovine semen that a Member State (here: Sweden) may not obstruct the use in its territory of the semen of pure-bred bulls (Belgian Blue) where they have been accepted for artificial insemination in another Member State on the basis of tests carried out in accordance with Union law.[74] The characteristics mentioned by the Swedish national authorities are likely to entail suffering for bovine animals of the Belgian Blue breed or to affect their behaviour are inherent in their genetic heritage. In particular, it is the specific muscular hypertrophy gene which produces a muscular mass which is large in comparison to the animal's internal organs or bones and results in the more frequent use of Caesarean sections in calving. These characteristics were taken into consideration when the genetic value of the Belgian Blue breed was assessed in accordance with the method laid down in the relevant Union instrument. Sweden was therefore not allowed to obstruct the use of semen of bulls of the Belgian Blue breed on grounds of animal protection.

96. A judgment in the same vein is *Compassion in World Farming*[75] where the CJEU was asked whether the UK could impose, as was contended by the animal welfare organization Compassion in World Farming, a ban on the exportation of calves to another Member State in order to prevent these animals from being treated badly (rearing in veal crates). Again, harmonization at the EU level prevented the UK to ban exportation on the basis of more animal-friendly national rules.[76]

6. The Protection of National Treasures Possessing Artistic, Historic or Archaeological Value

97. Obviously, the exception for the protection of national treasures possessing artistic, historic or archaeological value is more relevant in the context of exports (Article 35 TFEU). What is meant by a 'national treasure' is open to interpretation, but Directive 2014/60/EU[77] on the return of objects unlawfully removed from the territory of a Member State mentions that this could include items listed in the inventories of museums, books and pictures, paintings and sculptures.

---

73. Judgment of 19 November 1998, *Gunnar Nilsson*, C-162/97, EU:C:1998:554.
74. *Gunnar Nilsson*, para. 51.
75. Judgment of 19 March 1998, *Compassion in World Farming*, C-1/96, EU:C:1998:113.
76. *Ibid.*, para. 47.
77. Directive 2014/60/EU of the European Parliament and of the Council of 15 May 2014 on the return of cultural objects unlawfully removed from the territory of a Member State and amending Regulation (EU) No 1024/2012, *OJ* L 159, 28.5.2014, p. 1.

7.   The Protection of Industrial and Commercial Property

98.   Industrial property, the old term for IPR, includes patents, trade marks, designs and models, and copyright[78] and neighbouring rights. Designations of origin qualify as commercial property.[79] In constant case law, the Court has made a distinction between the *existence* of an IPR (which is not affected by the rules on free movement unless there is an element of discrimination in the national rules[80]) and its *exercise*, which has to be consistent with *inter alia* Articles 34–36 TFEU, meaning that not every exercise of an IPR benefits from the exception laid down in Article 36 TFEU. The key criterion to decide whether a right holder can rely on his right to restrict trade (e.g., importation in a given Member Sate from another) is whether he has given his consent for the marketing of the good in the EU. Once consent has been given, the IPR is exhausted, meaning that the holder can no longer exercise his right to stop further sales in the EU, relying on national law which would grant him that right (national exhaustion). To a large extent, this case law has become irrelevant: Union law in the area of copyright and trade mark law now provides for Union exhaustion not only of IPR that have a Union dimension (such as the Community trade mark) but also of national IPR.[81] The jurisprudence remains relevant for those IPR that are not harmonized at the EU level, notably patents, and for trade marks where a third party has interfered with the goods (*see* hereafter).

99.   That case law has been established since *Centrafarm v. Sterling Drug*,[82] where the Court decided that the holder of parallel patents for two Member States could not rely on his patent to block importation in one Member Sate (the Netherlands) of a medicine which a parallel importer had bought in another Member State (the UK) where the medicine was cheaper and imported in the first Member State, while the medicine was marketed by the holder in the two Member States (under parallel national patents).

100.   In later judgments, the CJEU had to deal with goods that had been marketed in the exporting Member State by the right holder but were subsequently altered (e.g., repackaged) by a parallel importer while importing the goods into the territory of another Member State. The *Boehringer Ingelheim* judgment,[83] handed down after the entry into force of the first Trade Mark Directive, summarizes this jurisprudence. First, a trade mark proprietor may rely on its trade mark rights in order to prevent a parallel importer from repackaging pharmaceutical products unless the exercise of those rights contributes to artificial partitioning of the markets between Member States. Second, replacement packaging of pharmaceutical products is objectively necessary within the meaning of the Court's case law if,

---

78. Judgment of 8 June 1971, *Deutsche Grammophongesellschaft*, 78/70, EU:C:1971:59.
79. Judgment of 9 June 1990, *Delhaize v. Promalvin*, C-47/90, EU:C:1992:250.
80. Judgment of 18 February 1992, *Commission v. Italy*, Case C-235/89, EU:C:1992:73, paras 13–14.
81. *See* Art. 15 Trade Marks Directive 2015/2430.
82. Judgment of 31 October 1974, *Centrafarm v. Sterling Drug*, 15/74, EU:C:1974:114.
83. Judgment of 23 April 2002, *Boehringer Ingelheim*, C-143/00, EU:C:2002:246.

without such repackaging, effective access to the market concerned, or to a substantial part of that market, must be considered to be hindered as the result of strong resistance from a significant proportion of consumers to relabelled pharmaceutical products.[84] Third, a parallel importer must, in any event, in order to be entitled to repackage trade-marked pharmaceutical products, fulfil the requirement of prior notice.[85] If he fails to satisfy that requirement, the trade mark proprietor may oppose the marketing of the repackaged pharmaceutical product. Furthermore, it is incumbent on the parallel importer himself to give notice to the trade mark proprietor of the intended repackaging. In the event of dispute, it is for the national court to assess, in the light of all the relevant circumstances, whether the proprietor had a reasonable time to react to the intended repackaging.[86] In *Wellcome v. Paranova*,[87] the Court clarified that where it is established that repackaging of the pharmaceutical product is necessary for further marketing in the Member State of importation, the presentation of the packaging should be assessed only against the condition that it should not be such as to be liable to damage the reputation of the trade mark or that of its proprietor.[88] It is for the parallel importer to furnish to the proprietor of the trade mark the information which is necessary and sufficient to enable the latter to determine whether the repackaging of the product under that trade mark is necessary in order to market it in the Member State of importation.[89]

B. Article 36 TFEU, Second Sentence: No Arbitrary Discrimination or a Disguised Restriction of Trade

101. Arbitrary discrimination actually means discrimination, i.e., an equal treatment that is not objectively justified. A measure that treats goods originating in a particular Member State differently (an import ban) can be justified, e.g., for reasons of public health. In that case, the measure discriminates formally, but not arbitrarily, because it is objectively justified. A disguised restriction of trade means that although the restriction can be justified, for instance for the protection of public health, its real goal is to protect local industry.[90]

---

84. *Ibid.*, para. 52.
85. *Ibid.*, para. 61.
86. *Ibid.* para. 67.
87. Judgment of 22 December 2008, *Wellcome v. Paranova*, C-276/05, EU:C:2008:756.
88. *Ibid.*, para. 30.
89. *Ibid.*, para. 37.
90. *See*, e.g., Judgment of 15 July 1982, *Commission v. United Kingdom*, Case 40/82, EU:C:1984:33 (disguised restriction: 'Newcastle disease').

IV. The 'Rule of Reason' or 'Mandatory Requirements' Case Law

A. 'Dassonville' *and* 'Cassis de Dijon'

102. In its landmark judgment *Dassonville*,[91] the Court of Justice gave a very broad definition of the notion measures having an effect equivalent to import restrictions: 'all trading rules enacted by Member States which are capable of hindering, actually or potentially, directly or indirectly, intra-Community trade, are to be considered as measures having an effect equivalent to quantitative restrictions'. As already indicated above, the term 'trading rules' covers a wide variety of regulations.[92]

103. Measures that fall within its scope are prohibited unless they can benefit from an exception. Article 36 TFEU discussed above contains an exhaustive list of grounds of justification. Consumer protection and environmental protection, just to name a few, are not mentioned in that provision.

104. However the Court developed a so-called rule of reason, to the effect that Article 34 TFEU does not apply to national 'trading rules' that are equally applicable to imported and domestic goods, provided they are necessary for the attainment of an objective of general interest.

105. Already in *Dassonville*, the Court accepted that Member States can take 'reasonable restrictions' to protect consumers.[93] In *Cassis de Dijon*[94] the Court held, in the line of *Dassonville*, that 'in the absence of common rules obstacles to movement within the Community resulting from disparities between the national laws relating to the marketing of the products in question must be accepted in so far as those provisions may be recognized as being necessary in order to satisfy mandatory requirements relating in particular to the effectiveness of fiscal supervision, the protection of public health, the fairness of commercial transactions and the defense of the consumer'.[95]

106. It is obvious from this judgment that the rule of reason, i.e., the possibility to justify obstacles to imports on other grounds than those mentioned in Article 36 TFEU, requires the fulfilment of four conditions that will be discussed in the following paragraphs.

---

91. Judgment of 11 July 1974, *Dassonville,* 8/74, EU:C:1974:82.
92. *See* para. 80 above.
93. *Dassonville,* para. 6.
94. Judgment of 20 February 1979, in *Rewe Zentral v. Bundesmonopolverwaltung für Branntwein* (Cassis de Dijon), 120/78, EU:C:1979:42.
95. *Ibid.,* para. 8.

1. Absence of Union Law Rules

107. Where the matter has been fully harmonized at EU level, such as, today, business-to-consumer (B2C) unfair commercial practices, the rule of reason does no longer apply and the legality of import restrictions has to be appraised solely in the light of the relevant regulation or directive.[96]

2. The Obstacle Results from Disparities

108. The obstacle to free movement must be due to differences in legislation between Member States and cannot result from an unequal treatment by the importing Member State. Where imported goods are subject to different rules than those applicable to domestic goods the rule of reason cannot be invoked. In other words, only measures that apply equally ('without distinction') to domestic and imported goods are eligible. Yet, measures that do not satisfy this condition can possibly be justified under Article 36 TFEU (*see* above). Examples in case law where this condition was not fulfilled are the '*Buy Irish*' case[97] (a campaign sponsored by the Irish authorities to buy Irish goods) and the '*Irish souvenirs*' case[98] (a legal requirement for souvenirs sold in Ireland that were not domestically manufactured to be labelled 'foreign').

3. The Measure Is Necessary in Order to Satisfy *Mandatory Requirements in the General Interest*

109. In *Cassis de Dijon*, the Court mentioned fiscal supervision, consumer protection and fairness in commercial transactions as examples, but the list of general interest objectives that are acceptable has been gradually extended in consecutive cases. Other examples are the protection of the environment,[99] cultural policy objectives,[100] safeguarding the freedom of expression,[101] social, cultural, religious and philosophical values of society, and the maintenance of press diversity.[102] The Court has consistently held that objectives of a purely economic nature cannot amount to a mandatory requirement in the general interest.[103]

---

96. *See*, e.g., Judgment of 12 October 1993, *Vanacker and Lesage*, C-37/92, EU:C:1993:836, para. 9.
97. Judgment of 26 February 1981, *Commission v. Ireland*, 249/81, EU:C:1982:402.
98. Judgment of 17 June 1981, *Commission v. Ireland*, 113/80, EU:C:1981:139.
99. Judgment of 26 September 1988, *Commission v. Denmark*, 302/86, EU:C:1988:421 (containers for beer and soft drinks).
100. Judgment of 11 July 1985, *See Cinéthèque c. Fédération des cinémas français*, 60 and 61/84, EU:C:1985:329.
101. Judgment of 25 March 2004, *Karner v. Troostwijk,* C-71/02, EU:C:2004:181.
102. Judgment of 26 June 1997, *Vereinigte Familiapress v. Heinrich Bauer*, C-368/95, EU:C:1997:325.
103. *See*, e.g., Judgment of 10 July 1984, *Campus Oil et al. v. The Minister for Industry and Energy et al.*, 72/83, EU:C:1984:256, para. 35; Judgment of 28 April 1998, *Decker*, C-120/95, EU:C:1998:167, para. 39; Judgment of 30 January 2000, *TK-Heimdienst*, C-254/98, EU:C:2000:12, para. 33.

4.   The Measure Must Be Necessary to Attain the Objective

110. In order to be justified the measure must be necessary, i.e., appropriate (suitable) to attain the stated objective and it must be proportionate to that objective.

111. Under the appropriateness or suitability test the Court verifies whether the means employed are appropriate to attain the ends.

112. The necessity requirement also implies that the same result cannot be achieved with a less restrictive measure (proportionality). The Court has consistently held that a product ban cannot be justified to protect the economic interests of consumers when the same result can be achieved, e.g., with labelling requirements.[104] The first example thereof was already given in *Cassis de Dijon* itself. The German administration opposed to the importation into Germany of the French liquor made from black current because it did not attain the minimum alcohol level (32°) required by German law. Before the Court of Justice, the German government defended the rule by referring to the interests of consumers not to be misled. Indeed, so it was contended, the German consumer expects a fruit liquor to satisfy the minimum requirement. The Court did not accept this reasoning and found that deception of the consumer could be attained by a less restrictive measure: adequate labelling of the alcohol content. Another 'cas célèbre' is the '*Reinheitsgebot*' (or purity law for beer) case, *Commission v. Germany* rendered in 1987,[105] where the Court refuted Germany's argument that the purity law (prohibition of other ingredients in beer than those that correspond to an old German tradition) was necessary to protect consumers against being misled about the quality of the product. Again, adequate labelling requirements could have solved that issue.

113. The necessity test plays a key role in this case law. Other telling examples are the judgments in *Rau v. De Smedt*[106] (compulsory cubical form of margarine package is disproportionate to protect consumers against being induced to believe that it is butter) and *Buet*[107] (a ban on doorstep selling of educational material is proportionate to protect consumers who, in case of such material, are generally particularly vulnerable).

B.   *The Hesitations in the Case Law after* Cassis de Dijon

114. The very broad concept of measures having equivalent effect in Article 34 TFEU led to a flood of case law on a great variety of national regulations, including

---

104. *See*, e.g., Judgments of 26 June 1980, *Criminal Proceedings Against Herbert Gilli and Paul Andres*, 788/79, EU:C:1980:171, paras 7–8; of 23 February 1998, *Commission v. France*, 216/84, EU:C:1988:81, para. 10; of 2 February 1989, *Commission v. Germany (Meat Products)*, 274/87, EU:1989:51, para. 13.
105. Judgment of 12 March 1987, *Commission v. Germany,* 178/84, EU:C:1987:126.
106. Judgment of 10 November 1982, *Rau v. De Smedt*, 261/81, EU:C:1982:382.
107. Judgment of 16 May 1989, *Buet*, 382/87, EU:C:1989:189.

advertising and sales promotions. In *Yves Rocher*,[108] the Court ruled that Article 34 TFEU precluded the application of a provision of the former German Law on Unfair Competition which prohibited a seller established in Germany, for mail order sales by catalogue or sales brochure of goods imported from another Member State, to advertise with a certain form of price comparison.

115.   In other cases the Court avoided to apply Article 34 TFEU to national measures it found to have insufficient internal market relevance. In this regard, one should mention *Krantz*.[109] The case concerned a Dutch legal provision to the effect that a reservation of property by a seller could not be invoked against the tax receiver. It was argued before the Court that such a rule could deter a seller established in another Member State from selling to a company in the Netherlands. The Court however observed that 'the national provision referred to by the national court applies without distinction to both domestic and imported goods, and does not seek to control trade with other Member States'[110] and that 'the possibility that nationals of other Member States would hesitate to sell goods on instalment terms to purchasers in the Member State concerned because such goods would be liable to seizure by the collector of taxes if the purchasers failed to discharge their Netherlands tax debts is *too uncertain and indirect* to warrant the conclusion that a national provision authorizing such seizure is liable to hinder trade between Member States [the author stresses]'.[111] This test has also been applied to typical rules of private law, like in *CMC Motorradcenter*.[112] It would seem that the Court takes a reserved approach when confronted with questions of private law.[113] Moreover, the pre-*Keck Krantz* ('too uncertain and too indirect')-test has survived *Keck*, as can be seen in *Corsica Ferries*[114] (an obligation on shipping companies to have recourse to the services of a local mooring company) and *BASF*[115] (on the application of a language provision for patents).

C. Keck & Mithouard

116.   And then came *Keck*. The Court wanted to restrain the scope of Article 34 TFEU. And it did so (short after *Yves Rocher*[116]) in a case concerning another legal provision on sales promotions, namely the French prohibition of resale at a loss. By making a carve out for 'certain selling arrangements' (*see* hereafter), the Court avoided to have to rule on the (probably very problematic) justification of such a

---

108. Judgment of 18 May 1993, *Yves Rocher*, C-126/91, EU:C:1993:191.
109. Judgment of 7 March 1990, *Krantz*, C-69/88, EU:C:1990:583.
110. *Ibid.*, para. 10.
111. *Krantz*, para. 11. The author stresses.
112. Judgment of 13 October 1993, *CMC Motorradcenter*, C-93/92, EU:C:1993:838.
113. *See* J. Stuyck, *The Court of Justice as a Motor or Private Law*, in *The Cambridge Companion to European Union Private Law* 101 et seq. (C. Twigg-Flesner ed., Cambridge University Press 2010).
114. Judgment in *Corsica Ferries*, C-266/96, EU:C:1998:306 at para. 13.
115. Judgment of 12 September 1999, *BASF*, C-44/98, BASF EU:C:1999:440, at para. 16.
116. *See* para. 113 above.

prohibition. Today a prohibition of resale at a loss, at least in B2C relations, comes under the scope of Directive 2005/29/EC[117] that has fully harmonized B2C unfair commercial practices, at least insofar as these provisions aim at the protection of consumers.[118]

117. In *Keck & Mithouard,*[119] the Court partially overruled *Dassonville/Cassis.* In paragraph 16, it held:

> By contrast, contrary to what has previously been decided, the application to products from other Member States of national provisions restricting or prohibiting certain selling arrangements is not such as to hinder directly or indirectly, actually or potentially, trade between Member States, within the meaning of the *Dassonville* judgment, so long as such provisions apply to all relevant traders operating within the national territory and so long as they affect in the same manner, in law and in fact, the marketing of domestic products and of those from other Member States.

118. The Court gave the reasons for this new rule in the next paragraph (17) of the judgment:

> Provided that those conditions are fulfilled, the application of such rules to the sale of products from another Member State meeting the requirements laid down by that state is not by nature such as to prevent their access to the market or to impede access any more than it impedes the access of domestic products, such rules therefore fall outside the scope of [Article 34 TFEU].

119. In *Keck & Mithouard,* the CJEU thus abandoned the strict standard of *Dassonville* and *Cassis de Dijon* for national regulations on 'certain selling arrangements'. Basically, this case law concerns rules on the circumstances (place, time, sales methods, advertising, price regulations,[120] etc.) in which goods are marketed. Henceforth such rules are immune for scrutiny under Article 34 TFEU on import restrictions if, in essence, they do not discriminate in law and in fact between imported goods and domestic goods. At the same time, the Court maintained its *Dassonville/Cassis de Dijon* case law with respect to rules that lay down requirements to be met by goods (designation, form, size, weight, composition, presentation, labelling and packaging).

---

117. Directive 2005/29/EC of the European Parliament and of the Council of 11 May 2005 concerning unfair business-to-consumer commercial practices in the internal market and amending Council Directive 84/450/EEC, Directives 97/7/EC, 98/27/EC and 2002/65/EC of the European Parliament and of the Council and Regulation (EC) No 2006/2004 of the European Parliament and of the Council ('Unfair Commercial Practices Directive'), *OJ* L 149, 11.6.2005, pp. 22–39.
118. *See* Order of 15 December 2011, *Inno v. Unizo,* EU:C:2011:851.
119. Judgment of 24 November 1993, *Keck & Mithouard,* C-267/91 and C-268/91, EU:C:1993:905.
120. *See* Judgment of 30 April 2009, *Fachverband der Buch- und Medienwirtschaft/LIBRO Handelsgesellschaft,* C-531/07, EU:C:2009:276; already in the1970s, in a 'pure' Dassonville and pre-Keck era, the CJEU applied consistently a mere non-discrimination test (and not a broader 'restrictions' test) regarding national price regulations.

D. *The Aftermath of* Keck

120. Increasingly, the Court had to deal with cases that did not fit in the *Cassis/Keck* dichotomy. Examples are commercial monopolies, authorization systems, and conditions under which goods can be used. The case law showed hesitations, but the Court basically stood firm on *Keck*.

121. Cases like *Mars*[121] and *Vereinigte Familiapress*[122] made it clear that it is not so much its nature (e.g., an advertising or sales promotions rule) that qualifies a rule as a selling arrangement, but the fact whether it does, in its application, affect the good itself or not. If it does (e.g., because the labelling of a good is not in conformity with a prohibition on misleading advertising or a rule on sales promotions) it is not a 'selling arrangement', but a requirement to be met by the goods within the meaning of *Cassis*.

122. Other judgments, like *Gourmet,*[123] stressed the importance of the second condition for application of the *Keck* 'immunity', namely that the measure does not discriminate in law or *in fact* imported goods. Since the consumption of alcohol is linked to traditional social practices and local habits, the Swedish ban on magazine advertising for alcohol was found to have a greater negative impact on the marketing of imported alcohol than on the marketing of domestic alcohol and therefore to impede access to the Swedish market of foreign alcohol.[124]

123. Interestingly, in order to determine whether a rule on selling arrangements, in particular in cases concerning advertising restrictions, falls outside the scope of Article 34 TFEU, the Court refers, since *De Agostini,*[125] to paragraph 17 of *Keck*. It examines whether a measure is not by nature such as to *prevent the access* of goods originating in other Member States *to the market* or to *impede access any more* than it impedes the access of domestic products. This formula contains two alternatives, the latter being a non-discrimination test, the former referring to an impediment to market access for imported goods, without any comparison with the fate of domestic goods.[126] This can be seen as the seed for the new case law developed in 2009, discussed hereafter.

124. Finally it should be stressed that although natural provisions on B2C advertising and sales promotions have been qualified as 'selling arrangements' that can

---

121. Judgment of 6 July 1995, *Mars,* C-470/93, EU:C:1995:224.
122. Judgment of 26 June 1997, *Vereinigte Familiapress* 368/95, EU:C:1997:325.
123. Judgment of 8 March 2001, *Gourmet,* C-405/98, EU:C:2001:135; *see* J. Stuyck, 'Gourmet une nouvelle brèche dans la jurisprudence "Keck"?' in *CDE,* 2011, 683 et seq.
124. *Gourmet,* C-405/98, para. 21.
125. Judgment of 9 July 1997, *de Agostini,* C-34/95, EU:C:1997:344.
126. *See* P. Oliver, *Oliver on Free Movement of Goods in the European Union* (Hart, Oxford, 2010).

benefit from the *Keck* 'immunity', for this type of rules *Keck* is not relevant anymore since they have been fully harmonized by Directive 2005/29 on B2C unfair commercial practices, at least insofar as these provisions aim at the protection of consumers.[127]

E. *Mickelsson & Roos*

125. Eventually, being confronted constantly with rules that were neither product-related (requirements to be met by goods), within the meaning of *Cassis de Dijon*, nor selling arrangements, within the meaning of *Keck & Mithouard*, the Court developed its new case law as expressed for the first time in *Commission v. Italy*[128] (hereafter 'Italian Trailers'), soon followed by *Mickelsson and Roos*.[129] The first case concerned a prohibition in Italy to use trailers for motorcycles (for road safety reasons); the second a ban on the use of jet-skis on public waterways in Sweden, except those waterways specifically designated by the authorities (basically for environmental reasons), which amounted at the time of the reference to a (quasi) absolute impossibility to use these engines in the country. In *Italian Trailers*, A.G. Léger proposed a strict *Cassis* approach. In *Mickelsson*, A.G. Kokott suggested to decide the case on the basis of *Keck* (in view of the similarity of the kind of regulation in issue with selling arrangements), but stressed the access to the market aspect.

126. In paragraph 24 of *Mickelsson and Roos* the Court said:

> It must be born in mind that measures taken by a Member State, the aim or effect of which is to treat goods coming from other Member States less favourably and, in the absence of harmonization of national legislation, obstacles to the free movement of goods which are the consequence of applying, to goods coming from other Member States where they are lawfully manufactured and marketed, rules that lay down requirements to be met by such goods, even if those rules apply to all products alike, must be regarded as 'measures having equivalent effect to quantitative restrictions on import' for the purposes of Article [34 TFEU] (with reference to Cassis de Dijon and other judgments). Any other measure which hinders access of products originating in other Member States to the market of a Member State is also covered by that concept (see Case C-110/05) Commission v. Italy … §37).

127. In these cases, the Court did not abandon *Keck*, but partly integrated *Keck*, without referring to it, in a broader category of discriminatory measures and it formulated a third category of measures that do fit neither in the category of discriminatory measures (including non-discriminatory selling arrangements) nor in that of

---

127. *See* Order of 15 December 2011, *Inno v. Unizo*, EU:C:2011:851.
128. Judgment of 10 February 2009, *Commission v. Italy*, C-110/05, EU:2009:66.
129. Judgment of 4 June 2009, *Aklagaren v. Percy Mickelsson and Joakim Roos*, C-142/05, EU:C:2009:336.

product-related rules (*Cassis*), i.e., all other measures that hinder access to the market for goods originating in another Member State and in which it classified conditions under which goods can be used.

In both cases (*Italian Trailers* and *Mickelsson & Roos*), the measure in issue was very likely to deter consumers to buy the goods, the importation of which was allowed but the use of which was banned or heavily restricted. The regulations thus hindered access of the products to the national market.

128. It should be noted that half a year before *Italian Trailers*, namely in *Commission v. Portugal*,[130] the Court had already ruled that a national provision (prohibition in Portugal to affix a dark film on car windows, a 'modality of use') affected the marketing in that country of all tinted film legally manufactured and sold in other Member States to be affixed to the windows of motor vehicles and therefore constituted a measure having equivalent effect.

129. Since *Mickelsson & Roos*, there are now clearly three categories of measures that fall within the scope of Article 34 TFEU, and which can be justified under Article 36 TFEU or, where they make no formal distinction between domestic goods and imported goods, under the 'rule of reason' of *Cassis de Dijon*:

(1) measures that treat goods coming from other Member States less favourably than domestic goods (be they selling arrangements or something else) (all discriminatory rules);
(2) obstacles to the free movement of goods which are the consequence of applying, to goods coming from other Member States where they are lawfully manufactured and marketed, rules that lay down requirements to be met by such goods, even if those rules apply to all products alike (product-related rules); and
(3) any other measure which hinders access of products originating in other Member States to the market of a Member State (a residuary category that encompasses non-discriminatory rules on modalities of use of goods).

It can be observed that *Keck & Mithouard* has not been formally overruled. However, the Keck-rule seems to be included in the first of the three categories of *Mickelsson* (all rules that treat goods imported from other Member States less favourably).

F. After Mickelsson, *Back to* Dassonville?

130. In some more recent case law, such as the judgments in *Ker-Optika bt*[131] and *Ascafor*,[132] the CJEU makes a further move towards making market access the

---

130. Judgment of 10 April 2008, *Commission v. Portugal*, C-265/06, EU:C:2008:210.
131. Judgment of 2 December 2010, *Ker-Optika bt*, C-108/09, EU:C:2010:721.
132. Judgment of 1 March 2012, *Ascafor*, C-484/10, EU:C:2012:113.

central test of Article 34 TFEU. In *Ker-Optika bt*, the Court had to rule on a pro-hibition in Hungarian law to sell contact lenses via the internet. The Court confirms that this concerns a selling arrangement.[133] It first refers to *Dassonville*,[134] but immediately adds, with reference to *Italian Trailers,* that its case law reflects the obligation to comply with the principles of non-discrimination, mutual recognition and access of EU products to national markets.[135] Finally, it refers to *Keck*, and states that a national rule on selling arrangements, unless it does not discriminate, is by nature such as to prevent the access of the imported goods to the market or to impede such access more than it impedes the access of domestic goods.[136] The negative formula of paragraph 17 of the *Keck* judgment (provided that the selling arrangement does not discriminate it does not impede access to the market) is reversed to a positive formula: a discriminatory selling arrangement that does indeed impede access to the market. In his opinion, A.G. Mengozzi had referred to *Keck* and came to the conclusion that the requirements laid down by Hungarian law for the marketing of lenses affected to a greater degree the selling of products from other Member States (the comparison test in *Keck*).[137]

131. Ascafor, rendered without opinion by the A.G. (Bot), concerned Spanish regulations on certification for reinforcing steel for concrete. Both Spanish and non-Spanish certification bodies granting a quality label to these products had to fulfil all the conditions laid down by the regulations. The Court again started with a ref-erence to the *Dassonville* formula,[138] quoting *Dassonville* and *Ker-Optika,* fol-lowed by a reference to the obligation to comply with the principles of non-discrimination and of mutual recognition (with reference to *Italian Trailers* and *Ker-Optika*).[139] The Court found that the imposition of all the requirements may result in the rejection of an application for recognition of quality certificates granted in another Member State, which in its turn can discourage economic operators in Spain from importing reinforced steel produced elsewhere in the EU.[140]

132. There is a tendency in the Court's case law to refer straightforwardly to *Dassonville* in cases that would seem to belong to the *Cassis* category of restric-tions, i.e., restrictions affecting directly the importation of goods as such, as can be seen in the recent Grand Chamber's judgment in *Alands Vindkraft*.[141]

133. In a recent judgment, referring to the 'Dassonville' formula, the Court held that Article 34 TFEU does not preclude Spanish legislation which provides that the

---

133. *Ker-Optika bt*, para. 45.
134. *Ibid.*, para. 47.
135. *Ibid.*, para. 48; *see also* Judgment of 4 June 2009, *Aklagaren v. Percy Mickelsson and Joakim Roos*, C-142/05, EU:C:2009:336, para. 24.
136. *Ker-Optika bt*, para. 51.
137. EU:C:2010:341, para. 64.
138. *Ascafor*, para. 52.
139. *Ibid.*, para. 53.
140. *Ibid.*, para. 57.
141. Judgment of 1 July 2014, *Alands Vindkraft AB v. Energimyndigheten*, C-573/12, EU:C:2014:2037, para. 66 (on production requirements for delivering green electricity certificates).

sales designation 'ibérico de cebo' may be granted only to products that comply with certain conditions imposed by that legislation, where that legislation permits the importation and marketing of products from other Member States under the designations they bear pursuant to the rules of the Member State of origin, even if they are similar, comparable or identical to the designations provided for in the Spanish legislation.[142]

In other words: back to the roots. In any event, *Cassis de Dijon* case law is still the leading case for justifications in the general interest of measures having equivalent effect within the meaning of *Dassonville*.

§5. MEASURES HAVING AN EFFECT EQUIVALENT TO QUANTITATIVE EXPORT RESTRICTIONS (ARTICLES 35 AND 36 TFEU)

134. The case law on Article 35 TFEU developed later, slower and differently from the case law on Article 34 TFEU. Before the CJEU rendered its first judgment on the matter (*see* next paragraph), W. H. Roth[143] described very precisely the background of export restrictions which, as one can imagine, is quite different from that of import restrictions. Member States (or the States within the US) are of course not naturally inclined to restrict exports to the other (Member) States, but will often try to restrict imports to protect their own industry. However, production regulations that restrict exports can also have as their object or effect to protect local producers.[144]

135. The first question on export restrictions (Article 35 TFEU) came to the Court in 1979 in the *Groenveld* case.[145] A Dutch court asked whether a national regulation on processing and preparation of meat, which prohibited, subject to express exceptions, any manufacturer of sausages from having in stock or processing horsemeat, was compatible with Article 35 TFEU. The regulation was adopted for the purpose of protecting Dutch exports of meat products both to Member States and to non-member countries which constitute important export markets and where there are objections to the consumption of horsemeat or indeed where the importation of products containing horsemeat is prohibited. As it is practically impossible to determine the presence of horsemeat in meat products,[146] the sole means of ensuring that such products do not contain horsemeat is to prohibit manufacturers of meat products from having in stock, preparing or processing horsemeat. The file further

---

142. Judgment of 14 June 2018, *Asociacion Nacional de Productores de Ganado Porcino*, C-169/17, EU:C:2018:440.
143. W.-H. Roth, *Freier Warenverkehr und staatliche Regelungsgewalt in einem Gemeinsamen Markt* (Beck 1977).
144. On p. 175, Roth gives an interesting example from the Supreme Court case law (334 U.S. 385(1948)): *Toomer v. Witsell*. In this judgment, the Supreme Court declared unlawful a South Carolina regulation requiring all shrimps fished in S.C. waters to be packed in a S.C. port before they could be further transported (cf. the EU *Rioja* cases mentioned hereafter).
145. Judgment of 8 November 1979, *Groenveld*, 15/79, EU:C:1979:253.
146. As was confirmed by the scandal, some years ago, about horsemeat in lasagne (and other prepared food), that occurred notwithstanding the much tougher control that is exercised these days on the food chain.

established that the regulation in question does not affect imports or re-exports of horsemeat originating in other Member States or non-member countries.

136. The Court answered that Article 35 TFEU concerns 'national measures which have as their specific object or effect the restriction of patterns of exports and thereby the establishment of a difference in treatment between the domestic trade of a Member State and its export trade in such a way as to provide a particular advantage for national production or for the domestic market of the state in question at the expense of the production or of the trade of other Member States'.[147] The Court found that a prohibition like the one in issue, which is applied objectively to the production of goods of a certain kind without drawing a distinction depending on whether such goods are intended for the national market or for export, does not fall within the scope of Article 35 TFEU.[148] The Court added that this assessment is not affected by the circumstance that the regulation in question has as its objective, *inter alia*, the safeguarding of the reputation of the national production of meat products in certain export markets within the Union and in non-member countries where there are obstacles of a psychological or legislative nature to the consumption of horsemeat when the same prohibition is applied identically to the product in the domestic market of the State in question.[149] Finally, the objective nature of that prohibition is not modified by the fact that the regulation in force in the Netherlands permits the retail sale of horsemeat by butchers.[150] In fact, that concession at the level of local trade does not have the effect of bringing about a prohibition at the level of industrial manufacture of the same product regardless of its destination.

137. Soon afterwards, the Court had to deal with a completely different type of restrictions to exports, in *Oebel*.[151] A German law provided that on working days, subject to certain exceptions, no person shall be permitted to work on the making of ordinary or fine baker's wares at night between 10 p.m. and 4 a.m. Another provision of that law prohibited the transport of ordinary or fine baker's wares for delivery to consumers or retail outlets between 10 p.m. and 5.45 a.m. According to the German government, that legislation was designed mainly to protect workers in small and medium-sized bakeries, which do not have enough staff to be able to arrange work in shifts, against permanent night-work likely to damage their health. The purpose of extending the prohibition to the large undertakings in the industry which are able to organize work in shifts was to protect the small family businesses against commercial competition. There were questions as to the import and export restrictive effect of these measures. With regard to the restriction on exports, the Court referred to the *Groenveld* formula and found that Article 35 TFEU did not

---

147. *Groenveld,* para. 7.
148. *Ibid.*
149. *Ibid,* para. 8.
150. *Ibid.*
151. Judgment of 14 July, *Oebel,* 155/80, EU:C:1981:177.

apply to the national rules at stake.[152] In his opinion, A.G. Capotorti warned that the abandonment of a single concept of what constitutes measures having equivalent effect would give rise to confusion.[153]

138. Again, reiterating the *Groenveld* formula, the CJEU ruled in *Syndicat National des Fabricants Raffineurs d'Huile de Graissage Usagé (Waste Oil* case)[154] that Article 35 TFEU does not allow a Member State to organize a system for the collection and disposal of waste oils within its territory in such a way as to prohibit exports to an authorized disposal or regenerating undertaking in another Member State.[155] In *Waste Oil* and in later judgments, the Court seems to have abandoned the last part of the third condition of *Groenveld,* namely that the particular advantage conferred on national production by the measure in question must be at the expense of the production or of the trade of other Member States.[156] It is submitted that this does not change the nature of the *Groenveld* test, which encompasses a difference in treatment (discrimination) to the advantage of the national production or the domestic market, which of course supposes a disadvantage for the production or the trade of other Member States.

139. Another example of a national provision that the Court found to be discriminatory, but justified on the basis of Article 36 TFEU (protection of industrial and commercial property), is the second Rioja-case, *Belgium v. Spain.*[157] Like in the first Rioja-case, *Delhaize,*[158] the Court found that Article 35 TFEU applies to a national provision that disqualifies Rioja wine to carry the '*denominación de origen calificada Rioja*' if it is transported in bulk (typically outside the country). However, the Court found that the measure was necessary for the protection of the designation of origin. The Court was convinced by the arguments put forward by Spain to justify the restriction, namely that for Rioja wines transported and bottled in the region of production, the controls are far-reaching and systematic and are the responsibility of the totality of the producers themselves, who have a fundamental interest in preserving the reputation acquired, and that only consignments which have been subjected to those controls may bear the '*denominación de origen calificada*'.[159] Hence, the risk to which the quality of the product finally offered to consumers is exposed is greater where it has been transported and bottled outside the

---

152. *Oebel,* 155/80, paras 15–16.
153. Opinion of AG Capotorti in *Oebel,* EU:C:1981:123.
154. Judgment of 10 March 1983, *Syndicat National des Fabricants Raffineurs d'Huile de Graissage,* 172/82, EU:C:1983:69.
155. *Ibid.,* para. 16.
156. *See* A.G. Mengozzi, Opinion in *Kakavetsos,* C-161/09, EU:C:2010:531, para. 47.
157. Judgment of 16 May 2000, *Belgium v. Spain,* C-388/95: EU:C:2000:244; the first was a preliminary ruling in which the Court had come to the opposite conclusion as to the compatibility with Art. 36: Judgment of 9 June 1990, *Delhaize v. Promalvin,* C-47/90, EU:C:1992:205.
158. *Ibid.*
159. *Belgium v. Spain,* para. 73. An interesting argument in the light of what, as a practitioner, the author found out when dealing with a similar export restriction for wine of another Spanish region. Evidence was found that what the 'Consejo Regulador' was doing was not more than rubber stamping an agreement between producers. This brought the whole story under the scope of Art. 101 TFEU

region of production than when those operations have taken place within the region. Be that as it may be, it could not be contested that the measure protects the local bottling industry to the detriment of the bottling industry in the importing countries.[160]

140.   The Spanish rule in the *Rioja* cases is a good example of 'local grab' legislation (favouring local users at the expense of users in other States), a type of legislation that is caught by the US Commerce Clause, which according to L.W. Gormley[161] may have influenced the *Groenveld*-doctrine.[162]

141.   From the beginning, the Court made one exception to *Groenveld* and applied *Dassonville* to exports. For goods covered by the common organization of the markets, any measure likely to impede, directly or indirectly, actually or potentially, intra-Union trade constitutes a measure having equivalent effect to a quantitative restriction on exports.[163] As rightly observed by A.G. Mengozzi,[164] the Court justified this difference on the ground that Articles 34 and 35 TFEU form an integral part of the common organization of the markets. Once the Union has adopted legislation in a given sector, Member States are under an obligation to refrain from taking any measure which might undermine or create exceptions to it.[165]

142.   The Court maintained this narrow discrimination criterion for almost thirty years, until it added a second criterion in *Gysbrechts*.[166]

143.   *Gysbrechts* concerned a Belgian law that prohibited distant sellers from requiring consumers to pay or to communicate the number of their payment card as a guarantee before expiry of the 'cooling off period' during which the consumer can exercise his right of withdrawal.[167]

144.   At the time when several Advocates General questioned *Keck* (and its 'access to the market' approach), A.G. Trstenjak[168] argued in favour of a new test

(prohibition of restrictive agreements, *see* paras 379 et seq. below). If that was the real nature of the Rioja regulation, Art. 36 TFEU, which eventually saved it, would have been of no avail.

160. The two Rioja cases started because a Spanish exporter, Promalvin, was prevented by law to execute a contract for supply of Rioja in bulk it had concluded with Delhaize, a Belgian supermarket chain that has its own bottling facilities in Belgium.

161. L. Gormley, *EU Law of Free Movement of Goods and Customs Union* 285 (Oxford University Press 2009).

162. *See also* W.M. Roth, footnote 141 above.

163. Judgment of 16 February 1980, *Vriend*, 94/79, EU:C:1980:50, para. 8, and Judgment of 15 April 1997, *Deutsches Milch-Kontor*, C-272/95, EU:C:1997:191, para. 24.

164. In his opinion in *Kasavetsos-Fragkopoulos*, C-161/09, EU:C:2010:531, para. 49.

165. Judgment of 17 October 1995, *Fishermen's Organisations and Others*, C-44/94, EU:C:1995:325, para. 52 and the case law cited.

166. Judgment of 16 December 2008, *Gysbrechts*, C-205/07, EU:C:2008:427.

167. The Court found the prohibition to require payment proportionate to the goal of consumer protection invoked. In the meantime, both the prohibitions have been repealed. At the EU level, *see* now Art. 9(3)Directive 2011/83 on Consumer Rights: Member States may not maintain such prohibitions for distant contracts.

168. Opinion in *Gysbrechts,* C-205/07, EU:C:2008:730.

for export restrictions in *Gysbrechts*. Drawing a parallel with the two conditions of *Keck* (a selling arrangement does not fall within the *Dassonville* formula where it: (1) applies equally to all operators active on the national market, and (2) does not discriminate in law or in fact between domestic trade and trade from/(here:) to other Member States), she nevertheless proposed to examine whether that provision or the interpretation thereof is an obstacle to *leaving the market*, in spite of the fact that it does not give rise to discrimination in law or in fact.[169] She submitted that Article 35 TFEU also applies to national measures (in that case a prohibition on a distant seller to require a payment or a consumer's payment card number before the expiry of the period for the exercise of the right of withdrawal) that are applicable to all traders active in the national territory, but the factual effect of which is greater on goods leaving the market of the exporting State than on marketing of goods in the domestic market of that Member State. In other words, Article 35 TFEU applies not only to measures that make a formal distinction between export and domestic trade, but also to those that have a discriminatory effect on exports. In her opinion, A.G. Trstenjak made a parallel between the access to the market test of *Keck* and what she called 'exit of the market' in case of exports. The Advocate General stressed however that certain selling arrangements restrict exit from the market even though they do not discriminate either in law or in fact.[170]

145.   The Court did not follow the Advocate General in extending, as such, *Keck* to exports but applied the de facto discrimination test of *Keck* by holding the contested measure to be an obstacle within the meaning of Article 35 TFEU in that its consequences are generally more significant for cross-border sales made directly to consumers than for domestic sales (in particular where the seller has to sue abroad consumers who keep the goods without paying them). Even though such a prohibition applies to all traders active in the national territory, its actual effect is nonetheless greater on the goods leaving the market of the exporting State.[171]

146.   Until *Gysbrechts*, the case law on Articles 34 and 35 TFEU was fundamentally different. Article 34 TFEU applied, and still applies, both to discriminatory and non-discriminatory measures. The rule of reason of *Cassis de Dijon* however only applies to measures that are equally applicable to imported and domestic goods, while measures that formally discriminate against imported goods might be justified on one of the grounds mentioned in Article 36 TFEU (on condition that the discrimination is not 'arbitrary'). In contrast, before *Gysbrechts*, Article 35 TFEU only applied to formally discriminatory measures to the advantage of national production or the domestic market and hence the only grounds of justification that could

---

169. Paragraph 73 of the Opinion.
170. Paragraph 59 of the Opinion.
171. *Gysbrechts*, para. 43.

be invoked were those of Article 36 TFEU (the other grounds of justification, recognized in *Dassonville* and *Cassis de Dijon* can only be invoked with respect to measures that apply 'without distinction'). This lack of coherence was heavily criticized.[172]

Gysbrechts has completely changed the picture. *Groenveld* was maintained but the Court accepted that also non-discriminatory measures can be caught by Article 35 TFEU.

147. The approach of the Court in *Gysbrechts* can be compared to its approach in *Deutscher Apothekerverband*,[173] which concerned Article 34 TFEU (import restrictions). German law prohibited the internet sale of medicines. In Germany, the sale of medicines is a monopoly of pharmacies, in contrast to, e.g., the Netherlands, where non-prescription drugs can be sold in ordinary shops and of course on the internet. The Court acknowledged that the German measure was a 'selling arrangement' and verified whether the conditions of *Keck* were satisfied. It found that the second condition of *Keck*, that is, no discrimination in law or in fact, was not satisfied. The prohibition is more of an obstacle to pharmacies outside Germany than to those within it. German pharmacies are still able to sell the products in their dispensaries. In addition, for pharmacies not established in Germany, the internet provides a more significant way to gain direct access to the German market. A prohibition which has a greater impact on pharmacies established outside German territory could impede access to the market for products from other Member States more than it impedes access for domestic products. Accordingly, the prohibition does not affect the sale of domestic medicines in the same way as it affects the sale of those coming from other Member States.

148. In *Gysbrechts*, the Court introduced a new test for export restrictions. Not only formal discriminatory measures that provide an advantage to local production can be caught by Article 35 TFEU, but also measures that discriminate de facto against exported goods fall within its scope. The Court did not however formally overrule *Groenveld*. The *Groenveld* test still exists and is the most simple of the two currently existing tests: a measure that formally discriminates against exports is prohibited without need to assess the effects of the measure (as under the *Gysbrechts* test).

149. In other words, since *Gysbrechts* there is a certain degree of convergence in the case law on Articles 34 and 35 TFEU: national measures that affect imports respectively exports more heavily than domestic trade are to be qualified as a measures having equivalent effect. Or, in the words of the first part of the first sentence (first category) of paragraph 24 of *Mickelsson & Roos*,[174] the notion of measures having equivalent effect covers 'measures taken by a Member State, the aim or

---

172. Among the fiercest opponents of the *Groenveld* case law, *see* L. Gormley, *inter alia* in *Landmark Cases of Consumer Law* 285 (Intersentia 2013), stressing that the essential evil which is prohibited by Arts 34–36 TFEU is not discrimination itself but rather interference with the essential unity of the internal market.
173. Judgment of 11 December 2003, *Deutscher Apothekerverband*, C-322/01, EU:C:2003:664.
174. *See* above at para. 124.

effect of which is to treat goods coming from other Member States (or *exported* to other Member States) less favourably' [the author stresses].

150. The broad scope of Article 35 has been confirmed. More recently in *New Valmar*[175] the Court ruled that Article 35 precludes legislation of a federated entity of a Member State (here the Flemish Community) which requires every undertaking that has its place of establishment within the territory of the entity concerned to draw all the details on invoices relating to cross-border transactions exclusive in the official language of that region, failing which those invoices are to be declared null and void. Such legislation is likely to have an impact, however, minor (but not a merely indirect or uncertain one)[176] on contractual relations. It can also be mentioned here that the Court confirmed its jurisprudence concerning goods that come under a common organization of the markets in *Kakavetsos-Fragkopoulos* (concerning dried grapes).[177] For such goods, Article 35 TFEU automatically applies to any measure likely to impede, directly or indirectly, actually or potentially, intra-Union trade constitutes a measure having equivalent effect to a quantitative restriction on exports.[178]

§6. STATE TRADING MONOPOLIES

151. Article 37 TFEU reads as follows:

1. Member States shall adjust any State monopolies of a commercial character so as to ensure that no discrimination regarding the conditions under which goods are procured and marketed exists between nationals of Member States.

   The provisions of this Article shall apply to any body through which a Member State, in law or in fact, either directly or indirectly supervises, determines or appreciably influences imports or exports between Member States. These provisions shall likewise apply to monopolies delegated by the State to others.
2. Member States shall refrain from introducing any new measure which is contrary to the principles laid down in paragraph 1 or which restricts the scope of the articles dealing with the prohibition of customs duties and quantitative restrictions between Member States.
3. If a State monopoly of a commercial character has rules which are designed to make it easier to dispose of agricultural products or obtain for them the best return, steps should be taken in applying the rules contained in this Article to ensure equivalent safeguards for the employment and standard of living of the producers concerned.

---

175. Judgment of 21 June 2016 (Grand Chamber), *New Valmar*, C-15/15, EU:C:2016:464.
176. *See Krantz*, above footnote 108.
177. Judgment of 3 March 2011, *Kakavetsos-Fragkopoulos*, C-161/09, EU:C:2011:110.
178. *Ibid.* para. 27.

152. The significance of this Article is limited. It only applies to State monopolies for the sale of goods, which existed, and still exist, in a limited number of Member States (formerly e.g., tobacco and now still, for e.g., alcohol and medicines in Sweden). Production monopolies and services monopolies must be assessed on the basis of the competition rules (in particular Article 106 TFEU).[179]

153. The Court of Justice ruled that Article 37(1) TFEU must be interpreted as meaning that as from 31 December 1969 (the end of the original transitional period for the establishment of the common market) every national monopoly of a commercial character must be adjusted so as to eliminate the exclusive right to import from other Member States.[180] This ruling also applies to export monopolies.[181]

154. In *Franzén*,[182] the Court of Justice found that aspects of the Swedish alcohol monopoly were contrary to the Treaty, but it did not find an infringement of Article 37 TFEU because the monopoly (held by the company Systembolaget, *see* hereafter) was not discriminatory.

155. Under Swedish law, the production of alcoholic beverages is subject to the holding of a 'production licence' whilst wholesale trade in spirits, wine and strong beer is subject to the holding of a 'wholesale licence'. However, persons holding a production licence are allowed to engage in wholesale trade in the products covered by the licence. Swedish legislation also makes the importation of wine, strong beer or spirit drinks into Sweden subject to the possession of a production or a wholesale licence. Licences are issued by the Alkoholinspektion (Alcohol Inspectorate), upon applications accompanied by supporting documents, pursuant to decisions of the inspectorate. Applicants have to show that they have sufficient storage capacity to engage in his activity, and provide a bank guarantee to cover payment of excise duties. Finally, each year the holder of a licence must pay a charge for the monitoring of his premises, the rates of which are set by the State. The Law on Alcohol has made Systembolaget Aktiebolag (hereinafter 'Systembolaget'), a company wholly owned by the State and specially constituted for this purpose, responsible for the retail of wine, strong beer and spirits.

156. As to the question whether Systembolaget's monopoly infringed Article 37 TFEU, the Court stated that it is clear not only from the wording of that provision but also from the position which it occupies in the general scheme of the Treaty that the provision is designed to ensure compliance with the fundamental principle that goods should be able to move freely throughout the common market, in particular by requiring quantitative restrictions and measures having equivalent effect on trade

---

179. Discussed hereafter in paras 564 et seq.
180. Judgment of 3 February 1976, *Pubblico Ministero v. Manghera et al.*, 59/75, EU:C:1976:91.
181. Kapteyn – VerLoren van Themaat – Gormley, at p. 409.
182. Judgment of 23 October 1997, *Franzén*, C-189/95, EU:C:1997:504.

between Member States to be abolished, and thereby to ensure maintenance of normal conditions of competition between the economies of Member States in the event that a given product is subject, in one or other of those States, to a national monopoly of a commercial character.[183]

157. The Court reminded in that context that Article 37 TFEU does not require national monopolies having a commercial character to be abolished, but requires them to be adjusted in such a way as to ensure that no discrimination exists between nationals of Member States regarding the conditions under which goods are procured and marketed.[184] Restrictions on trade which are inherent in the existence of the monopoly are not caught by this provision. Thus, Article 37 TFEU requires that the organization and operation of the monopoly be arranged so as to exclude any discrimination, i.e., making sure that trade in goods from other Member States is not put at a disadvantage, in law or in fact.[185] In aiming to protect public health against the harm caused by alcohol, a domestic monopoly on the retail of alcoholic beverages, such as that conferred on Systembolaget, pursues a public-interest aim.[186] Next, it must be examined whether the criteria and methods of selection used by Systembolaget are discriminatory or likely to put imported products at a disadvantage.[187] The Court finds that this is not the case. Systembolaget has a balanced purchase plan and the selection of drinks is made on the basis of purely commercial criteria (price competitiveness of the product, commercial history, etc.) or qualitative criteria ('blind' tasting), which are not apt to put domestic products at an advantage.[188] Moreover, traders whose offers are not selected may ask for their products to undergo a second qualitative test, and they are entitled to be told the reasons for decisions taken regarding the selection of beverages.[189] Finally, it does not appear that the number of sales outlets is limited to the point of compromising consumers' procurement of supplies of domestic or imported alcoholic beverages.[190]

158. On the other hand, the Court found that the system of production and wholesale licences constitutes a measure having equivalent effect within the meaning of Article 34 TFEU, because it imposes additional costs on such beverages, such as intermediary costs, payment of charges and fees for the grant of a licence, and costs arising from the obligation to maintain storage capacity in Sweden. These obstacles were not necessary for the protection of public health (Article 36 TFEU).[191]

---

183. *Franzén,* para. 37. With reference to *Manghera,* quoted above and other judgments.
184. *Franzén,* para. 38.
185. *Ibid.,* para. 40.
186. *Ibid.,* para. 41.
187. *Ibid.,* para. 42.
188. *Ibid.,* paras 46–48.
189. *Ibid.,* paras 50–51.
190. *Ibid.,* para. 54.
191. *Ibid.,* para. 76.

159. In *Kirster Hanner,*[192] the Court ruled that the Swedish State monopoly for the retail of medicines (Apoteket) was contrary to Article 37 TFEU.[193] It referred to its standing case law (including *Franzén)* that State monopolies of a commercial nature are not as such contrary to Article 37 TFEU, but that they need to be organized in such a way so as to avoid that trade in goods from other Member States is put at a disadvantage, in law or in fact.[194] In the case at hand, the Court found that Apoteket was entirely free in principle to select a product range of its choice;[195] there was no purchasing plan or a system of 'calls for tenders' within the framework of which producers whose products are not selected would be entitled to be apprised of the reasons for the selection decision,[196] nor was there any opportunity to contest such decisions before an independent supervisory authority. Thus, unlike the situation in *Franzén*, the selection system of the sales monopoly was not based on criteria that are independent from the origin of the products, and it was not transparent by providing both for an obligation to state reasons for decisions and for an independent monitoring procedure.

160. More recently, in *ANETT,*[197] the Court ruled that a Spanish law that prohibits tobacco retailers from importing tobacco products from other Member States violates Article 34 TFEU. Contrary to the Commission's opinion, the Court found that Article 37 TFEU did not apply.[198] The prohibition in issue was separable from the rules governing the tobacco monopoly.

---

192. Judgment of 31 May 2005, *Kirster Hanner,* C-438/02, EU:C:2005:352.
193. *Ibid.*, para. 49.
194. *Ibid.*, para. 36.
195. *Ibid.*, para. 42.
196. *Ibid.*
197. Judgment of 26 April 2012, *ANETT,* C-456/10, EU:C:2012:241.
198. *ANETT,* para. 30.

Chapter 3. Freedom of Establishment and Freedom to Provide Services

§1. Introduction

161. Article 20 TFEU establishes citizenship of the Union. It provides that 'Every person holding the nationality of a Member State shall be a citizen of the Union.' Moreover, 'Citizens of the Union shall enjoy the rights and be subject to the duties provided for in the Treaties. They shall have, inter alia the right to move and reside freely within the territory of the Member States.'

162. This general freedom did not exist under the original EEC Treaty. It will not be discussed in this monograph on commercial and economic law.

163. Provisions on free movement of workers and self-employed persons (including the right of residence) and companies laid down in Part I, Title IV TFEU already existed in the EEC Treaty and have remained largely unchanged.

164. Articles 45 TFEU et seq. relates to the free movement of workers, whereas for self- employed persons and companies there are two sets of rules, i.e., those on the right of establishment in Articles 49 TFEU et seq. and those on the freedom to provide services in Articles 56 TFEU et seq.

165. The freedom of movement for workers will not be discussed in this monograph. Reference is made to the IEL Labour Law.

§2. Distinction Between the Right of Establishment and the Freedom to Provide Services and Principles Common to Both Freedoms

166. The Treaty provisions on the right of establishment and the freedom to provide services are based on common principles. There are even a few provisions in the Treaty that apply to both freedoms. The Treaty basically prohibits discriminations on the basis of nationality, but the CJEU has condemned all restrictions to these freedoms that cannot be justified in the general interest, following the same strand as for the free movement of goods (*Dassonville, Cassis de Dijon*). In *Gebhard*,[199] while discussing the freedom of establishment, the Court ruled in very general terms that national measures liable to hinder or make less attractive the exercise of fundamental freedoms guaranteed by the Treaty (i.e., the free movement of goods, persons, services and capital) must fulfil four conditions: they must be applied in a non-discriminatory manner; they must be justified by imperative

---

199. Judgment of 30 November 1995, *Gebhard*, C-55/94, EU:C:1995:441.

requirements in the general interest; they must be suitable for securing the attainment of the objective which they pursue; and they must not go beyond what is necessary in order to attain it.[200]

167.   Nevertheless, there are differences in degree of liberalization under the right (or freedom) of establishment and the freedom to provide services. This is also evidenced by secondary Union law, in particular Directive 2006/123 on Services in the Internal Market,[201] which will be discussed further in this chapter.[202] Hence, the two freedoms should be well distinguished.

168.   As to the right of establishment Article 49(1) TFEU states that, within the framework of the provisions set out below, restrictions on the freedom of establishment of nationals of a Member State in the territory of another Member State shall be prohibited. Such prohibition shall also apply to restrictions on the setting-up of agencies, branches or subsidiaries by nationals of any Member State established in the territory of any Member State. The second paragraph of Article 49 TFEU adds that the freedom of establishment shall include the right to take up and pursue activities as self-employed persons and to set up an d manage undertakings, in particular companies or firms within the meaning of Article 54(2) TFEU, under the conditions laid down for its own nationals by the law of the country where such establishment is effected, subject to the provisions of the Chapter relating to capital.

169.   Pursuant to Article 56 TFEU, within the framework of the provisions set out below, restrictions on freedom to provide services within the Union shall be prohibited in respect of nationals of Member States who are established in a Member State other than that of the person for whom the services are intended. Article 57 TFEU states that 'services' are normally provided for remuneration, and that the freedom to provide services applies insofar as they are not governed by the provisions relating to freedom of movement for goods, capital and persons. They shall in particular include:

(a) activities of an industrial character;
(b) activities of a commercial character;
(c) activities of craftsmen;
(d) activities of the professions.

170.   The notion of services and the different types of cross-border provision of services that come within the scope of the Treaty will be discussed in more detail hereafter in §6, B. The question that has to be answered first is how the provision of a cross-border service is to be distinguished from a situation where the service provider makes use of the right of establishment. The CJEU has distinguished the

---

200. *Ibid.*, para. 39.
201. Directive 2006/123/EC of the European Parliament and of the Council of 12 December 2006 on services in the internal market, *OJ* 2006, L 376/36.
202. *See* paras 288 et seq.

right of establishment from the freedom to provide services. The concept of establishment within the meaning of the Treaty is a very broad one, allowing a Union national to participate, *on a stable and continuous basis*, in the economic life of a Member State other than his State of origin and to profit therefrom, so contributing to economic and social interpenetration within the Union in the sphere of activities as self-employed persons.[203] By contrast, when exercising the freedom to provide services a service provider may be temporarily present in another Member State (*see* Article 57(3) TFEU) (i.e., not on a stable and continuous basis). In *Gebhard*, the Court of Justice explained that:[204]

– the temporary nature of the provision of services, envisaged in Article 57(3) TFEU, is to be determined in the light of its duration, regularity, periodicity and continuity;
– the provider of services, within the meaning of the Treaty, may equip himself in the host Member State with the infrastructure necessary for the purposes of performing the services in question;
– a national of a Member State who pursues a professional activity on a stable and continuous basis in another Member State where he holds himself out from an established professional base to, amongst others, nationals of that State comes under the provisions of the chapter relating to the right of establishment and not those of the chapter relating to services.

§3. The Right of Establishment of Natural Persons

171. Article 49(1) TFEU prohibits restrictions on the freedom of establishment of nationals of a Member State in the territory of another Member State. Such prohibition shall also apply to restrictions on the setting-up of agencies, branches or subsidiaries. Pursuant to the second paragraph of Article 49, the freedom of establishment includes the right to take up and pursue activities as a self-employed person and to set up and manage undertakings, in particular companies or firms within the meaning of the Article 54(2) TFEU, under the conditions laid down for its own nationals by the law of the country where such establishment is affected, subject to the provisions of the Chapter relating to capital. The freedom of establishment of companies and firms poses specific problems that will be discussed hereafter.[205]

172. Only Member State nationals are the beneficiaries of the right of establishment, but nationals of third countries might benefit from this right by virtue of an agreement between the Union and the third country. Furthermore, if Article 49 TFEU limits the right to establishment of nationals of a Member State to the establishment in 'other' Member States, the Court of Justice has recognized the right of a national of a Member State to establish in the Member State of which he is a

---

203. Judgment of 21 June 1974, *Reyners,* 2/74, EU:C:1974, para. 21; Judgment of 30 November 1995, *Gebhard,* C-55/94, EU:C:1995:441, para. 25.
204. Judgment in *Gebhard*, C-55/94, EU:C:1995:441, para. 39.
205. *See* at paras 142 et seq.

national. An example is the *Dieter Kraus* ruling,[206] dealing with a German citizen having obtained an LLM degree in an English university, and who was denied the right to use the title in the exercise of his profession in Germany. The Court of Justice found this denial to be an infringement of Article 49 TFEU.

173. In its landmark judgment in *Reyners*,[207] the Court of Justice ruled that since the end of the transitional period Article 52 of the EEC Treaty (now Article 49 TFEU) is a directly applicable provision, despite the absence, in a particular sphere, of the directives prescribed by Articles 54(2) and 57(1) of the EEC Treaty (now Articles 50 and 53 TFEU). In other words, since 1 January 1970 the freedom of establishment is directly effective. The case concerned Mr Reyners, a lawyer of Dutch nationality, who was refused admittance to the Brussels bar by the Belgian authorities because Belgian law at that time required the possession of the Belgian nationality for such admittance. Soon after *Reyners*, in *Van Binsbergen*, the Court also recognized the direct effect of Article 56 TFEU laying down the freedom to provide services.[208] The possibility for an individual to invoke a Treaty provision against the State is called 'vertical direct effect'. Much later, in *Viking*,[209] the Court ruled that the freedom of establishment can also be invoked against certain private parties (horizontal direct effect).

174. The *Reyners* case dealt with a straightforward, direct, discrimination in the basis of nationality. In later judgments, the Court has extended the protection of Article 49 TFEU, first to situations of indirect discriminations on the basis of nationality and later to non- discriminatory restrictions of the right of establishment that cannot be justified in the general interest ('rule of reason', *see* judgment in *Gebhard,* quoted above[210]).

175. A first extension related to indirect discriminations on the basis of nationality. An example is the *Thieffry*[211] case. Mr Thieffry, a Belgian citizen, was refused admittance to the Paris bar, not because of his nationality, but for the sole reason that he did not possess a French law degree, although he possessed a Belgian law degree that had been declared equivalent to a French law degree by the French academic authorities as well as the certificate which was required for the exercise of the legal profession ('*certificat d'aptitude à la profession d'avocat*'). The Court found that this was a restriction incompatible with Article 49 TFEU.

176. In a later case, *Klopp*,[212] the CJEU applied Article 49 TFEU to the following situation: Mr Onno Klopp, a lawyer who already held chambers in Germany wanted to open second chambers in Paris, but he was prevented from doing so

---

206. Judgment of 31 March 1993, *Dieter Kraus,* 19/92, EU:C:1993:125.
207. Judgment of 21 June 1974, *Reyners,* 2/74, EU:C:1974:68.
208. Judgment of 3 December 1974, *van Binsbergen,* 33/74, EU:C:1974:131; discussed hereafter, at para. 171.
209. Judgment of 11 December 2007, *Viking,* C-438/05, EU:C:2007:772; *see* hereafter para. 155.
210. *See* at para. 164.
211. Judgment of 28 April 1977, *Thieffry,* 71/76, EU:C:1977:65.
212. Judgment of 6 June 1984, *Klopp,* 107/83, EU:C:1984:270.

because this would infringe the then existing French bar rule that a lawyer (*avocat*) may have his chambers in one place only. That rule was based on the need for lawyers to genuinely practise before a court in order to ensure their availability to both the court and their clients. The Court accepted that in the absence, at that time, of Union rules on the exercise of the legal profession, each Member State was free to regulate the exercise of the legal profession in its territory.[213] Nevertheless, a Member State may not require a lawyer to have only one establishment throughout the Union territory.[214] Such a restricted interpretation of the right of establishment would mean that a lawyer, once established in a particular Member State, would be able to enjoy the freedom of the Treaty to establish himself in another Member State only at the price of abandoning the establishment he already had.[215]

177. Finally, in *Gebhard*,[216] the Court ruled that every obstacle to the right of establishment comes under the scope of application of Article 49 TFEU unless it is justified in the general interest. The Court ruled that all national measures liable to hinder or make less attractive the exercise of fundamental freedoms guaranteed by the Treaty (i.e., the free movement of goods, persons, services and capital) must fulfil four conditions: they must be applied in a non-discriminatory manner; they must be justified by imperative requirements in the general interest; they must be suitable for securing the attainment of the objective which they pursue; and they must not go beyond what is necessary in order to attain it.

The protection of public health is one of the overriding reasons of public interest recognized by EU law. Member States have a wide discretion in this area.[217] In *Memoria and Dall'Antonia*[218] the Court ruled that 49 TFEU precludes national legislation, which prohibits, even despite the express wishes of the deceased, the recipient of a cinerary urn from entrusting its safekeeping to a third party, and requires him to store the urn in his home, unless it is entrusted to a municipal cemetery, and furthermore prohibits any activity carried out for profit relating, even non-exclusively, to the safekeeping of cinerary urns, on whatever basis and for whatever period. Since that legislation prohibits EU nationals from providing those services in the Member State concerned it hinders those nationals to establish themselves in that Member State for the purpose of performing those services. The Court rejected the argument that the measure was justified for the protection of public health, because that objective cannot justify the restriction at issue in so far as cremation ashes, unlike corpses, are biologically inert, since they have been sterilized by heat, and accordingly their safekeeping cannot amount to a constraint imposed by public health considerations. In contrast the objective of protection of the respect owed to

---

213. *Ibid.*, para. 17.
214. *Ibid.*, para. 18.
215. *Ibid. See also,* Judgment of 21 April 2005, *Commission v. Greece*, C-140/03, EU:C:2005:242: a national law prohibiting an optician to operate more than one optician's shop is contrary to Art. 49 TFEU.
216. *See* above at para. 164.
217. *See i.a.* Judgment of 1 June 2010, *Blanco Pérez*, C-570/07 and 571/07, EU:C:2010:300.
218. Judgment of 14 November 2018, *Memoria and Dall'Antonia*, C-342/17, EU:C:2018:906.

the memory of the deceased is capable of amounting to an overriding reason in the public interest, but in the case at hand the Court found that this objective could be pursued with less stringent measures.

178. In *Gebhard*, the Court also said that the possibility for a national of a Member State to exercise his right of establishment, and the conditions for his exercise of that right, must be determined in the light of the activities which he intends to pursue on the territory of the host Member State.[219] Where the taking up of a specific activity is not subject to any rules in the host State, a national of any other Member State will be entitled to establish himself on the territory of the first State and pursue that activity there.[220] On the other hand, where the taking up or the pursuit of a specific activity is subject to certain conditions in the host Member State, a national of another Member State intending to pursue that activity must in principle comply with them.[221] Likewise, Member States must take account of the equivalence of diplomas and, if necessary, proceed to a comparison of the knowledge and qualifications required by their national rules and those of the person concerned.[222]

179. Pursuant to Article 51 TFEU, the provisions of the chapter on the right of establishment shall not apply so far as any given Member State is concerned, to activities which in that State are connected, even occasionally, with the exercise of official authority. In *Reyners*,[223] the Court of Justice had to consider this exception since the Belgian government defended the nationality requirement for lawyers (*avocats*) by relying on this Treaty exception. The Court considered that, having regard to the fundamental character of the freedom of establishment and the rule on equal treatment with nationals in the system of the Treaty, the exceptions allowed cannot be given a scope which would exceed the objective for which this exemption clause was inserted.[224] The exceptions must enable Member States to exclude non-nationals from taking up functions involving the exercise of official authority which are connected with one of the activities of self-employed persons provided for in Article 49 TFEU. This need is fully satisfied when the exclusion of nationals is limited to those activities which, taken on their own, constitute a direct and specific connection with the exercise of official authority.[225] An extension of the exception allowed by Article 51 TFEU to a whole profession would be possible only in cases where such activities were linked with that profession in such a way that freedom of establishment would result in imposing on the Member State concerned the obligation to allow the exercise, even occasionally, by non-nationals of functions appertaining to official authority.[226] Professional activities involving contacts, even regular and organic, with the courts, including even compulsory cooperation in their

---

219. *Ibid.*, para. 32.6.
220. *Ibid.*, para. 36.
221. *Ibid.*
222. *Ibid.*, para. 38.
223. Judgment of 21 June 1974, *Reyners*, 2/74, EU:C:1974:68.
224. *Ibid.*, para. 43.
225. *Ibid.*, para. 45.
226. *Ibid.*, para. 46.

functioning, do not constitute, as such, connection with the exercise of official authority.[227] The most typical activities of the profession of lawyer, in particular, such as consultation and legal assistance and also representation and the defence of parties in court, even when the intervention or assistance of the *avocat* is compulsory or is a legal monopoly, cannot be considered as connected with the exercise of official authority.[228]

180. In seven Grand Chamber judgments of 24 May 2011 in actions brought by the Commission against different Member States, the CJEU found that a nationality requirement for notaries is also inconsistent with the Treaty.[229]

181. The Court reiterates that the exception to the fundamental rule of freedom of establishment laid down in Article 51 TFEU must be interpreted in a manner which limits its scope to what is strictly necessary to safeguard the interests it allows the Member States to protect. Moreover, the exception must be restricted to activities which in themselves are directly and specifically connected with the exercise of official authority.[230] To ascertain whether the activities entrusted to notaries involve a direct and specific connection with the exercise of official authority, account must be taken of the nature of the activities carried out by notaries. In this respect, the Court held that the various activities performed by notaries do not involve a direct and specific connection with the exercise of official authority within the meaning of Article 51 TFEU, despite the significant legal effects of their acts. In particular as regards authentic instruments, the only documents and agreements that are authenticated are those which the parties have freely entered into, whereas the notary cannot unilaterally alter the agreement he is called on to authenticate without first obtaining the consent of the parties.[231] Furthermore, as regards enforceability, while the notary's endorsement of the authority to enforce on the authentic instrument does give it enforceable status, that status is based on the intention of the parties to enter into a document or agreement, after its conformity with the law has been checked by the notary, and to make it enforceable.[232] The same applies to other activities entrusted to notaries, such as attachments of immovable property,[233] certain sales of immovable property,[234] activities concerning inventories of deceased persons' estates and property in joint ownership or co-ownership,[235] the affixing and

---

227. *Ibid.*, para. 51.
228. *Ibid.*, para. 52.
229. Judgments of 24 May 2011, Cases C-47/08, C-50/08, C-51/08, C-52/08, C-53/08, C-54/08 and C-61/08, *Commission v. Belgium, France, Luxembourg, Austria, Portugal, Germany and Greece*, EU:C:2011:C:334, 335, 336, 337, 338, 339, 340; Judgment of 15 March 2018, *Commission v. Czech Republic*, C-575/16, EU:C:2018:186; judgment of 1 February 2017, *Commission v. Hungary*, C-392/15, EU:C:2017:73.
230. Case C-47/08, at para. 85.
231. *Ibid.*, paras 90–91.
232. *Ibid.*, para. 103.
233. *Ibid.*, para. 105.
234. *Ibid.*, para. 108.
235. *Ibid.*, para. 109.

removal of official seals,[236] the judicial division of estates,[237] the procedure for ranking the creditors following a sale by auction,[238] acts such as gifts *inter vivos,* wills, marriage contracts and statutory cohabitation agreements,[239] acts constituting companies, associations and foundations and tax-collecting functions.[240]

182. Article 52 TFEU contains exceptions related to the general interest. It states that the provisions of the chapter on establishment shall not prejudice the applicability of provisions laid down by law, regulation or administrative action providing for special treatment for foreign nationals on grounds of public policy, public security or public health. The same exceptions apply to the free movement of workers and the freedom to provide services. In the context of the freedom of establishment, they do not, however, play a significant role.

§4. FREEDOM OF ESTABLISHMENT OF COMPANIES

183. Pursuant to Article 54 TFEU 'companies or firms formed in accordance with the law of a Member State and having their registered office, central administration or principal place of business within the Union shall, for the purposes of this Chapter, be treated in the same way as natural persons who are nationals of Member States. "Companies or firms" means companies or firms constituted under civil or commercial law, including cooperative societies, and other legal persons governed by public or private law, save for those which are non-profit-making'.

184. While as a matter of principle the Treaty grants companies the same right of establishment as natural persons, i.e., they may not be subject to restrictions on the setting-up of agencies, branches or subsidiaries and the right includes the right to take up and pursue activities and to set up and manage undertakings, in particular companies or firms (*see* Article 49 TFEU), the right of establishment of companies poses specific problems, as is evidenced by the case law of the Court of Justice, discussed in the following paragraphs.

I. Right of Primary Establishment of Companies

185. In a first case, *Daily Mail,*[241] the Court had to deal with the question whether national law can restrict the possibility for a company incorporated under its laws from moving its central management and control (principal place of establishment) to another Member State. Daily Mail wanted to change its seat from the UK to the Netherlands for tax reasons and thus had to ask for the consent of the UK tax administration. Dutch law accepted such a transfer of a company that would

---

236. *Ibid.*
237. *Ibid.,* para. 110.
238. *Ibid.,* para. 111.
239. *Ibid.,* para. 113.
240. *Ibid.,* para. 114.
241. Judgment of 27 September 1988, *Daily Mail,* 81/87, EU:C:1988:456.

continue to be incorporated under foreign law. The question arose whether the restriction of English law was compatible with Article 54 TFEU.

186.   The Court of Justice first confirmed that in the case of a company, the right of establishment is generally exercised by the setting-up of agencies, branches or subsidiaries, as is expressly provided for in the second sentence of the first paragraph of Article 49 TFEU.[242] Indeed, that is the form of establishment in which the applicant engaged in this case by opening an investment management office in the Netherlands. Next, it pointed out that the provision of UK law at issue does not stand in the way of a partial or total transfer of the activities of a company incorporated in the UK to a company newly incorporated in another Member State, if necessary after winding-up and, consequently, the settlement of the tax position of the UK company.[243] UK law requires Treasury consent only where such a company seeks to transfer its central management and control out of the UK while maintaining its legal personality and its status as a UK company.[244]

187.   The Court observed that certain States require that not merely the registered office but also the real head office, that is to say the central administration of the company, is situated on their territory, and that the removal of the central administration from that territory thus presupposes the winding-up of the company with all the consequences this entails in company law and tax law.[245] The legislation of other States permits companies to transfer their central administration to a foreign country but some of them, such as the UK, make that right subject to certain restrictions, and the legal consequences of a transfer, particularly in regard to taxation, vary from one Member State to another.[246] The Treaty has taken account of that variety in national legislation. In defining, in Article 54 TFEU, the companies which enjoy the right of establishment, the Treaty places on the same footing, as connecting factors, the registered office, central administration and principal place of business of a company.[247] The Court moreover held that the differences in national legislation concerning the required connecting factor and the question whether – and if so how – the registered office or real head office of a company incorporated under national law may be transferred from one Member State to another are problems which are not resolved by the rules concerning the right of establishment but must be dealt with by future legislation or conventions.[248] To conclude, Articles 46 and 54 TFEU cannot be interpreted as conferring on companies incorporated under the law of a Member State a right to transfer their central management and control and their central administration to another Member State while retaining their status as companies incorporated under the legislation of the first Member State.[249]

---

242. *Ibid.*, para. 17.
243. *Ibid.*, para. 18.
244. *Ibid.*
245. *Ibid.*, para. 20.
246. *Ibid.*
247. *Ibid.*, para. 21.
248. *Ibid.*, para. 23.
249. *Ibid.*, para. 24.

188.   *Daily Mail* thus denied reliance on the right of primary establishment in the context of transfer of the seat of a company. The obstacles to the transfer in the case at hand actually stemmed from differences in legislation between the Member State concerning the recognition of companies as legal persons. Later judgments have clarified that in other circumstances companies, just like natural persons, do enjoy a right of primary establishment. *Überseering*[250] concerned a firm incorporated under Dutch law as a 'besloten vennootschap' (a private limited company). It brought an action in court for payment of a sum of money against another company in execution of a contract. Under German law, Überseering was denied legal capacity because, although being incorporated and recognized under Dutch law, according to German law it had lost its legal capacity as a result of a share transaction that amounted to the transfer actual centre of administration to Germany. It thus became an irregular German company. Again, this problem stemmed from a difference between the law of two Member States regarding the recognition of companies (in the Netherlands, incorporation under Dutch law suffices, while Germany requires the presence of the real seat in Germany). Questioned by the German Supreme Court, the Court of Justice ruled that where a company formed in accordance with the law of a Member State (A) in which it has its registered office is deemed, under the law of another Member State (B), to have moved its actual centre of administration to Member State B, Articles 49 and 54 TFEU preclude Member State B from denying the company legal capacity and, consequently, the capacity to bring legal proceedings before its national courts for the purpose of enforcing rights under a contract with a company established in Member State B.[251] It can be noted that in this case it was the Member State to which the company was deemed to have moved its seat that denied the company legal capacity where according to the law under which it was and remained to be incorporated that legal capacity was not put into question.

189.   In *Cartesio,*[252] like in *Daily Mail,* the Court of Justice had to rule about a restriction imposed by the law of the Member State under the law of which the company was incorporated and where that company wanted to move its primary establishment to another Member State. Cartesio was formed as a limited partnership under Hungarian law. Its seat was established in Hungary. The company had two partners both of whom were natural persons resident in Hungary and holding Hungarian nationality: a limited partner, whose only commitment is to invest capital, and an unlimited partner, with unlimited liability for the company's debts. At a given moment, Cartesio filed an application with the regional court for registration of the transfer of its seat to Gallarate in Italy and, in consequence, for amendment of the entry regarding Cartesio's company seat in the commercial register. The application was rejected on the ground that the Hungarian law in force did not allow a company incorporated in Hungary to transfer its seat abroad while continuing to be subject to Hungarian law as its personal law.

---

250. Judgment of 5 November 2002, *Überseering*, C-208/00, EU:C:2002:632.
251. *Ibid.*, para. 52.
252. Judgment of 16 December 2008, *Cartesio,* C-210/06, EU:C:2008:723.

190. The Court of Justice ruled that this rejection was not in violation of Articles 49 and 54 TFEU. It held that a distinction must be made between the situation where the seat of a company incorporated under the law of one Member State is transferred to another Member State with no change as regards the law which governs that company, and the situation where a company governed by the law of one Member State moves to another Member State with an attendant change as regards the national law applicable.[253] In the latter situation, the company is converted into a form of company which is governed by the law of the Member State to which it has moved.

191. Thus, a Member State has the power to define both the connecting factor required of a company if it is to be regarded as incorporated under the law of that Member State and, as such, capable of enjoying the right of establishment and the connecting factor required if the company is to be subsequently able to maintain that status.[254] That power includes the possibility for a Member State not to permit a company governed by its law to retain that status if the company intends to reorganize itself in another Member State by moving its seat to the territory of the latter, thereby breaking the connecting factor required under the national law of the Member State of incorporation (as was the case in *Cartesio*).

II. The Right of Secondary Establishment of Companies

192. While the incorporation of a company is an act of primary establishment, the creation of a branch by that company (in another Member Sate) is an act of secondary establishment.

193. In *Centros*,[255] the Court ruled that it is contrary to Articles 49 and 54 TFEU for a Member State to refuse to register a branch of a company formed in accordance with the law of another Member State in which it has its registered office but in which it conducts no business where the branch is intended to enable the company in question to carry on its entire business in the State in which that branch is to be created, while avoiding the need to form a company there, thus evading application of the rules governing the formation of companies which, in that State, are more restrictive as regards the paying up of a minimum share capital.[256] That interpretation does not, however, prevent the authorities of the Member State concerned from adopting any appropriate measure for preventing or penalizing fraud, either in relation to the company itself, if need be in cooperation with the Member State in which it was formed, or in relation to its members, where it has been established that they are in fact attempting, by means of the formation of a company, to evade their obligations towards private or public creditors established in the territory of

---

253. *Ibid.*, para. 111.
254. *Ibid.*, para. 110.
255. Judgment of 9 March 1999, *Centros*, C-212/97, EU:C:1999:26.
256. *Ibid.*, para. 39.

the Member State concerned.[257] In the case at hand, two Danish citizens had created a limited company under English law with no intention to exercise a business activity through that company in the UK. The sole business intended was that of the Danish branch of the limited company for which the shareholders sought a registration in Denmark. The registration was refused because the Danish authorities considered that the creation of the English limited company followed by the creation of a Danish branch was a way to circumvent the stricter Danish rules on minimum capital of companies (than those applicable in England).

194. The Court accepted the right for natural persons to choose the Member State of incorporation of the company even if they do not pursue any economic activity in the Member State of the principal establishment and the ensuing right of secondary establishment of that company in other Member States. The exception relating to the evasion of their obligations towards creditors did not apply in the case at hand because creditors were perfectly informed of the limits on the possibility to recover their claim for the company by the disclosure of the legal form of Centros, i.e., a limited company under English law.

195. In *Inspire Art,*[258] the Court ruled that it is contrary to Articles 49 and 54 TFEU for national legislation (in this case of The Netherlands) such as the *Wet op de Formeel Buitenlandse Vennootschappen* (Law on Formally Foreign Companies) to impose on the exercise of freedom of secondary establishment in that State by a company formed in accordance with the law of another Member State certain conditions provided for in domestic company law in respect of company formation relating to minimum capital and directors' liability. The reasons for which the company was formed in that other Member State, and the fact that it carries on its activities exclusively or almost exclusively in the Member State of establishment, do not deprive it of the right to invoke the freedom of establishment guaranteed by the TFEU, save where the existence of an abuse is established on a case-by-case basis.[259]

§5. Horizontal Direct Effect of the Right of Establishment

196. The Treaty provisions on fundamental freedoms are addressed to the Member States, which have to refrain from introducing or maintaining obstacles to the exercise of those freedoms. Nevertheless in a certain number of judgments, the Court of Justice has recognized the right of individuals to rely on the personal freedoms (free movement of workers, right of establishment and freedom to provide services) against certain non-governmental bodies, and with regard to the free movement of workers, even the right of an employee to rely on the free movement of workers against a (potential) employer, where that employer is not the State or a public body.

---

257. *Ibid.*
258. Judgment of 30 September 2003, *Inspire Art,* C-167/01, EU:C:2003:512.
259. *Inspire Art,* para. 143.

197. The first judgment of the Court of Justice conferring horizontal effect on a Treaty provision addressed to Member States and conferring rights on employees was not one concerning free movement, but the judgment has inspired the Court to recognize horizontal effect in that area as well. In *Defrenne*,[260] the Court of Justice ruled with respect to what is now Article 157 TFEU (equal pay for equal work for men and women) that the fact that certain provisions of the Treaty are formally addressed to the Member States does not prevent rights from being conferred at the same time on any individual who has an interest in compliance with the obligations thus laid down, including in his or her relationship with another private person, such as a private employer.[261]

198. In the area of free movement, the Court ruled first in *Walrave & Koch*[262] that Article 43 TFEU on the free movement of workers, and Article 56 TFEU on the freedom to provide services can be invoked by an individual against a sport federation that sets the rules for the exercise of the professional activity. According to the rules of the *Union cycliste internationale* (UCI) on medium-distance world cycling championships behind motorcycles, the pacemaker (sitting on the motorbike) had to be of the same nationality as the stayer. The question arose whether these provisions apply to the rules of the UCI, which is a private body. The Court considers that together with Article 18 TFEU (discrimination on the basis of nationality) these provisions have in common the prohibition, in their respective spheres of application, of any discrimination on grounds of nationality. It then decides, for the first time, that the prohibition of such discrimination does not only apply to the action of public authorities but extends likewise to rules of any other nature aimed at regulating in a collective manner gainful employment and the provision of services. Indeed, the abolition between Member States of obstacles to freedom of movement for persons and to freedom to provide services, which are fundamental objectives of the Union, would be compromised if the abolition of barriers of national origin could be neutralized by obstacles resulting from the exercise of their legal autonomy by associations or organizations which do not come under public law.[263] Moreover, since working conditions in the various Member States are sometimes governed by means of provisions laid down by law or regulation or by agreements and other acts concluded or adopted by private persons, to limit the prohibitions in question to acts of a public authority would risk creating inequality in their application.[264] That case law was confirmed in *Donà & Mantera*[265] concerning a nationality requirement imposed on football players by the Italian Football Federation.

---

260. Judgment of 8 April 1976, *Defrenne v. Sabena*, 43/75, EU:C:1976:56.
261. *Ibid.*, para. 31.
262. Judgment of 12 December 1974, *Walrave & Koch*, 36/74, EU:C:1974:140.
263. *Walrave & Koch*, para. 18.
264. *Ibid.*, para. 19.
265. Judgment of 14 July 1976, *Donà & Mantera*, 13/76, EU:C:1976:115.

199. Two further judgments of the CJEU relating to the free movement of workers should be mentioned here. The first one is *Bosman*,[266] which confirms the 'collective horizontal direct effect' of the Treaty rules on free movement of persons (i.e., the possibility to invoke a Treaty provision against collective rules imposed by private bodies); the second one is *Angonese*,[267] relating to individual horizontal direct effect (i.e., the possibility for an individual to invoke the freedom against another individual) which is exceptional, in that it only applies to discriminations on the basis of nationality against employees or prospective employees.

200. In *Bosman*, the Court ruled that Article 43 TFEU on the free movement of workers precludes the application of rules laid down by sporting associations, under which: (i) a professional footballer who is a national of one Member State may not, on the expiry of his contract with a club, be employed by a club of another Member State unless the latter club has paid to the former club a transfer, training or development fee, (ii) in matches in competitions which they organize, football clubs may field only a limited number of professional players who are nationals of other Member States.[268] In this judgment, the Court gave that Treaty article horizontal direct effect (as against a sport organization) even with respect to a provision that did not discriminate on the basis of nationality, but which hindered the free, cross-border, movement of football players.

201. In *Angonese*,[269] the Court confirmed the applicability of Article 43 TFEU to the situation of an Italian national whose mother tongue is German, who was resident in the province of Bolzano (which is a bilingual area: Italian-German) and who had studied in Austria. Later he wanted to participate in a competition for a job with a private bank in Bolzano. One of the conditions for entry to the competition was possession of a type-B certificate of bilingualism (in Italian and German), which used to be required in the province of Bolzano for access to certain jobs in the public service. The certificate is issued by the public authorities of the province of Bolzano after an examination which is held only in that province. It is usual for residents of the province of Bolzano to obtain the certificate as a matter of course for employment purposes. Obtaining the certificate is viewed as an almost compulsory step as part of normal training. Mr Angonese was not in possession of the certificate, but he was perfectly bilingual. With a view to gaining admission to the competition, he had submitted a certificate showing completion of his studies as a draughtsman and certificates attesting to his studies of languages (English, Slovene and Polish) at the Faculty of Philosophy at Vienna University and had stated that his professional experience included practising as a draughtsman and translating from Polish into Italian. Mr Angonese was refused admittance to competition because he had not produced the certificate. The national judge found that non-residents of Bolzano may have difficulty obtaining the certificate in good time in view of the short period between the oral and the written part of the exam. Although

---

266. Judgment of 15 December 1995, *Bosman,* C-415/93, EU:C:1995:463.
267. Judgment of 6 June 2000, *Angonese,* C-281/98, EU:C:2000:296.
268. *Bosman,* paras 114 and 237.
269. *Angonese,* C-281/98, EU:C:2000:296.

Mr Angonese, being a resident of Bolzano, would not personally encounter that difficulty, the Court nevertheless took the question referred by the Italian judge and made an abstract ruling. Mr Angonese argued that the requirement of the certificate violated Article 43 TFEU. The CJEU first referred to its *Walrave* and *Bosman* judgments (*see* above) where it held that the prohibition of discrimination based on nationality applies not only to the actions of public authorities but also to rules of any other nature aimed at regulating in a collective manner gainful employment and the provision of services (*see* above).[270] Second, it recalled its *Defrenne* ruling (*see also* above) where it held that the fact that certain provisions of the Treaty are formally addressed to the Member States does not prevent rights from being conferred at the same time on any individual who has an interest in compliance with the obligations thus laid down.[271] In that judgment, the Court ruled, in relation to a provision of the Treaty which was mandatory in nature (i.e., the principle of equal pay for men and women), that it applied equally to all agreements intended to regulate paid labour collectively, as well as to contracts between individuals. Such considerations are, according to the Court in *Angonese, a fortiori*, applicable to Article 43 TFEU, which lays down a fundamental freedom and which constitutes a specific application of the general prohibition of discrimination contained in Article 18 TFEU.[272] In that respect, like Article 43 TFEU, it is designed to ensure that there is no discrimination on the labour market. Consequently, the prohibition of discrimination on grounds of nationality laid down in Article 43 TFEU must be regarded as applying to private persons as well. As to the existence of a discrimination on the basis of nationality the Court observed that since the majority of residents of the province of Bolzano are Italian nationals, the obligation to obtain the requisite certificate puts nationals of other Member States at a disadvantage by comparison with residents of the province.[273] In other words, there was an indirect discrimination on the basis of nationality, which even if imposed by a private employer violates the free movement of workers. Particularly revealing is that the Court expressly limited the application of what is now Article 43 TFEU to direct and indirect discrimination on the basis of nationality, and did not extend it, like in *Bosman*, to non-discriminatory restrictions. It should be reminded that *Bosman* concerned the collective organization of labour and not, as *Angonese*, a restriction imposed by an individual employer.

202. In *Viking*,[274] the Court had to deal with the applicability of the right of establishment with regard to restrictions imposed by a trade union. In the case law mentioned above, the Court had already decided in general terms that the personal freedoms of the Treaty apply to restrictions imposed by NGOs that regulate labour in a collective manner. *Viking* is the first, and so far the only, judgment where that case law was specifically applied to a situation of the right of establishment and

---

270. *Ibid.*, para. 31.
271. *Ibid.*, para. 34.
272. *Ibid.*, para. 35.
273. *Ibid.*, para. 40.
274. Judgment of 11 December 2007, *Viking*, C-438/05, EU:C:2007:772.

where the obstacles to that freedom are not imposed by a sporting federation, but by a trade union, the powers of which are somewhat different.

203.   Viking was a large ferry operator incorporated under Finnish law operating seven vessels, including the *Rosella* which, under the Finnish flag, plied the route between Tallinn (Estonia) and Helsinki (Finland). So long as the *Rosella* was under the Finnish flag, Viking was obliged under both Finnish law and the terms of a collective bargaining agreement to pay the crew wages at the same level as those applicable in Finland, which are higher than those applicable in Estonia. As a result, following direct competition from Estonian vessels operating on the same route with lower wage costs the *Rosella* was running at a loss. As an alternative to selling the vessel, Viking sought to reflag the Rosella by registering it in Estonia, where workers enjoy less rights than in Finland. In an attempt to prevent this from happening, the Finnish trade unions launched a strike in order to induce Viking to conclude a collective agreement under Finnish law. There upon Viking brought an action before an English court requesting it to declare the action taken by the trade unions contrary to Article 49 TFEU. The English Court referred questions to the CJEU.

204.   The Court of Justice refers to its settled case law, to the effect that Articles 43, 49 and 56 TFEU do not only apply to the actions of public authorities but also extend to rules of any other nature aimed at regulating in a collective manner gainful employment, self-employment and the provision of services (with reference to *inter alia Walrave and Koch, Donà*,[275] *Bosman*, and *Angonese*).[276] The Court adds that since working conditions in the different Member States are governed sometimes by provisions laid down by law or regulation and sometimes by collective agreements and other acts concluded or adopted by private persons, limiting application of the prohibitions laid down by these articles to acts of a public authority would risk creating inequality in its application (*see*, by analogy, *Walrave and Koch*, paragraph 19; *Bosman*, paragraph 84; and *Angonese*, paragraph 33).

205.   In the present case, the Court stated, first, that the organization of collective action by trade unions must be regarded as covered by the legal autonomy that those organizations, which are not public law entities, enjoy pursuant to the trade union rights accorded to them, *inter alia*, by national law. Second, as the trade unions submit, collective action such as that at issue in the main proceedings, which may be the trade unions' last resort to ensure the success of their claim to regulate the work of Viking's employees collectively, must be considered to be inextricably linked to the collective agreement the conclusion of which the trade unions are seeking. The Court of Justice concluded that Article 49 TFEU is to be interpreted to the effect that collective action which seeks to induce an undertaking whose registered office is in a given Member State to enter into a collective work agreement with a trade union established in that State and to apply the terms set out in that agreement to the employees of a subsidiary of that undertaking established in another Member

---

275. *See* above paras 151–154.
276. *Viking*, para. 33.

State, constitutes a restriction within the meaning of that article. That restriction may, in principle, be justified by an overriding reason of public interest, such as the protection of workers, provided that it is established that the restriction is suitable for ensuring the attainment of the legitimate objective pursued and does not go beyond what is necessary to achieve that objective.

§6. Freedom to Provide Services: Notion

206. Article 56(1) TFEU, which is the basic provision of the freedom to provide services reads: 'Within the framework of the provisions set out below, restrictions on freedom to provide services within the Union shall be prohibited in respect of nationals of Member States who are established in a Member State other than that of the person for whom the services are intended.' Pursuant to the second paragraph, 'the European Parliament and the Council, acting in accordance with the ordinary legislative procedure, may extend the provisions of the Chapter to nationals of a third country who provide services and who are established within the Union'.

I. The Notion of 'Service'

207. Pursuant to Article 57 TFEU, the notion of 'services' covers services that are normally provided for remuneration, insofar as they are not governed by the provisions relating to freedom of movement for goods, capital and persons. They shall in particular include:

(a) activities of an industrial character;
(b) activities of a commercial character;
(c) activities of craftsmen;
(d) activities of the professions.

208. The list is not exhaustive. The Treaty notion of services is very broad and includes *inter alia* the professions, (semi) professional sport (*see* hereafter), medical services and education for remuneration (*see* hereafter).

II. The Cross-Border Element

209. Pursuant to the third paragraph of Article 57 TFEU, 'without prejudice to the provisions of the Chapter relating to the right of establishment, the person providing a service may, in order to do so, temporarily pursue his activity in the Member State where the service is provided, under the same conditions as are imposed by that State on its own nationals'.

210. Articles 56–57 TFEU make it clear that in a situation where a service provider relies on a (primary or secondary) establishment (*see* above) the freedom to provide services does not apply. *Gebhard*,[277] discussed in the section on the right of establishment gives criteria to distinguish the mere provision of services from the exercise of the right of establishment. The third paragraph of Article 57 TFEU recognizes that the freedom to provide services may be exercised through the presence of the service provider in the Member State of the beneficiary – without having a permanent link with that Member State, in which case he exercises the right of establishment –, but this is not required for the application of Article 56 TFEU: a pure cross-border activity, without any presence in the host Member State, suffices.

211. The freedom to provide services only applies in cross-border situations. The Court of Justice has identified several situations where a service provider exercises the freedom to provide services:

(1) a service provider established in Member State A travels temporarily to Member State B in order to provide a service there to the benefit of a recipient (*see* Article 57 TFEU, last paragraph);
(2) a recipient of a service who resides in Member State A travels to Member State B where the service provider is established to benefit from services there;
(3) a service provider established in Member State A provides services to the benefit of recipients in Member State B, without travelling to Member State B;
(4) the service provider established in Member State A provides services in Member State B to the benefit of recipients who have their residence in Member State A.

212. The *first* situation, which is expressly mentioned in the Treaty (Article 57 TFEU, last paragraph), is to be distinguished from a situation of establishment. Where the link with the host Member State is permanent, the service provider is deemed to exercise the right of establishment rather than the freedom to provide services. An example of the mere provision of services (without establishment) is that of the lawyer who visits his client in another Member State or appears in court for him in another Member State, even if that is not the Member State of residence of the recipient.

213. In the *second* situation, it is the recipient who travels to the Member State where the service provider is established. An example is given in *Luisi and Carbone*.[278] Ms Luisi, an Italian citizen, travelled to Germany to see a doctor and Mr Carbone, an Italian citizen as well, travelled to Germany as a tourist. Both persons carried cash in excess of the amounts that, at that time, were allowed by Italy in the context of restrictions on the free movement of capital (restrictions that were still allowed then under Union law). To the extent that the money served for the payment of services to be received in another Member State, the Court found that the restrictions imposed by Italy amounted to an obstacle to the freedom to provide services. The case also shows that the freedom to provide services can be invoked by

---

277. Judgment in *Gebhard, see* above at para. 164.
278. Judgment of 31 January 1984, *Luisi & Carbone*, 286/82 and 26/83, EU:C:1984:35.

the recipient of the services who is prevented from benefiting from a service rendered by a service provider established in another Member State. In contrast, the *Steymann*[279] case shows that the right of recipients of services to freely move into another Member State is linked to the reception of specific services. Mr Steymann, a German national, settled in the Netherlands. For a short period, he was in paid employment as a plumber. Subsequently, he became a member of the religious community known as 'the Bhagwan Community', which supplies its material needs by means of commercial activities, including running a discothèque, a bar and a launderette. Mr Steymann's contribution to the life of the Bhagwan Community consisted in the performance of plumbing work on the community's premises and general household duties. He also took part in the community's commercial activity. The community provided for the material needs of its members in any event, irrespective of the nature and the extent of their activities. Mr Steymann applied for a Dutch residence permit in order to pursue an activity as an employed person. His application was turned down. The Court of Justice decided that Articles 56 and 57 TFEU do not cover the situation where a national of a Member State goes to reside in the territory of another Member State and establishes his principal residence there in order to provide or receive services for an indefinite period.[280] However, such a right may now be recognized under the right of residence.[281]

214. The *third* situation, where a service provider established in Member State A provides services to the benefit of recipients in Member State B, without being present in Member State B, is the one where the service is genuinely provided cross-border. Today one would think of online services. The case law of the CJEU gives examples of restrictions that were imposed in the past by certain Member States on the retransmission of television broadcasts. In *Bond van Adverteerders*,[282] the CJEU ruled that the distribution by operators of cable networks established in a Member State, of television programmes supplied by broadcasters established in other Member States and containing advertisements intended especially for the public in the Member State where the programmes are received, comprises a number of services within the meaning of Articles 59 and 60 of the Treaty.[283] National prohibitions of advertising and subtitling such as those existing in the Netherlands at the time entail restrictions on freedom to supply services contrary to Article 56 TFEU that could not be justified on grounds of public policy. This case law has been confirmed in later judgments. For example in *De Agostini*,[284] the Court of Justice reiterated the principle of *Bond van Adverteerders* and found that a Member State is not precluded from taking, on the basis of provisions of its domestic legislation, measures against an advertiser in relation to television advertising (in this case concerning

---

279. Judgment of 5 October 1988, *Steymann v. Staatsecretaris van Justitie*, 196/87, EU:C:1988:475.
280. *Ibid.*, para. 17.
281. *See* Directive 2004/38/EC on the right of citizens of the Union and their family members to move and reside freely within the territory of the Member States, (2004) *OJ* L 158/77.
282. Judgment of 26 April 1988, *Bond van Adverteerders*, 352/85, EU:C:1988:196.
283. *Ibid.*, para. 17.
284. Judgment of 9 July 1997, *De Agostini*, C-34/95, C-35/95 and C-36/95, EU:C:1997:344.

advertising directed at children).[285] However, it is for the national court to determine whether those provisions are necessary for meeting overriding requirements of general public importance or one of the aims stated in Article 52 TFEU, whether they are proportionate for that purpose and whether those aims or overriding requirements could be met by measures less restrictive of intra-Union trade (rule of reason, *see* hereafter).[286]

215.   Finally, the *fourth* situation, where a service provider provides services in another Member State to recipients residing in his Member State can be illustrated by the tourist guide cases of the CJEU. In *Commission v. France*,[287] the Court found that France had violated its obligations under Article 56 TFEU by making the provision of services by tourist guides travelling with a group of tourists from another Member State, where those services consist in guiding such tourists in certain places other than museums and historical monuments which may be visited only with a specialized professional guide, subject to possession of a licence which requires the acquisition of a specific qualification normally obtained by success in an examination. In *Commission v. Italy*[288] and *Commission v. Greece*,[289] the Court of Justice found that these Member States had violated the freedom to provide services by maintaining comparable requirements.

III. A Service for Remuneration

216.   Only services that are rendered for remuneration fall within the scope of the freedom to provide services.

217.   In *Humbel*,[290] the Court of Justice considered that even though the concept of remuneration is not expressly defined in Articles 56 et seq. TFEU, its legal scope may be deduced from the provisions of the second paragraph of Article 57 TFEU, which states that 'services' include in particular activities of an industrial or commercial character and the activities of craftsmen and the professions.[291] The essential characteristic of remuneration lies in the fact that it constitutes consideration for the service in question, and is normally agreed upon between the provider and the recipient of the service. State education or education that is (entirely or substantially) subsidized by the State is not a service within the meaning of Article 57 TFEU. First of all, the State, in establishing and maintaining such a system, is not seeking to engage in gainful activity but is fulfilling its duties towards its own population in the social, cultural and educational fields. Second, the system in question is, as a general rule, funded from the public purse and not by pupils or their parents.

---

285. *Ibid.*, para. 54.
286. *Ibid.*
287. Judgment of 26 February 1991, *Commission v. France*, C-154/89, EU:C:1991:76.
288. Judgment of 26 February 1991, *Commission v. Italy*, C-180/89, EU:C:1991:78.
289. Judgment of 26 February 1991, in *Commission v. Greece*, C-198/89, EU:C:1991:79.
290. Judgment of 27 September 1988, *Humbel*, 263/86, EU:C:1988:451.
291. *Ibid.*, para. 16.

The nature of the activity is not affected by the fact that pupils or their parents must sometimes pay teaching or enrolment fees in order to make a certain contribution to the operating expenses of the system.

218. Professional sport is a service for remuneration. Moreover, many other services for remuneration accompany professional sport events, including the exploitation of broadcast rights. In *Bacardi France*,[292] the Court found that the French prohibition of 'indirect' TV advertising (the appearance on screen of hoardings visible during the retransmission of binational sporting events taking place in other Member States) for alcohol entailed a restriction on freedom to provide advertising services insofar as the owners of the advertising hoardings must refuse, as a preventive measure, any advertising for alcoholic beverages if the sporting event is likely to be retransmitted in France.[293] They also impede the provision of broadcasting services for television programmes.[294] French broadcasters must refuse all retransmission of sporting events in which hoardings bearing advertising for alcoholic beverages marketed in France may be visible. Furthermore, the organizers of sporting events taking place outside France cannot sell the retransmission rights to French broadcasters if the transmission of the television programmes of such events is likely to contain indirect television advertising for those alcoholic beverages.[295]

219. In *Christelle Deliège*,[296] a case about restrictions imposed upon judokas to participate in competitions while this participation is not as such remunerated, the Court considered that sporting activities and, in particular, a high-ranking athlete's participation in an international competition, are capable of involving the provision of a number of separate but closely related services which may fall within the scope of Article 56 TFEU, even if some of those services are not paid for by those for whom they are performed with (a reference to *Bond van Adverteerders*).[297] For example, an organizer of such a competition may offer athletes an opportunity of engaging in their sporting activity in competition with others and, at the same time, athletes' participation in the competition enables the organizer to put on a sports event which the public may attend, which television broadcasters may retransmit and which may be of interest to advertisers and sponsors.[298] Moreover, the athletes provide their sponsors with publicity the basis for which is the sporting activity itself.[299]

220. Medical services paid by the patient are obviously services within the meaning of Article 67 TFEU. However, often they are not paid by the patient but by the social security system. In *Smits and Peerbooms*,[300] the Court recalled first that

---

292. Judgment of 13 July 2004, *Bacardi France*, C-429/02, EU:C:2004:432.
293. *Ibid.*, para. 35.
294. *Ibid.*
295. *Ibid.*
296. Judgment of 11 April 2000, *Christelle Deliège*, C-51/96 and C-191/97, EU:C:2000:199.
297. *Ibid.*, para. 56.
298. *Ibid.*, para. 57.
299. *Ibid.*
300. Judgment of 12 July 2001, *Smits and Peerbooms*, C-157/99, EU:C:2001:404.

Article 57 TFEU does not require that the service be paid for by those for whom it is performed (with reference to *inter alia Bond van Adverteerders*: not the viewer but the advertiser is paying for the broadcast).[301] Second, it pointed out that Article 57 TFEU applies to services normally provided for remuneration and that it has been held that, for the purposes of that provision, the essential characteristic of remuneration lies in the fact that it constitutes consideration for the service in question (*Humbel*, paragraph 17).[302] In the present cases, the payments made by the sickness insurance funds under the contractual arrangements provided for by the law, albeit set at a flat rate, are indeed the consideration for the hospital services and unquestionably represent remuneration for the hospital which receives them and which is engaged in an activity of an economic character.[303]

221. It is obvious from some of the judgments mentioned above that advertising is a service and that restrictions on advertising may form an obstacle to the freedom to provide the service advertised. However, in *Grogan*,[304] the Court of Justice ruled that Article 56 TFEU does not cover information distributed by student associations in Ireland about the identity and location of clinics in the UK where, contrary to Ireland, voluntary termination of pregnancy is lawfully carried out and the means of communicating with those clinics, where the clinics in question have no involvement in the distribution of the said information. The Court stressed that medical termination of pregnancy, performed in accordance with the law of the State in which it is carried out, constitutes a service within the meaning of Article 57 TFEU, but a restriction of the information about that service distributed by organizations that have no connection with the providers of these services is not a restriction to the freedom to provide services.[305]

§7. FREEDOM TO PROVIDE SERVICES: BENEFICIARIES

222. Article 56(1) TFEU reads: 'Within the framework of the provisions set out below, restrictions on freedom to provide services within the Union shall be prohibited in respect of nationals of Member States who are established in a Member State other than that of the person for whom the services are intended.'

223. The cross-border element has been discussed in §6. It has been seen that the Court of Justice has already accepted as falling within the ambit of the freedom to provide services the situation where the provider of the service and the recipient are established in one and the same Member State, but where the service is provided in another Member State (tourist guide cases). The beneficiaries of the freedom to provide services are nationals of Member States (and their clients, *see* above

---

301. *Ibid.*, para. 57.
302. *Ibid.*, para. 58.
303. *Ibid.*
304. Judgment of 4 October 1991, *The Society for the Protection of Unborn Children Ireland Ltd v. Stephen Grogan and Others*, C-159/90, EU:C:1991:378.
305. *Ibid.*, para. 32.

Luisi & Carbone). A third-country national, even where he is established in a Member State of the EU, cannot benefit from Article 56 TFEU.[306] The same holds true for the national of a Member State who is established outside the Union.

§8. Freedom to Provide Services: Types of Restrictions Caught by Article 56 TFEU and Grounds of Justification

224. From Article 56(1) TFEU, quoted in the preceding paragraph, it follows that only nationals of a Member State established in another Member State than the Member State where the service is provided can invoke the protection it grants. Quite naturally, the first type of restriction identified by the Court of Justice was discrimination on the basis of the place of establishment. In *van Binsbergen*,[307] the Court's first judgment on the freedom to provide services, it held that Articles 56 and 57 TFEU oppose to a national requirement of habitual residence within that State, in order to have the right to provide services, where the provision of services is not subject to any special condition under the national law applicable (here the profession of '*procureur*', i.e., the equivalent of a solicitor or *avoué*).[308] In this judgment, the Court of Justice also confirmed, as it did in *Reyners*[309] with respect to the freedom of establishment, that Article 56 TFEU has become directly effective as from the end of the transitional period (for the original Member States: 1 January 1970).[310]

225. Pursuant to Article 62 TFEU, the provisions of Articles 51–54 TFEU included in the chapter on establishment also apply to services. Article 51 TFEU[311] relates to the exercise of public authority and does not seem to be particularly relevant in the context of the freedom to provide services. Article 52 TFEU contains a limited list of express grounds of justification for a different treatment of nationals and foreigners.[312]

226. While the initial case law related to discrimination on the basis of nationality and place of establishment – for some of which a justification can be found in Article 52 TFEU –, in later judgments the Court of Justice has extended the scope of the restrictions that are prohibited by Article 56 TFEU. A first category are restrictions which do not take into account the evidence and guarantees already furnished by the provider of the services in his home Member State. Examples are the judgments in *Webb*[313] and *Commission v. Germany*[314] (insurance case).

---

306. Judgment of 3 October 2006, *FKP Scorpio*, C-290/04, EU:C:2006:630, para. 68.
307. Judgment of 3 December 1974, *van Binsbergen*, 33/74, EU:C:1974:131.
308. *Ibid.*, para. 17.
309. *See* above para. 171.
310. *van Binsbergen*, para. 23.
311. Discussed above at paras 177 et seq.
312. Discussed above at para. 179.
313. Judgment of 17 December 1981, *Webb*, 279/80, EU:C:1981:314.
314. Judgment in 4 December 1986, *Commission v. Germany*, 205/84, EU:C:1986:463.

227. In *Webb*, the Court of Justice ruled that Article 49 EC (now Article 56 TFEU) does not preclude a Member State which requires agencies for the provision of manpower to hold a licence from requiring a provider of services established in another Member State and pursuing such activities on the territory of the first Member State to comply with that condition even if he holds a licence issued by the State in which he is established. This is however subject to restrictions. In the first place, when considering applications for licences and in granting them the Member State in which the service is provided must make no distinction based on the nationality of the provider of the services or his place of establishment. In the second place, that Member State must take into account the evidence and guarantees already produced by the provider of the services for the pursuit of his activities in the Member State in which he is established.[315]

228. *Commission v. Germany* (insurance case) concerned the situation where in order to be allowed to operate in Germany insurance companies needed an authorization from the German authorities, even if they were established in another Member State, while e.g., in the UK, at the time, such an authorization regime did not apply. The Court ruled that the requirement of authorization may be maintained only insofar as it is justified on the grounds relating to the protection of policy-holders and insured persons.[316] The Court added that those grounds are not equally important in every sector of insurance, and that there may be cases where, because of the nature of the risk insured and of the party seeking insurance (e.g., large businesses), there is no need to protect the latter by the application of the mandatory rules of national law.[317] This landmark case was the basis for the first generation of EU directives on the freedom to provide insurance services.

229. There is a whole line of cases on tax provisions that restrict the free provision of services. In *Svensson and Gustavsson*,[318] the Court ruled that Articles 56 and 63 TFEU (on free movement of capital) are infringed where a Member State (here Luxembourg) makes the grant of a housing benefit, in particular an interest rate subsidy, subject to the requirement that the loans intended to finance the construction, acquisition or improvement of the housing which is to benefit from the subsidy have been obtained from a credit institution approved in that Member State, which implies that it must be established there.[319] This requirement clearly favoured credit institutions established in Luxembourg to the detriment of those established in other EU Member States. In *Asscher*,[320] the Court found to be contrary to Article 56 TFEU the fact of applying to a national of a Member State who pursues an activity as a self-employed person within its territory and at the same time pursues another activity as a self-employed person in another Member State, in which he resides, a higher rate of income tax than that applicable to residents pursuing the same activity where there is no objective difference between the situation of such

---

315. *Webb,* para. 21.
316. *Ibid.,* para. 39.
317. *Ibid.,* para. 49.
318. Judgment of 14 November 1995, *Svensson & Gustavsson,* C-484/93, EU:C:1995:379.
319. *Ibid.,* para. 19.
320. Judgment of 27 June, *Asscher,* C-107/94, EU:C:1996:251.

taxpayers and that of taxpayers who are resident or treated as such to justify that difference in treatment.[321] In *Danner*,[322] the Court of Justice ruled that Article 56 TFEU precludes a Member State's tax legislation from restricting or disallowing the deductibility for income tax purposes of contributions to voluntary pension schemes paid to pension providers in other Member States while allowing such contributions to be deducted when they are paid to institutions in the first-mentioned Member State, if that legislation does not at the same time preclude taxation of the pensions paid by the above-mentioned pension providers.[323]

230. Whereas the initial case law focused on discrimination on the place of establishment, and by extension substantive discrimination consisting in ignoring the equivalence of compliance with requirements in the home Member State (the Member State of establishment of the service provider), in later judgments the Court of Justice developed, in interpreting Article 56 TFEU, a full-fledged rule of reason, like the one it had already developed with regard to the free movement of goods,[324] meaning that the provision also prohibits restrictions that do not discriminate on the basis of nationality or place of establishment, but nevertheless form an obstacle to the freedom to provide services, unless they can be justified in the general interest.

231. The leading case is *Säger v. Dennemeyer*.[325] Germany reserved the provision of patent renewal services to patent agents authorized in that country. Hence a company established in another Member State could not provide such services for German patent holders. The clients of companies providing such services (in the EU or worldwide) are large companies that hold a series of patents. With regard to this restriction the Court of Justice said in very general terms that Article 56 TFEU requires not only the elimination of all discrimination against a person providing services on the ground of his nationality, but also the abolition of any restriction, even if it applies without distinction to national providers of services and to those of other Member States, when it is liable to prohibit or otherwise impede the activities of a provider of services established in another Member State where he lawfully provides similar services.[326] The Court added that in particular, a Member State may not make the provision of services in its territory subject to compliance with all the conditions required for establishment and thereby deprive of all practical effectiveness the provisions of the Treaty whose object is, precisely, to guarantee the freedom to provide services.[327] Such a restriction is all the less permissible where, as in the main proceedings, and unlike the situation governed by Article 57(3) TFEU, the service is supplied without it being necessary for the person providing it to visit the territory of the Member State where it is provided.[328] National legislation which makes the provision of certain services on the national territory

---

321. *Ibid.*, para. 62.
322. Judgment of 3 October 2002, *Danner*, C-136/00, EU:C:2002:558.
323. *Ibid.*, para. 57.
324. *See* above paras 94 et seq.
325. Judgment of 25 July 1991, *Säger v. Dennemeyer*, C-76/90, EU:C:1991:331.
326. *Ibid.*, para. 12.
327. *Ibid.*, para. 13.
328. *Ibid.*

by an undertaking established in another Member State subject to the issue of an administrative licence for which the possession of certain professional qualifications is required constitutes a restriction on the freedom to provide services within the meaning of Article 56 TFEU.[329] Finally, as a fundamental principle of the Treaty, the freedom to provide services may be limited only by rules which are justified by imperative reasons relating to the public interest and which apply to all persons or undertakings pursuing an activity in the State of destination, insofar as that interest is not protected by the rules to which the person providing the services is subject in the Member State in which he is established.[330] In particular, those requirements must be objectively necessary in order to ensure compliance with professional rules and to guarantee the protection of the recipient of services and they must not exceed what is necessary to attain those objectives.[331] These conditions – objective justification in the general interest and proportionality – can be compared to those which the Court developed earlier with respect to the free movement of goods.[332] In the case at hand, the Court found that there was no objective justification: the measure was disproportionate to the aim of protecting the recipients of the services.

232. The Court of Justice has consistently applied the 'rule of reason' developed *inter alia* in *Säger v. Dennemeyer* and refused to mitigate the broad scope of application of Article 56 TFEU, as it did, in *Keck & Mithouard*,[333] with regard to the free movement of goods, by excluding non-discriminatory rules on 'selling arrangements' from the scope of Article 34 TFEU. In *Alpine Investments*,[334] the Court of Justice decided that Article 56 TFEU does not preclude national rules (of the Netherlands) which, in order to protect investor confidence in national financial markets, prohibit the practice of making unsolicited telephone calls to potential clients resident in other Member States to offer them services linked to investment in commodities futures.[335] It had been argued before the Court that the prohibition of a sales method was a 'selling arrangement' and hence was not caught by Article 56 TFEU since it applied irrespective of the residence of the recipient (in the Netherlands or abroad), but the Court rejected that argument and confirmed the broad scope of Article 56 TFEU catching all restrictions to the cross-border provision of services that cannot be justified in the general interest.

233. The CJEU accepted several grounds of justification for impediments to the freedom to provide services, *inter alia* the coherence of the tax system.[336]

234. National rules on advertising can violate both Articles 34 and 56 TFEU, because both the movement of the advertised goods and the advertising in itself as

---

329. *Ibid.*, para. 14.
330. *Ibid.*, para. 15.
331. *Ibid.*
332. *See* above paras 108 et seq.
333. *See* above paras 116 et seq.
334. Judgment of 10 May 1995, *Alpine Investments,* C-384/93, EU:C:1995:126.
335. *Ibid.*, para. 56.
336. Judgment of 28 January 1992, *Bachmann,* C-204/90, EU:C:1992:35.

a (cross-border) service can be affected. This is particularly clear in case of TV broadcasting, where advertisers in the receiving Member State pay a broadcaster in another Member State for commercials directed at the public in the Member State of the advertisers. An example is *De Agostini*,[337] in which the Court confirmed *Alpine Investments* as to the freedom to provide services. This case related to a Swedish ban of TV advertising directed at children less than 12 years of age. The questions put to the Court of Justice related on the one hand to the interpretation of some provisions of the TV Without Frontiers Directive,[338] and on the other hand to the interpretation of Articles 34 and 56 TFEU.

With regard to Article 34 TFEU the Court applied the *Keck* test, i.e., the advertising ban is not covered by Article 34 TFEU, unless it is shown that the ban does not affect in the same way, in fact and in law, the marketing of national products and of products from other Member States.[339] The Court left it to the national judge to decide whether that was the case.[340] If so, the national judge would have to apply the rule of reason. However, as to Article 56 TFEU the Court only reiterated the rule of reason and again let it to the national judge to verify whether its conditions were satisfied. Likewise in *Gourmet*,[341] concerning a Swedish ban on advertising for alcoholic beverages in magazines, the Court of Justice found that neither the free movement of goods nor the freedom to provide services opposed to such a ban unless it was apparent that, in the circumstances of law and of fact which characterize the situation in the Member State concerned, the protection of public health against the harmful effects of alcohol can be ensured by measures having less effect on intra-Union trade. In this case, it can be reminded that with respect to the free movement of goods the Court found that the conditions of *Keck* were not satisfied, because the ban had a greater impact on imported goods than on domestic goods.[342] Hence the Court applied the rule of reason. In other words, the analysis under the free movement of goods and the freedom to provide services coincided.

235. In *Karner*,[343] the analysis under the free movement of goods and the freedom to provide services could possibly have led to different results since the Court came to the firm conclusion that the legislation at hand concerned a selling arrangement that was not discriminatory and hence not caught by Article 34 TFEU, while the analysis under Article 56 TFEU could have shown a restriction to an advertising service that (obviously) could not be justified in the general interest. The case concerned a provision of Austrian law prohibiting any public announcements or notices intended for a large circle of persons from making reference to the fact that the

---

337. Judgment of 9 July 1997, *Konsumentombudsmannen v. De Agostini and TV Shop*, C-34/95, C-35/95 and C-36/95, EU:C:1997:344.
338. Council Directive 89/552/EEC of 3 October 1989 on the coordination of certain provisions laid down by law, regulation or administrative action in Member States concerning the pursuit of television broadcasting activities, *OJ* 1989, L 298, p. 23; *see* now: Directive 2010/13 Audiovisual Media Services, *OJ* 210 L 95/7.
339. *De Agostini*, para. 40.
340. *Ibid.*, para. 45.
341. Judgment of 8 March 2001, *Gourmet*, C-405/98, EU:C:2001:135.
342. *See also* above para. 105.
343. Judgment of 24 March 2004, *Karner v. Trootstwijk*, C-71/02, EU:C:2004:181.

goods advertised originate from an insolvent estate when the goods in question, even though that was their origin, no longer form part of the insolvent estate. The Court ruled that where a national measure relates to both the free movement of goods and freedom to provide services, it will in principle examine the restriction in relation to only one of those two fundamental freedoms if it appears that, in the circumstances of the case, one of them is entirely secondary in relation to the other and may be considered together with it.[344] In the case at hand, the free movement of goods was definitely more important than the freedom to provide services (here: the provision of advertising services on behalf of the company that had made an announcement of the auction sale of goods from the estate of a bankruptcy).

236.   In a few judgments, the Court of Justice seems to apply a kind of *Keck*, or rather a *Krantz*[345] test to restrictions on the freedom to provide services. An example is *Viacom Outdoor*.[346] The case concerned a municipal tax on outdoor advertising. It was argued that such tax could deter advertisers established in other Member States from advertising in the commune and hence constituted an impediment incompatible with Article 56 TFEU. The Court first of all noted that such a tax is applicable without distinction to any provision of services entailing outdoor advertising and public bill-posting in the territory of the municipality concerned and that the rules on the levying of this tax do not, therefore, draw any distinction based on the place of establishment of the provider or recipient of the bill-posting services or on the place of origin of the goods or services that form the subject matter of the advertising messages disseminated.[347] In other words, the tax is not discriminatory. In this regard, it can be remembered that the Court of Justice generally applies a non-discrimination test when examining tax measures in the light of the freedom to provide services. But the Court goes on by considering that such a tax is applied only to outdoor advertising activities involving the use of public space administered by the municipal authorities and its amount is fixed at a level which may be considered modest in relation to the value of the services provided which are subject to it.[348] In those circumstances, the levying of such a tax is not on any view liable to prohibit, impede or otherwise make less attractive the provision of advertising services to be carried out in the territory of the municipalities concerned, including the case in which the provision of services is of a cross-border nature on account of the place of establishment of either the provider or the recipient of the services.[349]

237.   Recently, in *Cepelnik*,[350] the Grand Chamber of the Court found that Article 56 TFEU precludes national legislation under which the competent authorities can order a commissioning party established in that Member State to suspend payments to his contractor established in another Member State, or even to pay a security in

---

344. *Karner*, para. 46.
345. Judgment of 7 March 1990, *Krantz*, C-69/88, EU:C:1990:583; *see* above para. 114.
346. Judgment of 17 February 2005, *Viacom Outdoor*, C-134/03, EU:C:2005:94.
347. *Ibid.*, para. 37.
348. *Ibid.*, para. 38.
349. *Ibid.*
350. Judgment of 13 November 2018, *Cepelnik*, C-33/17, EU:C:2018:221.

an amount equivalent to the price still owed for the works in order to guarantee payment of the fine which might be imposed on that contractor in the event of a proven infringement of the labour law of the first Member State. Measures such as those provided for by the national legislation which are intended in particular to ensure the effectiveness of the penalties that might be inflicted on the service provider in the event of an infringement of the legislation on labour law may be regarded as appropriate for ensuring that those objectives are realized, but disproportionate to its aim, because (i) it makes it possible for the competent authorities to require the commissioning party to suspend his payments to the service provider and to pay a security in the amount of the price still owed for the works, on the basis of 'reasonable suspicion of an administrative offence' against the national rules in the field of labour law; the legislation thus allows such measures to be adopted even before a finding is made by the competent authority of an administrative offence disclosing fraud, in particular social security fraud, or abuse or a practice capable of affecting the protection of workers; (ii) it does not provide that the service provider against whom there is such reasonable suspicion can, before the adoption of those measures, put forward his observations on the acts of which he is accused and (iii) the amount of the security that may be required from the recipient of the services corresponds, in accordance with the national legislation at issue in the main proceedings, to the price still owed for the works at the time of the adoption of that measure; since the amount of the security may thus be fixed by the competent authorities without taking account of possible construction faults or other defective performance of the contract for works by the service provider, it could exceed, perhaps substantially, the amount that the commissioning party would in principle have to pay on completion of the works.

238. In *Vanderborght*[351] the Court ruled that Article 56 TFEU (and the provisions of a couple of directives) precludes national legislation (of Belgium) which imposes a general and absolute prohibition of any advertising relating to the provision of oral and dental care services. Again the measure was found to go beyond what is necessary for the protection of public health.

§9. THE SERVICES DIRECTIVE: THE GROUNDS OF JUSTIFICATION FOR
   RESTRICTIONS TO THE FREEDOM TO PROVIDE SERVICES REVISITED

239. Directive 2006/123 on Services in the Internal Market[352] (the Services Directive), which actually relates both to the right of establishment and the freedom to provide services, will be discussed systematically in a separate section hereinafter.[353] At this place it should however be stressed that, with regard to the service sectors that are not excluded from the scope of application of the Services Directive (especially those for which there are no specific Union rules) the case law of the

---

351. Judgment of 4 May 2017, *Luc Vanderborght*, C-339/15, EU:C:2017:335.
352. Directive 2006/123/EC of the European Parliament and of the Council of 12 December 2006 on services in the internal market, *OJ* 2006, L 376/36.
353. *See* paras 288 et seq.

Court of Justice analysed in the preceding paragraphs (in §8) should be put into context since the entry into force of that Directive. Interestingly, recital 40 explains that the concept of 'overriding reasons relating to the public interest', to which reference is made in certain provisions of this Directive, has been developed by the Court of Justice in its case law in relation to Articles 49 and 56 TFEU and may continue to evolve. The notion as recognized in the case law of the Court of Justice covers at least the following grounds: 'public policy, public security and public health; the maintenance of order in society; social policy objectives; the protection of the recipients of services; consumer protection; the protection of workers, including the social protection of workers; animal welfare; the preservation of the financial balance of the social security system; the prevention of fraud; the prevention of unfair competition; the protection of the environment and the urban environment, including town and country planning; the protection of creditors; safeguarding the sound administration of justice; road safety; the protection of I.P; cultural policy objectives, including safeguarding the freedom of expression of various elements, in particular social, cultural, religious and philosophical values of society; the need to ensure a high level of education, the maintenance of press diversity and the promotion of the national language; the preservation of national historical and artistic heritage; and veterinary policy.' A long list. However this list is not relevant anymore for the freedom to provide services under the Directive. According to Article 16 of Directive 2006/123, the freedom to provide services can only be restricted on one of the following grounds: public policy, public security, public health or the protection of the environment; and, where the service provider moves to the host Member State, also the imposition rules on employment conditions, including those laid down in collective agreements. In other words, all other grounds of justification recognized by the Court and listed in recital 40 of the Directive do no longer apply to services that are not excluded from its scope.

§10. Free Provision of Services in the Field of Transport, Banking and Insurance

240. Article 58(1) TFEU provides that the freedom to provide services in the field of transport shall be governed by the provisions of the Title relating to transport (Title VI, Articles 90–100 TFEU). Pursuant to Article 58(2) TFEU, the liberalization of banking and insurance services connected with movements of capital shall be effected in step with the liberalization of movement of capital. Free movement of capital (that has been liberalized gradually) will be discussed in the next chapter. For financial services, such as banking, insurance and investment services, there exists, nowadays, a comprehensive body of rules at the EU level, based on mutual recognition of licences delivered by the home State (the Member State where the institution holds its head office) as well as, increasingly, supervision at the EU level. These very elaborate sector-specific rules will not be discussed in the present general monograph. As to transport, Article 58(1) TFEU means that there is no directly effective principle of free provision of services in this sector of economic activity. The now existing liberalization of transport is the result of Union legislation that will be discussed in a separate chapter.[354]

---

354. Discussed hereafter Part II, Chapter 5.

Chapter 4. Free Movement of Capital and Payment

§1. INTRODUCTION

241. The provisions on the free movement of capital and payments can be found in Articles 63–66 TFEU. Whereas the Treaty articles concerning the other freedoms (of goods, persons end services) discussed above have not changed since the original EEC Treaty (except for some minor terminological and procedural matters) the provisions on the free movement of capital and payments are new since the Treaty of Maastricht (1994). They are now governed by the same principles and dealt with in the same chapter of the TFEU and not separately and differently like under the EEC Treaty.

§2. HISTORY

242. Pursuant to the original Article 67 EEC the free movement of capital was only liberalized to the extent required for the functioning of the common market, i.e., the other freedoms, such as the free movement of persons (workers and establishment) and services. In other words, the freedom was conditional and hence not directly effective (it could not be invoked by private individuals in national courts).[355] The First Directive of 11 May 1961[356] and Directive 72/156 on international capital flows[357] contained a very limited liberalization.

243. In contrast, in *Luisi and Carbone*[358] the Court ruled that since restrictions on the freedom to provide services were to be abolished as from the end of the transitional period, any restrictions on payments relating to the provision of services must disappear.[359] Consequently, payments relating to tourism and travel for the purposes of business, education or medical treatment have been liberalized since the end of the transitional period. The case concerned restrictions on the exportation of bank notes. In its judgment, the Court distinguished the free movement of payments, which was liberalized, from the free movement of capital, which was not. Current payments are transfers of foreign exchange which constitute the consideration within the context of an underlying transaction, whilst movements of capital are financial operations essentially concerned with the investment of the funds in question rather than remuneration for a services. Under the TFEU, the distinction between capital movement and the movement of payments is less crucial because both freedoms are now basically treated the same way. In certain respects, there are still differences (*see* below) and for that reason this case law remains relevant.

---

355. *See* Judgment of 11 November 1981, *Casati,* 203/80, EU:C:1981:261.
356. First Directive of 11 May 1960 for the implementation of Art. 67 of the Treaty, *OJ* 1960, L 43/921.
357. Council Directive 72/156/EEC of 21 March 1972 on regulating international capital flows and neutralizing their undesirable effects on domestic liquidity, *OJ* 1972, L 91/13.
358. Judgment of 31 January 1984, *Luisi and Carbone*, 286/82 and 26/83, EU:C:1984:35.
359. *Ibid.*, para. 37.

244. A first real liberalization of capital movements was achieved with Council Directive 88/361[360] of 24 June 1988 for the implementation of Article 67 of the Treaty. The Directive has not been formally repealed. Its provisions are now superseded by the more liberal provisions of the TFEU, but its Annex, containing the nomenclature of capital movements remains relevant. The Court regularly refers to it when interpreting the free movement of capital under the Treaty provisions. Directive 88/361 established full liberalization of capital movements with some meaningful exceptions (safeguard measures, measures to prevent infringements of tax and prudential supervision law, special provisions for Spain, Portugal and Greece, secondary residences, etc.).

§3. Free Movement of Capital Since Maastricht: The Principles

245. The present Treaty Articles were introduced by the Treaty of Maastricht in 1993. Article 63(1) TFEU reads: 'within the framework of the provisions set out in this Chapter, all restrictions on the movement of capital between Member States and between Member States and third countries shall be prohibited'. Likewise Article 63(2) TFEU provides that 'within the framework of the provisions set out in this Chapter, all restrictions on payments between Member States and between Member States and third countries shall be prohibited'. Hence both the free movement of capital and the free movement of payments are now, as a matter of principle, fully liberalized.

246. Pursuant to Article 64(1) TFEU, the provisions of Article 63 TFEU shall be without prejudice to the application to *third countries* of any restrictions which exist on 31 December 1993 under national or Union law adopted in respect of the movement of capital to or from third countries involving direct investment – including in real estate –, establishment, the provision of financial services or the admission of securities to capital markets. In respect of restrictions existing under national law in Bulgaria, Estonia and Hungary, the relevant date shall be 31 December 1999. Pursuant to Article 64(2) TFEU, the Union legislature, acting in accordance with the ordinary legislative procedure, shall adopt the measures on the movement of capital to or from third countries involving direct investment – including investment in real estate – establishment, the provision of financial services, or the admission of securities to capital markets. Pursuant to Article 64(3) TFEU, the Council can even, acting with unanimity, adopt measures which constitute a step backwards in Union law as regards the liberalization of the movement of capital to or from third countries. In addition, pursuant to Article 65(4) TFEU, in the absence of measures pursuant to Article 64(3) TFEU, the Commission or, in the absence of a Commission decision within three months from the request of the Member State concerned, the Council, may adopt a decision stating that restrictive tax measures adopted by a Member State concerning one or more third countries are to be considered compatible with the Treaties insofar as they are justified by one of the objectives of the Union and

---

360. Council Directive 88/361/EEC of 24 June 1988 for the implementation of Art. 67 of the Treaty, *OJ* 2008, L 178/5.

compatible with the proper functioning of the internal market (on the latter notion *see* hereafter). The Council shall act unanimously on application by a Member State. Finally, Article 66 TFEU provides that where, in exceptional circumstances, movements of capital to or from third countries cause, or threaten to cause, serious difficulties for the operation of EMU, the Council, on a proposal from the Commission and after consulting the ECB, may take safeguard measures with regard to third countries for a period not exceeding six months if such measures are strictly necessary.

247. It should thus be noted that, contrary to the other internal market freedoms, the free movement of capital not only applies to the internal market but also in relation to third countries, although international capital movements can be subject to restrictions imposed by the EU. Capital movements within the Union can only be restricted by Member States for reasons of general interest discussed hereafter.

248. Indeed, pursuant to Article 65(1) TFEU, the provisions of Article 63 TFEU shall be without prejudice to the right of Member States:

(a) to apply the relevant provisions of their tax law which distinguish between taxpayers who are not in the same situation with regard to their place of residence or with regard to the place where their capital is invested;
(b) to take all requisite measures to prevent infringements of national law and regulations, in particular in the field of taxation and the prudential supervision of financial institutions, or to lay down procedures for the declaration of capital movements for purposes of administrative or statistical information, or to take measures which are justified on grounds of public policy or public security.

Furthermore, pursuant to Article 65(2) TFEU the provisions of this Chapter shall be without prejudice to the applicability of restrictions on the right of establishment which are compatible with the Treaties. Finally, the measures and procedures referred to in paragraphs 1 and 2 shall not constitute a means of arbitrary discrimination or a disguised restriction on the free movement of capital and payments as defined in Article 63 TFEU (Article 65(3) TFEU).

§4. CASE LAW OF THE COURT OF JUSTICE

249. There is an obvious link between the free movement of capital and the right of establishment. If an individual who is the national of a Member State or a company that is incorporated in a Member State wants to establish a company (e.g., a subsidiary) in another Member State, it may want to invest capital that it transfers from the first Member State. It should be stressed that also the acquisition of an existing company in another Member State, i.e., by obtaining control over that company (e.g., by buying the majority its shares) is considered an act of establishment. The acquisition of a minority stake in a company rather qualifies as a 'mere' capital movement, but restrictions on the possibility to buy shares in a company may amount to a restriction of capital movements as well as of the right of establishment, where the acquisition of control is made impossible. The case law on 'golden shares' discussed hereinafter illustrates this point perfectly. There is also quite a strong link between free movement of capital and the freedom to provide services, as the judgment in *Svensson & Gustavson*, already discussed here above in relation to the freedom to provide services illustrates.[361] The Court of Justice ruled that it was not compatible with Articles 59 and 67 of the Treaty (now Articles 56 and 63 TFEU) for a Member State to make the grant of a housing benefit, in particular an interest rate subsidy, subject to the requirement that the loans intended to finance the construction, acquisition or improvement of the housing which is to benefit from the subsidy have been obtained from a credit institution approved in that Member State, which implies that it must be established there.

250. In *Sanz de Lera*,[362] the Court of Justice had to interpret for the first time the new provisions on capital movement inserted by the Maastricht Treaty. It ruled that Articles 63(1) and 65(1)(b) TFEU preclude rules which make the export of coins, banknotes or bearer cheques conditional on prior authorization but do not by contrast preclude a transaction of that nature being made conditional on a prior declaration.[363] The Court expressly accepted the need to ensure effective fiscal supervision and the prevention of illegal activities such as tax evasion and money laundering as a ground of justification, hence departing from a strict reading of Article 65(1) TFEU that does not mention these grounds of justification.[364] In other words, the Court construes a kind of rule of reason for capital movements, as it did for the other internal market freedoms.

251. An issue on which the Court of Justice has been called regularly to render a preliminary ruling is that of so-called golden shares. Where a Member State partly privatizes a State-owned company and remains minority shareholder, it typically wants to maintain veto right on strategic issues. The State is then granted a 'golden share', i.e., the right to oppose to certain decisions although according to the normal rules of company law it would not have this right in view of its minority shareholding.

252. In three judgments of the same day in 2002, *Commission v. Belgium*,[365] *Commission v. France*,[366] and *Commission v. Portugal*[367] the Court set the principles. Points I and III in the nomenclature set out in Annex I to Directive 88/361,[368] and the explanatory notes appearing in that annex, indicate that direct

---

361. *See* above para. 226.
362. Judgment of 14 December 1995, *Sanz de Lera*, C-163/94, C-165/94 and C-250/94, EU:C:1995:451.

363. *Ibid.*, para. 30.
364. *Ibid.*, para. 22.
365. Judgment of 4 June 2002, *Commission v. Belgium*, C-503/99, EU:C:2002:328.
366. Judgment of 4 June 2002, *Commission v. France*, C-483/99, EU:C:2002:327.
367. Judgment of 4 June 2002, *Commission v. Portugal*, C-367/98, EU:C:2002:326.
368. *See* above footnote 349.

investment in the form of participation in an undertaking by means of a shareholding or the acquisition of securities on the capital market constitute capital movements within the meaning of Article 65 TFEU. The explanatory notes state that direct investment is characterized, in particular, by the possibility of participating effectively in the management of a company or in its control. The free movement of capital, as a fundamental principle of the Treaty, may be restricted only by national rules which are justified by reasons referred to in Article 67(1) TFEU or by overriding requirements of the general interest and which are applicable to all persons and undertakings pursuing an activity in the territory of the host Member State.[369] Furthermore, in order to be so justified, the national legislation must be suitable for securing the objective which it pursues and must not go beyond what is necessary in order to attain it, so as to accord with the principle of proportionality (with reference to *inter alia. Sanz de Lera,* discussed above).[370] In *Commission v. France,* the Court found that these conditions were not fulfilled in view notably of the extensive powers given to the government.[371] In *Commission v. Belgium,* the Court accepted that the conditions were fulfilled. The objective pursued by the legislation at issue, namely the safeguarding of energy supplies in the event of a crisis, falls undeniably within the ambit of a legitimate public interest.[372]Furthermore, a negative measure such as a right of opposition cannot guarantee adequate supplies by contrast with positive measures such as planning designed to encourage natural gas undertakings to conclude long-term supply contracts and to diversify their sources of supply, or a system of licences. By the same token, the existence of infrastructures for the conveyance of energy products could be ensured not by a general right of opposition but by rules precisely defining the standards required of the undertakings concerned. Moreover, the rights attaching to the golden shares in issue preclude the conclusion of long-term contracts and diversification of sources of supply. Similarly, the remedies available to contest the measures in issue are inadequate, on account of the length and cost of the procedure involved.

253. In a number of later judgments,[373] golden shares were found not to be justified. A famous case is the *Volkswagen* case[374] where the Court decided that by maintaining in force legislation which, in derogation from ordinary company law, combines a limitation of the voting rights of every shareholder in a given company to 20% of that company's share capital with the requirement of a majority of over 80% of the company's capital for the adoption of certain decisions by the general assembly, and which, in derogation from the general law, allows a Member State

---

369. *Commission v. Belgium*, para. 45.
370. *Ibid.*
371. *Commission v. France*, C-483/99, para. 51.
372. *Commission v. Belgium*, para. 46.
373. Judgment of 13 May 2003, in *Commission v. Spain*, C-463/00, EU:C:2003:272; Judgment of 6 December 2007, *Federconsumatori*, C-463/04, EU:C:2007:752; Judgment of 28 September 2005, *Commission v. The Netherlands,* C-282/04 and C-283/04, EU:C:2005:712; Judgment of 8 July 2010, *Commission v. Portugal,* C-171/08., EU:C:2010:412; Judgment of 10 November 2010, *Commission v. Portugal,* C-543/08, EU:C:2010:669; Judgment of 10 November 2011, *Commission v. Greece,* C-212/09, EU:C:2011:717.
374. Judgment of 23 October 2007, *Commission v. Germany*, C-112/05, EU:C:2007:623.

and a territorial entity of that State each to appoint two representatives to the company's supervisory board, Germany failed to fulfil its obligations under Article 56(1) EC.

254.　The fixing of the threshold of the required majority at more than 80% of the capital, being a requirement derogating from general law and imposed by way of specific legislation, affords any shareholder holding 20% of the share capital a blocking minority and in this case creates an instrument enabling the public authorities to procure for themselves a blocking minority allowing them to oppose important resolutions, on the basis of a lower level of investment than would be required under general company law. By capping voting rights at the same level of 20%, the specific legislation supplements a legal framework which enables the said public authorities to exercise considerable influence on the basis of such a reduced investment. By limiting the possibility for other shareholders to participate in the company with a view to establishing or maintaining lasting and direct economic links with it which would make possible effective participation in the management of that company or in its control, such a situation is liable to deter direct investors from other Member States, thereby diminishing the interest in acquiring a stake in the capital of that company and thus constituting a restriction on the movement of capital.

255.　The same applies to the right to appoint two representatives to the company's supervisory board, being a specific right, in derogation from general company law, laid down by a national legislative measure for the sole benefit of the public authorities. By enabling those authorities to participate in a more significant manner in the activity of the supervisory board than their status as shareholders would normally allow, that measure thus establishes an instrument which gives the public authorities the possibility of exercising influence which exceeds their levels of investment.

256.　In *Sanz de Lera*,[375] the Court found a system of prior authorization for the export of banknotes to be disproportionate to the public policy objectives pursued. Not all prior authorization systems however are unjustified in the light of Article 63 TFEU. An example is *Margaretha Ospelt*.[376] The case concerned a transaction whereby Ms Ospelt wanted to transfer the property of land in Austria to a Liechtenstein Anstalt. The court found that the rules applicable to the relationship between the EU and Liechtenstein (the EEA Agreement) coincided with those of the TFEU chapter on free movement of capital. The relevant Austrian administrative law provision required a prior authorization for the transfer in question, essentially to preserve the agricultural and landscape destination of the land. The Court emphasized that measures such as that at issue entail, by their very purpose, a restriction on the free movement of capital, but may nevertheless be permitted provided that, first, they pursue in a non-discriminatory way an objective in the public interest and, second, they are appropriate for ensuring that the aim pursued is achieved and do not

---

375. *See* above para. 246.
376. Judgment of 23 September 2003, *Margaretha Ospelt*, C-452/01, EU:C:2003:493.

go beyond what is necessary for that purpose (with reference to former judgments). Furthermore, where the granting of prior authorization is concerned, such measures must be based on objective criteria which are known in advance and which allow all persons affected by a restrictive measure of that type to have a legal remedy available to them. So far as concerns the condition as to the aims of the national measure in issue, there is no doubt that the measure pursues public-interest objectives which are such as to justify restrictions on the free movement of capital. First, preserving agricultural communities, maintaining a distribution of land ownership which allows the development of viable farms and sympathetic management of green spaces and the countryside as well as encouraging a reasonable use of the available land by resisting pressure on land, and preventing natural disasters are social objectives are clearly objectives of general interest. Second, those objectives are consistent with the objectives of the CAP which, aims 'to ensure a fair standard of living for the agricultural community' in the working-out of which, account must be taken 'of the particular nature of agricultural activity, which results from the social structure of agriculture and from structural and natural disparities between the various agricultural regions'. As to the principle of proportionality, the Court considers that a system of prior authorization may, in certain circumstances, be necessary and proportionate to the aims pursued, if the same objectives cannot be attained by less restrictive measures, in particular by a system of declarations. That is the case where national authorities seek to control the development of agricultural land ownership by laying down objectives such as those in the Austrian law. Indeed, the objective of sustaining and developing viable agriculture on the basis of social and land planning considerations entails keeping land intended for agriculture in such use and continuing to make use of it under appropriate conditions. In that context, prior supervision by the competent authorities does not merely reflect a need for information but is intended to ensure that the transfer of agricultural land will not lead to their ceasing to be used as intended or to a use which might be incompatible with their long-term agricultural use.

Chapter 5. Completing the Internal Market

§1. Basic Rules

I. Treaty Provision

257. Chapters 1–4 were dedicated to the basic internal market freedoms: free movement of goods, persons, services and capital, as they generally flow from directly effective Treaty provisions. It has been seen that obstacles to free movement can often be accepted as being necessary for the protection of a general interest recognized by Union law. This means that these Treaty provisions cannot in themselves guarantee the functioning of the internal market, i.e., an area without internal frontiers in which free movement is ensured. To put it differently; 'negative integration', i.e., the striking down of national obstacles because they are incompatible with one of the basic freedoms, is insufficient to complete the internal market. Therefore, in addition, 'positive integration' is required: a set of legislative measures at the EU level aiming at the achievement of the internal market. The most prominent form of such action is through 'harmonization' of the laws of the Member States.

258. The TFEU contains general and specific provisions on harmonization of legislation. These provisions will be discussed in the following section (II). The most general one is Article 114 TFEU (ex Article 95 EC), which reads as follows:

1. Save where otherwise provided in the Treaties, the following provisions shall apply for the achievement of the objectives set out in Article 26.[377] The EP and the Council shall, acting in accordance with the ordinary legislative procedure and after consulting the Economic and Social Committee, adopt the measures for the approximation of the provisions laid down by law, regulation or administrative action in Member States which have as their object the establishment and functioning of the internal market.
2. Paragraph 1 shall not apply to fiscal provisions, to those relating to the free movement of persons nor to those relating to the rights and interests of employed persons.
3. The Commission, in its proposals envisaged in paragraph 1 concerning health, safety, environmental protection and consumer protection, will take as a base a high level of protection, taking account in particular of any new development based on scientific facts. Within their respective powers, the EP and the Council will also seek to achieve this objective.
4. If, after the adoption of a harmonisation measure by the EP and the Council, by the Council or by the Commission, a Member State deems it necessary to maintain national provisions on grounds of major needs referred

---

377. Article 26 TFEU: '*(1) The Union shall adopt measures with the aim of establishing or ensuring the functioning of the internal market, in accordance with the relevant provisions of the Treaties; (2) The internal market shall comprise an area without internal frontiers in which the free movement of goods, persons, services and capital is ensured in accordance with the provisions of the Treaties ... .*'

to in Article 36, or relating to the protection of the environment or the working environment, it shall notify the Commission of these provisions as well as the grounds for maintaining them.

5. Moreover, without prejudice to paragraph 4, if, after the adoption of a har-monisation measure by the European Parliament and the Council, by the Council or by the Commission, a Member State deems it necessary to introduce national provisions based on new scientific evidence relating to the protection of the environment or the working environment on grounds of a problem specific to that Member State arising after the adoption of the harmonisation measure, it shall notify the Commission of the envisaged provisions as well as the grounds for introducing them.

6. The Commission shall, within six months of the notifications as referred to in paragraphs 4 and 5, approve or reject the national provisions involved after having verified whether or not they are a means of arbitrary discrimi-nation or a disguised restriction on trade between Member States and whether or not they shall constitute an obstacle to the functioning of the internal market.

    In the absence of a decision by the Commission within this period, the national provisions referred to in paragraphs 4 and 5 shall be deemed to have been approved.

    When justified by the complexity of the matter and in the absence of danger for human health, the Commission may notify the Member State concerned that the period referred to in this paragraph may be extended for a further period of up to six months.

7. When, pursuant to paragraph 6, a Member State is authorised to maintain or introduce national provisions derogating from a harmonisation measure, the Commission shall immediately examine whether to propose an adap-tation to that measure.

8. When a Member State raises a specific problem on public health in a field which has been the subject of prior harmonisation measures, it shall bring it to the attention of the Commission which shall immediately examine whether to propose appropriate measures to the Council.

9. By way of derogation from the procedure laid down in Articles 258 and 259, the Commission and any Member State may bring the matter directly before the Court of Justice of the European Union if it considers that another Member State is making improper use of the powers provided for in this Article.

10. The harmonisation measures referred to above shall, in appropriate cases, include a safeguard clause authorising the Member States to take, for one or more of the non-economic reasons referred to in Article 36, provisional measures subject to a Union control procedure.

259. The different branches of Article 114 TFEU will briefly be discussed here-inafter. The corresponding Article 95 in the TEC was originally Article 100a, before renumbering of the Articles of that Treaty. It was inserted in 1967 to supplement the already existing Article 100 EEC that is now Article 115 TFEU, but which does not play a role anymore. That Article reads:

Without prejudice to Article 114, the Council shall, acting unanimously in accordance with a special legislative procedure and after consulting the European Parliament and the Economic and Social Committee, issue directives for the approximation of such laws, regulations or administrative provisions of the Member States as directly affect the establishment or functioning of the internal market.

260. The unanimity requirement in Article 100 EEC was one of the reasons why in 1967 the SEA introduced a new Article 100a that required a qualified majority only (now the 'ordinary legislative procedure'). The other reason was that the requirement that the provisions of the Member States directly affected the internal market (at that time the 'common market') restricted the possibilities of harmonization. The new article was a central piece in the programme to complete the internal market by 1992.[378]

II. Legal Grounds for Harmonization of Legislation

261. The content of Article 114 TFEU has been given above and its genesis has been situated. Obviously Article 115 TFEU is one of the other provisions on harmonization, but without practical significance today. The Treaty contains some other general harmonization provisions as well as more specific ones that only apply with respect to certain freedoms or certain issues.

262. There are three more general harmonization provisions in the TFEU, Articles 116, 117 and 118. Pursuant to Article 116 where the Commission finds that a difference between the provisions laid down by law, regulation or administrative action in Member States is distorting the conditions of competition in the internal market and that the resultant distortion needs to be eliminated, it shall consult the Member States concerned. If such consultation does not result in an agreement eliminating the distortion in question, the European, Parliament and the Council, acting in accordance with the ordinary legislative procedure, shall issue the necessary directives. Any other appropriate measures provided for in the Treaties may be adopted. This is also a historic provision from the EEC Treaty which, as far as we know, is not applied anymore. Article 117 complements Article 116. Both articles will be disregarded here. Finally Article 118 TFEU is new. It was introduced by the Lisbon Treaty, because the existing provisions were insufficient to create specific EU legislation in the field of IPR. Article 118 reads: In the context of the establishment and functioning of the internal market, the EP and the Council, acting in accordance with the ordinary legislative procedure, shall establish measures for the creation of European IPR to provide uniform protection of IPR throughout the Union and for the setting-up of centralized Union-wide authorization, coordination and supervision arrangements. The Council, acting in accordance with a special legislative procedure, shall by means of regulations establish language arrangements

---

378. *See* below paras 215 et seq.

for the European IPR. In this latter respect, the Council shall act unanimously after consulting the EP. This new provisions was the basis for The Unitary Patent Regulation.[379]

Some chapters of the Treaty on various policies (environment, social policy, consumers, health …) contain specific provisions on measures that can be adopted by the EU legislature. These measures may include harmonization or may focus on cooperation with a limited possibility of harmonization (e.g., health policy), or may provide for specific consequences of harmonization (e.g., Article 169(4) TFEU: measures adopted under this article in the field of consumer protection do not prevent Member States to adopt further reaching measures, while normally Member States only have this possibility if it is expressly provided for in the harmonization directive).[380]

III. Article 114(1) TFEU: Broad Legal Basis

263. Under Article 114(1) TFEU (on 'approximation of laws'), the EU legislature shall adopt the measures for the approximation of the provisions laid down by law, regulation or administrative action in Member States which have as their object the establishment and functioning of the internal market.

The scope of this provision is rather broad. Admittedly in the first *Tobacco Advertising* case,[381] the ECJ quashed a directive because it regulated a matter that had no sufficient link with the internal market (i.e., advertising for tobacco on items such as umbrellas in pubs), but in a more recent judgment, *Vodafone*[382] which it held the Roaming Regulation to be valid, the Court ruled:

> 32. According to consistent case-law the object of measures adopted on the basis of Article 95(1) EC must genuinely be to improve the conditions for the establishment and functioning of the internal market … . While a mere finding of disparities between national rules and the abstract risk of infringements of fundamental freedoms or distortion of competition is not sufficient to justify the choice of Article 95 EC as a legal basis, the Community legislature may have recourse to it in particular where there are differences between national rules which are such as to obstruct the fundamental freedoms and thus have a direct effect on the functioning of the internal market (Case C-380/03 Germany v Parliament and Council [2006] ECR I-11573, paragraph 37 and the case-law cited) or to cause significant distortions of competition (Case C-376/98 Germany v Parliament and Council [2000] ECR I-8419, paragraphs 84 and 106).
>
> 33. Recourse to that provision is also possible if the aim is to prevent the emergence of such obstacles to trade resulting from the divergent development of national laws. However, the emergence of such obstacles must be likely

---

379. Regulation 1257/2012 implementing enhanced cooperation in the area of unitary patent protection, *OJ* 2011, L 361/1.
380. This provision will not be discussed here (and it is hardly used in practice).
381. Judgment of 5 October 2000, *Germany v. Parliament and Council,* C-376/98, EU:C:2000: 544.
382. Judgment of 8 June 2010, *Vodafone,* C-58/08, EU:C:2010:321.

and the measure in question must be designed to prevent them (Germany v Parliament and Council, paragraph 38 and the case-law cited …).

36. Moreover, provided that the conditions for recourse to Article 95 EC as a legal basis are fulfilled, the Community legislature cannot be prevented from relying on that legal basis on the ground that consumer protection is a decisive factor in the choices to be made (see, regarding public health protection, Germany v Parliament and Council, paragraph 88 … .

In other words, the existence of potential obstacles to trade that are not hypothetical but likely to occur are sufficient to justify harmonization on the basis of Article 114 TFEU.

IV. Article 114(2): The Exceptions

264. Pursuant to Article 114(2) TFEU paragraph 1 shall not apply to fiscal provisions, to those relating to the free movement of persons nor to those relating to the rights and interests of employed persons.

Fiscal provisions can only be harmonized by unanimity. Article 113 TFEU reads: The Council shall, acting unanimously in accordance with a special legislative procedure and after consulting the EP and the Economic and Social Committee, adopt provisions for the harmonization of legislation concerning turnover taxes, excise duties and other forms of indirect taxation to the extent that such harmonization is necessary to ensure the establishment and the functioning of the internal market and to avoid distortion of competition.

As to the free movement of persons, specific provisions apply: Article 46 for the free movement of workers (according to the normal legislative procedure) and Article 50 (*see* next section VI) for the right of establishment.

V. Article 114(4) to (8): Member States Powers after Harmonization

265. As a matter of principle, any harmonization measure at the EU level preempts the Member States from adopting or maintaining legislative or administrative measures that contradict the measures adopted at the EU level. This principle does not apply where a matter has not been fully harmonized (e.g., in case of minimum harmonization).[383]

266. Paragraphs (4)–(8) of Article 114 contain two additional cases in which Member States can maintain or introduce, diverging national provisions after harmonization but under strict conditions and according to strict procedural rules.[384]

---

383. *See* hereafter para. 275.
384. *See* Judgment of 21 January 2003, *Germany v. Commission*, C-512/99, EU:C:2003:40; Judgment of 13 September 2007, *Land Oberösterreich*, C-439/05P, EU:C:2007:510.

VI. Articles 50 and 53 TFEU

267. The Treaty contains two delegations of powers to the EU legislature to adopt measures with a view to facilitate the freedom of establishment: Articles 50 and 53. The latter also applies to the freedom to provide services. Article 50 refers to the adoption of directives according to the ordinary legislative procedure, in particular:

(a) by according, as a general rule, priority treatment to activities where freedom of establishment makes a particularly valuable contribution to the development of production and trade;

(b) by ensuring close cooperation between the competent authorities in the Member States in order to ascertain the particular situation within the Union of the various activities concerned;

(c) by abolishing those administrative procedures and practices, whether resulting from national legislation or from agreements previously concluded between Member States, the maintenance of which would form an obstacle to freedom of establishment;

(d) by ensuring that workers of one Member State employed in the territory of another Member State may remain in that territory for the purpose of taking up activities therein as self-employed persons, where they satisfy the conditions which they would be required to satisfy if they were entering that State at the time when they intended to take up such activities;

(e) by enabling a national of one Member State to acquire and use land and buildings situated in the territory of another Member State, insofar as this does not conflict with the principles laid down in Article 39(2);

(f) by effecting the progressive abolition of restrictions on freedom of establishment in every branch of activity under consideration, both as regards the conditions for setting-up agencies, branches or subsidiaries in the territory of a Member State and as regards the subsidiaries in the territory of a Member State and as regards the conditions governing the entry of personnel belonging to the main establishment into managerial or supervisory posts in such agencies, branches or subsidiaries;

(g) by coordinating to the necessary extent the safeguards which, for the protection of the interests of members and others, are required by Member States of companies or firms within the meaning of the second paragraph of Article 54 with a view to making such safeguards equivalent throughout the Union;

(h) by satisfying themselves that the conditions of establishment are not distorted by aids granted by Member States. Article 53 on the other hand (which also applies to the freedom to provide service) provides for the adoption of directives for the mutual recognition of diplomas, certificates and other evidence of formal qualifications and for the coordination of the provisions laid down by law, regulation or administrative action in Member States concerning the taking-up and pursuit of activities as self-employed persons. In the case of the medical and allied and pharmaceutical professions, the progressive abolition of restrictions shall be dependent upon coordination of the conditions for their exercise in the various Member States. On the basis of both provisions, several generations of directives to facilitate the freedom of establishment and the freedom to provide services for certain activities have seen the light. Today there are two major horizontal directives, i.e., directives that apply to all sectors of economic life, with the exception of those expressly excluded, and for which there might exist specific rules. These two directives are Directive 2005/36 on the recognition of professional qualifications (as amended by Directive 2013/55) and Directive 2006/123 in Services in the Internal Market, and they will be discussed in separate sections.[385]

§2. Forms and Methods of Harmonization

I. Fields in Which Harmonization Measures Have Been Adopted

268. Harmonization directives have seen the light in various fields of national law: labour law, social security law, including patients' rights, international private law, insurance law, bank supervision law, company and securities law, consumer law, commercial agency, competition law, public procurement law, social policy, law of establishment, IP law, etc. These directives are not discussed in this monograph. The rules they enact have or should have been transposed into national law. The reader is referred to the relevant monographs of the Member States of the EU.

II. Different Types of Harmonization

269. Harmonization of laws of the Member States can be more or less comprehensive. Some directives only harmonizes some aspects of a given issue, e.g., certain rights of the commercial agent, guarantees in consumer sales, only private enforcement (and not other aspects) of competition law etc. In order to determine whether Member States retain the right to maintain or to introduce unilaterally legal rules on a given issue or in a given field, it is therefore, first and foremost, important, to verify what has exactly been harmonized. Outside the harmonized field, the Member States are free to enact legislation, provided it does not run counter the general Treaty provisions, i.e., in the first place the internal market freedoms, discussed above.

270. Once the harmonized field is determined, the degree of harmonization has to be determined. In case of *full (or 'maximum') harmonization*, the directive sets the minimum as well as the maximum. In case of *minimum harmonization* the directive only sets the minimum, mostly the minimum level of protection. For example in consumer law traditionally directives contained a minimum harmonization. A good example is Directive 93/13/EEC on Unfair Terms in Consumer Contracts. Member States are allowed to maintain a higher level of consumer protection than the minimum provided for by the Directive (e.g., they can extend the protection to negotiated terms, they can maintain or introduce a list of terms that are deemed to

---

385. *See* hereafter paras 281–287 respectively 288–319.

be unfair in all circumstances, while the Directive only contains a general fairness clause and criteria to determine the unfair character of a contract term in a consumer contract). An example of full harmonization is Directive 2005/29/EC on B2C Unfair Commercial Practices. The Directive contains an exhaustive list of practices that are unfair in all circumstances: Member States cannot prohibit a given practice in all circumstances, i.e., without a case-by-case appraisal, if it is not on that list.[386]

271. It should be emphasized that for 'minimum harmonization' it is required that the Union Act (Directive) expressly provides for the possibility for Member States to legislate beyond the level of the act. If that is not the case, the harmonization is exhaustive or 'full'.

272. In the past the EU legislature also had recourse, often as a transitional measure, to so-called *optional harmonization*: Member States were allowed to continue to apply their national rules to domestic goods (e.g., foodstuffs) while they could not apply these rules to goods imported from other Member States. Full or minimum harmonization directives sometimes also contain options on topical issues. In the full harmonization Consumer Rights Directive 2011/83/EU, e.g., it is provided that where a distance contract is to be concluded by telephone, Member States may provide that the trader has to confirm the offer to the consumer who is bound only once he has signed the offer or has sent his written consent. Finally directives often have a mix of full and minimum harmonization: Article 3(9) of Directive 2005/29/EC e.g., provides that for real estate and financial services the harmonization is only minimum, while for all other sectors it is full. Likewise in Directive 2011/83/EU on consumer rights, which is as a matter of principle a full harmonization directive, the provision on pre-contractual consumer information for contracts other than distant and off premise contracts only sets a minimum.

273. Sometimes harmonization is limited to cross-border situations, e.g., in tax law, social security of migrant workers or private international law (*see* Brussels I*bis* Regulation 1215/2012 on mutual recognition and enforcement of judgments in civil and commercial matters).

274. Not harmonization in the strict sense, but a technique to remove obstacles as a result of disparities in legislation between Member States, is the system of mutual recognition. Mutual recognition is a general principle of EU law as developed by the Court of Justice in *Cassis de Dijon*.[387] Under this case law, goods legally marketed in a Member State have to be recognized by other Member States as complying with their own rules, unless these rules are mandated by an overriding general interest.[388] EU legislation can impose mutual recognition, often on the basis of harmonization of essential requirements. Examples are the single licence for banks or insurance companies (a European passport) – Member States have to trust a license granted by another Member State since the essential requirements for

---

386. Judgment of 23 April 2009, *VTB-VAB*, C-261/07 and C-299/07, EU:C:2009:244.
387. Judgment of 20 February 1979, *Cassis de Dijon*, C-120/78, EU:C:1979:42.
388. *See* above, paras 94 et seq.

granting such licences have been harmonized – or for TV broadcasters and the mutual recognition of diplomas and professional qualifications.[389]

III. Consequences of Harmonization

275. The consequences for the Member States of harmonization at the EU level depend on the degree of harmonization, i.e., full or minimum harmonization, as already discussed in the preceding section. In *Deutscher Apothekerverband*[390] and in *Gysbrechts*,[391] the Court of Justice ruled that a national measure in an area which has been the subject of exhaustive harmonization at Union level must be assessed in the light of the provisions of that harmonizing measure and not those of the Treaty. This also means that in case of full harmonization, the 'rule of reason' of '*Cassis de Dijon*' does not apply anymore. If a national measure conflicts with a directive and forms an obstacle to the internal market, there is no scope to justify that measure on the basis of mandatory requirements in the general interest. Furthermore, where the directive does not (as some directives do) contain a safeguard provision (referring to, e.g., the grounds mentioned in Article 36) recourse to Treaty exceptions to free movement is also excluded.

276. Harmonization, even 'full harmonization', does however not prevent the application to a given situation of general provisions of national law that are not aimed at regulating the harmonized field. An example is the *De Agostini* case.[392] While the then TV Without Frontiers Directive did not allow for the authorities of a Member State to control broadcasts from broadcasters licensed by another Member State, the Court of Justice ruled that the Directive does not preclude a Member State from taking, pursuant to general legislation on protection of consumers against misleading advertising, measures against an advertiser in relation to television advertising broadcast from another Member State, provided that those measures do not prevent the retransmission, as such, in its territory of television broadcasts coming from that other Member State.

§3. THE '1992 PROGRAMME'

I. Introduction

277. While according to the original EEC Treaty the 'common market' should have been completed by 31 December 1969 (after a transitional period of 12 years) many legal and practical obstacles for the free movement of goods, persons, services and capital remained. One of the main reasons was that legislation at the EC

---

389. *See* hereafter para. 220.
390. Judgment of 11 December 2003, *Deutscher Apothekerverband*, C-322/01, EU:C:2003:664, at para. 64.
391. Judgment of 16 December 2008, *Gysbrechts*, C-205/07, EU:C:2008:730, at para. 33.
392. Judgment of 9 July 1979, *Konsumentombudsmannen v. De Agostini and TV Shop*, C-34/95, C-35/95 and C-36/96, EU:C:1997:344, at para. 38.

level required unanimity within the Council, pursuant to Article 100 EEC.[393] In 1985, the European Commission presented its White Paper on 'Completing the Internal Market',[394] which was approved by the Council in June 1985.[395] The White Paper provides for the removal of internal barriers between Member States and distinguishes three kinds of barriers: physical, tax and technical barriers. Physical barriers relate to controls on goods (customs controls and veterinary and plant health controls) and persons (which were eventually abolished as between the Schengen countries only). Tax barriers result from differences in direct and indirect taxation. Technical barriers take several forms, such as technical requirements and standards, rules on public procurement, restrictions on the movement of workers, services and capital movements, differences in company law regimes and in the legal protection of industrial and IP, etc.

278. This programme could only be realized, thanks to an amendment of the EEC Treaty by the SEA 1987, which introduced the notion of 'internal market', a notion that eventually, in the Lisbon Treaty, replaced that of 'common market'. The Single European also replaced the existing unanimity requirement for directives by a qualified majority within the Council. Henceforth the adoption of harmonization measures could not be blocked by a single Member State (or even by a small minority of votes by several Member States). The unanimity rule has however been maintained for certain fields, in particular tax legislation.[396] Consequently tax law is still largely national in nature, which is one of the main hiatuses in the internal market.

II. The New Approach on Technical Harmonization and Standards

279. One of the main achievements of the White Paper and the Council Resolution endorsing it is the so-called new approach on harmonization and standards. It is based on four guiding principles: (i) harmonization limited to essential safety requirements; (ii) technical specifications implementing these essential requirements have to be drawn up by standardization organizations (CEN – CENELEC) and to the extent possible standards should be harmonized at the European level; provisionally national standards apply; (iii) the standards have a voluntary character; and (iv) there is a legal presumption that standards comply with essential safety requirements. Conformity with a standard is proven by a certificate issued by a certification body. Directives that have been adopted under the 'new approach'[397] have implemented these four principles. They sometimes contain safeguard measures that

---

393. *See* above para. 257.
394. COM(1985) 310 def.
395. Council Resolution 85/C of 7 May 1985 on a new approach to technical harmonisation and standards, *OJ* 1985, C 136/1.
396. *See* above para. 261.
397. Early examples of such directives: toys (Directive 88/378/EEC, (1988) *OJ* L 187/1), construction products: (Directive 89/106 EEC, (1989) *OJ* L 40/12), electromagnetic compatibility: (Directive 89/336/EEC, (1989) *OJ* L 139/19), water boilers (Directive 92/42/EEC, (1992) *OJ* L 167/17), medical devices: Directive 93/42/ EEC, (1993) *OJ* L 169/&), lifts (Directive 95/16/EC, (1995) *OJ* L 213/1), satellite earth station equipment (Directive 93/97/EC, (1993) L 290/1).

allow Member States to restrict importation of goods originating in other Member States, for e.g., safety reasons (where the level of protection is different or to cope with a specific hazard. In this respect, it should be mentioned that there is legislation at the EU level on the safety of goods[398] providing for coordination at the EU level, and a Rapid Alert System enables quick exchange of information between thirty-one European countries and the European Commission about dangerous non-food products posing a risk to health and safety of consumers.

III. Information Procedure on Technical Rules and Standards

280. With a view to facilitate the free movement of goods, Directive 83/139, which has been replaced by Directive 98/34, lays down a procedure for the provision of information in the field of technical standards and regulations and, since an amendment of 2006 also of rules on information society services. The Directive has proven to be very important. The Directive imposes on Member States the duty to inform the Commission and the other Member States of the introduction of any new technical regulation. In *CIA Security*,[399] the Court ruled that that individuals may rely on the Directive before the national court which must decline to apply a national technical regulation which has not been notified in accordance with the directive.

§4. The Internal Market for Services

I. Introduction

281. While there is no general horizontal directive to establish the internal market for goods (apart from the information procedure discussed in the preceding paragraph), there being separate directives and regulations for a large number of goods, in contrast, for the exercise of professional activities by way of establishment of by way of cross-border provision of services there is, since 1989 a general Directive on the mutual recognition of professional qualifications, now Directive 2005/36, and since more recently, the EU legislature adopted an overarching Directive to accelerate the creation of a single market for services: Directive 2006/123 on Services in the Internal Market. Both directives will be discussed hereafter.

---

398. There are sector-specific directives and Directive 2001/95/EC of the European Parliament and of the Council of 3 December 2001 on general product safety *OJ* 2002, L 11/4.
399. Judgment of 30 April 1996, *CIA Security*, C-194/94, EU:C:1996:172; *see also* Judgment of 6 June 2002, *Sapod Audic*, C-159/00, EU:C:2002:343.

II. The Directive on Recognition of Professional Qualifications

282. Directive 2005/36 EC of 7 September 2005 on the recognition of professional qualifications,[400] is based on what is now Articles 46, 53(1) and 62 TFEU (free movement of workers, freedom of establishment and freedom to provide services). The Directive replaces previous directives, i.e., specific directives for certain professions, like doctors, architects, nurses, veterinarians, dental practitioners, midwives, that coordinated qualifications and contained a system of mutual recognition of diplomas, as well as general Directives 89/48 and 92/51 on the mutual recognition of diplomas in the other sectors, all these directives being repealed.

283. Article 2(1) determines the scope of application of the Directive: both employed and self-employed nationals of Member States in relation to regulated professions.

284. Article 4 grants access in a host Member Sate for an activity for which one is qualified in his or her home Member State in order to pursue it in the first Member State under the same conditions as nationals of that Member State.

285. Articles 5–9 relate to the free provision of services. The principle is: freedom to provide services for a service provider legally established in a Member State for the purpose of pursuing the same profession, on a temporary basis in another Member State, provided he has pursued that profession in the Member Sate of establishment for at least two years during the ten years before, if the profession is not regulated in that Member State. There shall be no requirement of authorization, and no registration or membership of a professional organization or body may be imposed.

286. Articles 10 et seq. relate to the right of establishment. The principle is equal treatment for applicants possessing the attestation of competence or evidence of formal qualifications required by another Member Sate in order to gain access to and pursue that profession on the territory of the host Member State. In the following three situations, the host M.S. may require the applicant to complete an adaptation period of up to three years, or to take an aptitude test (Article 14):

(1) when the duration of the education and training in the home Member State is at least one year less;
(2) when matters differ substantially;
(3) when the regulated profession in the host M.S. comprises one or more regulated professional activities which do not exist in the corresponding profession in its applicant's home M.S. The applicant may choose between the adaptation period or the aptitude test, but there is no free choice in case of legal professions (Article 14(3)).

---

400. *OJ* 2005, L 255/22.

287. For lawyers there are additional specific Union rules on establishment and provision of services. A first directive is Directive 77/249 to facilitate the effective exercise by lawyers of the freedom to provide services,[401] which basically allows lawyers legally established (and registered) in a Member State to represent clients in or out of court in other Member States. The Directive on recognition of professional qualifications also applies to lawyers. But in addition Directive 98/5 facilitates practice of the profession of lawyer on a permanent basis in a Member State other than that in which the qualification was obtained.[402] Pursuant to this Directive, a lawyer can obtain the right to establish himself in another Member State and use the professional title usual in that Member State without having to pass the aptitude test required under the professional qualifications Directive, on condition that he has practised in that Member State, on a permanent basis during at least three years effectively and regularly pursued for a period of at least three years an activity in the host Member State in the law of that State including Union law (Article 10(1)).

III. The Services Directive

A. General

288. Directive 2006/123 on Services in the Internal Market relates to both the right of establishment and the freedom to provide services. It applies to services supplied by providers established in a Member State (Article 2(1)).

289. The Directive applies to all sectors, except those expressly excluded from its scope and they are numerous. Article 2(2) excludes:

a. Non-economic services of general interest;
b. Financial services (banking, credit, payments, investment services, insurance);
c. Electronic communications;
d. services in the field of transport, including port services;
e. Temporary work agencies;
f. Healthcare;
g. Audiovisual services;
h. Gambling;
i. Activities connected with official authority (Art. 45 EC);
j. Social services (housing, childcare and support of families);
k. Private security;
l. Notaries and bailiffs.

---

401. *OJ* 1977, L 172/14.
402. *OJ* 1998, L 77/36.

290. The exclusion of services in the field of transport can be related to the provision of Article 58(1) TFEU that freedom to provide services in the field of transport shall be governed by the provisions of the Title relating to transport. Hence the directly effective Treaty provision of Article 56 TFEU on freedom to provide services does not apply to services in the field of transport.[403]

291. In two judgments of 2015, *Trijber*[404] *Itevelesa*,[405] and in one of 2017 *Asociacion Profesional Elte Taxi v. Uber Spain*,[406] the CJEU has clarified this exception. In the first judgment, it ruled that an activity which consists in providing, for payment, a service carrying passengers on a boat for a waterway tour of a city (here: Amsterdam) for event-related purposes, does not constitute a service in the field of 'transport' within the meaning of the Services Directive. The fact that the activity contains a transport service is not enough to qualify the service as such as a transport service. In contrast to *Itevelesa*, the Court ruled that vehicle roadworthiness testing activities, because they are indispensable to the transport activity, are transport services. Finally in *Asociación Profesional Elite Taxi* the Court ruled that an intermediation service such as that of Uber the purpose of which is to connect, by means of a smartphone application and for remuneration, non-professional drivers using their own vehicle with persons who wish to make urban journeys, must be regarded as being inherently linked to a transport service and, accordingly, must be classified as 'a service in the field of transport' within the meaning of Article 58(1) TFEU. Consequently, such a service must be excluded from the scope of Article 56 TFEU, Directive 2006/123 and Directive 2000/31 (on services of the information society).

292. In *Gebhart Hiebler*,[407] the CJEU interpreted the exclusion of activities which are connected with the exercise of official authority (as set out in Article 51 TFEU) by insisting that the exception should be interpreted strictly and by referring to its case law on the basis of Article 51 TFEU,[408] that the exception does not cover the trade of chimney sweep, even though that trade entails the performance not only of private economic activities but also of fire safety regulation tasks.

293. Article 3(1) adds that if the provisions of this Directive conflict with a provision of another Union act governing specific aspects of access to or exercise of a service activity in specific sectors or for specific professions, the provision of the other Union act shall prevail and shall apply to those specific sectors or professions.

---

403. *See* hereafter Part 3, Chapter 5.
404. Judgment of 1 October 2015, *Trijber*, C-340/14 and C-341/14, EU:C:2015:641.
405. Judgment of 15 October 2015, *Grupo Itevelesa*, C-168/14, EU:C:2015:685.
406. Judgment of 20 December 2017, *Asociación Profesional Elite Taxi v. Uber Spain*, C-434/15, EU:C:2017:981.
407. Judgment of 23 December 2015, *Gebhart Hiebler*, C-293/14, EU:C:2015:843.
408. *See* above paras 177 et seq.

B. Administrative Simplification

294. The first branch of the Directive relates to administrative simplification. The most important provision in this respect is the obligation on Member States to provide for a point of single contact. Member States shall ensure that it is possible for providers to complete the following procedures and formalities through points of single contact:

(a) all procedures and formalities needed for access to his service activities;
(b) any applications for authorization needed to exercise his service activities. The establishment of points of single contact shall be without prejudice to the allocation of functions and powers among the authorities within national systems.

C. The Right of Establishment

295. With regard to the right of establishment, the Directive codifies (and refines) the case law of the Court of Justice. Most of the provisions of this section relate to the conditions under which Member States may subject the exercise of an activity on their territory by way of establishment to an authorization.

296. Article 9 relates to *authorization schemes*. Member States shall not make access to a service activity or the exercise thereof subject to an authorization scheme unless the following conditions are satisfied:

(a) the authorization scheme does not discriminate against the provider in question;
(b) the need for an authorization scheme is justified by an overriding reason relating to the public interest;
(c) the objective pursued cannot be attained by means of a less restrictive measure, in particular because an a posteriori inspection would take place too late to be genuinely effective.

297. Article 10 relates to the conditions for the granting of authorizations.

(1) Authorization schemes shall be based on criteria which preclude the competent authorities from exercising their power of assessment in an arbitrary manner.
(2) The criteria referred to in paragraph 1 shall be:
　　(a) non-discriminatory;
　　(b) justified by an overriding reason relating to the public interest;
　　(c) proportionate to that public-interest objective;
　　(d) clear and unambiguous;
　　(e) objective;
　　(f) made public in advance;
　　(g) transparent and accessible.

(3) The conditions for granting authorization for a new establishment shall not duplicate requirements and controls which are equivalent or essentially comparable as regards their purpose to which the provider is already subject in another Member State or in the same Member State. The liaison points referred to in Article 28(2) and the provider shall assist the competent authority by providing any necessary information regarding those requirements.

(4) The authorization shall enable the provider to have access to the service activity, or to exercise that activity, throughout the national territory, including by means of setting-up agencies, subsidiaries, branches or offices, except where an authorization for each individual establishment or a limitation of the authorization to a certain part of the territory is justified by an overriding reason relating to the public interest.

(5) The authorization shall be granted as soon as it is established, in the light of an appropriate examination, that the conditions for authorization have been met.

(6) Except in the case of the granting of an authorization, any decision from the competent authorities, including refusal or withdrawal of an authorization, shall be fully reasoned and shall be open to challenge before the courts or other instances of appeal.

(7) This Article shall not call into question the allocation of the competences, at local or regional level, of the Member States' authorities granting authorizations.

298. In *Trijber*,[409] the CJEU interpreted that provision as precluding a national measure, under which the grant of an authorization for the exercise of an activity, consisting in the operation of window prostitution business by renting rooms out in shifts is subject to the condition that the service provider is able to communicate with the recipients of this service, in this case prostitutes, where that condition is such as to ensure that the legitimate objective of general interest pursed – namely the prevention of criminal offences related to prostitution – is secured, and does not go beyond what is necessary to achieve that objective, which is for the referring court to determine.

299. Article 11 relates to the duration of the authorization.

An authorization granted to a provider shall not be for a limited period, except where:

a. the authorization is being automatically renewed or is subject only to the continued fulfilment of requirements;

b. the number of available authorizations is limited by an overriding reason relating to the public interest;[410] or

---

409. Judgment of 1 October 2015, *Trijber*, C-340/14 and C-341/14, EU:C/2015:641.
410. In Judgment of 1 October 2015, *Trijber*, C-340/14 and C-341/14, EU:C/2015:641, the CJEU interpreted that provision as precluding the grant of authorizations for an unlimited period, where the number of authorizations is limited for reasons of public interest.

    c. a limited authorization period can be justified by an overriding reason relating to the public interest (see Article 11(1)).

This provision shall not concern the maximum period before the end of which the provider must actually commence his activity after receiving authorization (Article 11(2)).

Member States shall require a provider to inform the relevant point of single contact provided for in Article 6 of the following changes:

(a) the creation of subsidiaries whose activities fall within the scope of the authorization scheme;
(b) changes in his situation which result in the conditions for authorization no longer being met (Article 11(3)).

This Article shall be without prejudice to the Member States' ability to revoke authorizations, when the conditions for authorization are no longer met (Article 11(4)).

300. Article 12 relates to the selection from among several candidates:

(1) Where the number of authorizations available for a given activity is limited because of the scarcity of available natural resources or technical capacity, Member States shall apply a selection procedure to potential candidates which provides full guarantees of impartiality and transparency, including, in particular, adequate publicity about the launch, conduct and completion of the procedure.
(2) In the cases referred to in paragraph 1, authorization shall be granted for an appropriate limited period and may not be open to automatic renewal nor confer any other advantage on the provider whose authorization has just expired or on any person having any particular links with that provider.

Subject to paragraph 1 and to Articles 9 and 10, Member States may take into account, in establishing the rules for the selection procedure, considerations of public health, social policy objectives, the health and safety of employees or self-employed persons, the protection of the environment, the preservation of cultural heritage and other overriding reasons relating to the public interest, in conformity with Community law. In *Promoimpresa*,[411] the CJEU ruled that Article 12(1) and (2) must be interpreted as precluding a national measure which permits the automatic extension of existing authorizations of State-owned maritime and lakeside property for tourist and leisure-oriented business activities, without any selection procedure for potential candidates.

301. Article 13 concerns authorization procedures:

---

411. Judgment of 14 July 2016, *Promoimpresa*, C-458/14 and C-67/15, EU:C:2016:558.

(1) Authorization procedures and formalities shall be clear, made public in advance and be such as to provide the applicants with a guarantee that their application will be dealt with objectively and impartially.

(2) Authorization procedures and formalities shall not be dissuasive and shall not unduly complicate or delay the provision of the service. They shall be easily accessible and any charges which the applicants may incur from their application shall be reasonable and proportionate to the cost of the authorization procedures in question and shall not exceed the cost of the procedures.[412]

(3) Authorization procedures and formalities shall provide applicants with a guarantee that their application will be processed as quickly as possible and, in any event, within a reasonable period which is fixed and made public in advance. The period shall run only from the time when all documentation has been submitted. When justified by the complexity of the issue, the time period may be extended once, by the competent authority, for a limited time. The extension and its duration shall be duly motivated and shall be notified to the applicant before the original period has expired.

(4) Failing a response within the time period set or extended in accordance with paragraph 3, authorization shall be deemed to have been granted. Different arrangements may nevertheless be put in place, where justified by overriding reasons relating to the public interest, including a legitimate interest of third parties.

(5) All applications for authorization shall be acknowledged as quickly as possible. The acknowledgement must specify the following:
  (a) the period referred to in paragraph 3;
  (b) the available means of redress;
  (c) where applicable, a statement that in the absence of a response within the period specified, the authorization shall be deemed to have been granted.

(6) In the case of an incomplete application, the applicant shall be informed as quickly as possible of the need to supply any additional documentation, as well as of any possible effects on the period referred to in paragraph 3.

(7) When a request is rejected because it fails to comply with the required procedures or formalities, the applicant shall be informed of the rejection as quickly as possible.

302. Certain requirements are prohibited in relation to establishment. They are enumerated in Article 14 and generally concern types of restrictions that had already been found by the Court of Justice to contravene the right of establishment. They include: *inter alia* discriminatory requirements based directly or indirectly on nationality or, in the case of companies, the location of the registered office,[413] a

---

412. In Judgment of 16 November 2016, *Hemming et.al.*, C-316/15, EU:C:2016:879, the CJEU interpreted Art. 13(2), as precluding the requirement for the payment of a fee, at the time of submitting an application for the grant or renewal of authorization, part of which corresponds to the costs relating to the management and enforcement of the authorization scheme concerned, even if that part is refundable if that application is refused.

413. *See* Judgment of 16 June 2015, *Rina Services*, C-593/13. EU:C:2015:399. The Services Directive does not permit national legislation under which certification bodies must have their registered office in national territory.

prohibition on having an establishment in more than one Member State, restrictions on the freedom to choose between a principal or secondary establishment, conditions of reciprocity with the Member State in which the provider already has an establishment, save in the case of conditions of reciprocity provided for in Community instruments concerning energy; the case-by-case application of an economic test making the granting of authorization subject to proof of the existence of an economic need or market demand, the direct or indirect involvement of competing operators, including within consultative bodies, in the granting of authorizations or in the adoption of other decisions of the competent authorities, with the exception of professional bodies and associations or other organizations acting as the competent authority, an obligation to provide or participate in a financial guarantee or to take out insurance from a provider or body established in their territory.

303. Pursuant to Article 15(1), other requirements that are not prohibited in all circumstances, namely:

(a) quantitative or territorial restrictions, in particular in the form of limits fixed according to population or of a minimum geographical distance between providers;
(b) an obligation on a provider to take a specific legal form;
(c) requirements which relate to the shareholding of a company;
(d) requirements, other than those concerning matters covered by Directive 2005/36/EC[414] or provided for in other Community instruments, which reserve access to the service activity in question to particular providers by virtue of the specific nature of the activity;
(e) a ban on having more than one establishment in the territory of the same State;
(f) requirements fixing a minimum number of employees;
(g) fixed minimum and/or maximum tariffs with which the provider must comply;
(h) an obligation on the provider to supply other specific services jointly with his service;

are to be evaluated in the light of the following criteria: non-discrimination (requirements must be neither directly nor indirectly discriminatory according to nationality nor, with regard to companies, according to the location of the registered office), necessity: (requirements must be justified by an overriding reason relating to the public interest) and proportionality (requirements must be suitable for securing the attainment of the objective pursued; they must not go beyond what is necessary to attain that objective and it must not be possible to replace those requirements with other, less restrictive measures). This provision shall apply to legislation in the field of services of general economic interest only insofar as the application of these paragraphs does not obstruct the performance, in law or in fact, of the particular task assigned to them (*see* Article 15(4)).

---

414. *See* above para. 281.

304. Regarding the type of restrictions referred to in Article 15(1) (*see* (a)) (quantitative or territorial restrictions), the CJEU clarified in *Gebhart Hiebler*[415] that this provision precludes legislation which limits, in all respects, a licence to trade as chimney sweep to a particular geographical area, if that legislation does not seek to attain, in a consistent and systematic manner, the objective of public health protection (a matter to be determined by the national court).

305. With regard to the provision of Article 15(1)(b), namely an obligation on a provider to take a specific legal form, the CJEU ruled in *Commission v. Hungary*[416] that it opposes to several provisions of Hungarian law subjecting the granting of benefits in kind to employees to companies to certain companies formed in accordance to Hungarian law.

306. In *CMVRO*[417] the Court ruled that Article 15 does not preclude national legislation (Romania) under which veterinary practitioners have an exclusive right to retail and use organic products, special purpose anti-parasitic products and veterinary medicinal products, in that it complies with the third condition laid down in Article 15(3)(proportionality), but that it does preclude the rule under which shares in establishments retailing veterinary medicinal products must be owned exclusively by one or more veterinary practitioners, for lack of proportionality. Indeed the Court considered that while a Member State may lawfully prevent economic operators who are not veterinary practitioners from being in a position to exert decisive influence over the operation of establishments retailing veterinary medicinal products, the objective referred to in that paragraph cannot justify a provision that totally precludes such operators from holding shares in such establishments, as it is perfectly plausible that veterinary practitioners will be able to monitor such establishments effectively even if they do not hold all the shares in those establishments, given the fact that a limited number of those shares are held by persons who are not veterinary practitioners will not necessarily make such monitoring impossible.

D. The Freedom to Provide Services

307. While the Services Directive codifies more or less the case law of the Court of Justice on the right of establishment, it constitutes a further step in the liberalization of services. In effect Article 16 reduces the grounds of justification for restrictions to the freedom to provide services. Not all grounds of justification that had been recognized by the Court of Justice have been maintained, only those that are in the Treaty (Article 51 TFEU) and a few others. Consumer protection, e.g., is not any more a ground of justification on under the Directive. Article 16(1) contains

---

415. Judgment of 23 December 2015, *Gebhart Hiebler*, C-293/14, EU:C:2015:843.
416. Judgment of 23 February 2016 (Grand Chamber), *Commission v. Hungary*, C-179/14, EU:C:2015:843.
417. Judgment of 1 March 2018, *CMVRO*, C-297/16, EU :C :2018 :141.

a general provision: Member States shall not make access to or exercise of a service activity in their territory subject to compliance with any requirements which do not respect the following principles.

308. Non-discrimination: the requirement may be neither directly nor indirectly discriminatory with regard to nationality or, in the case of legal persons, with regard to the Member State in which they are established;

309. Necessity: the requirement must be justified for reasons of public policy, public security, public health or the protection of the environment;

310. Proportionality: the requirement must be suitable for attaining the objective pursued, and must not go beyond what is necessary to attain that objective.

311. Article 16(2) contains types of requirements that may not be imposed on service providers established in other Member States: (a) an obligation on the provider to have an establishment in their territory, (b) an obligation to obtain an authorization from the competent authorities, (c) a ban on the provider setting-up a certain infrastructure in their territory, (d) the application of certain contractual arrangements between the provider and the recipient which prevent or restrict service provision by the self-employed, (e) an obligation on the provider to possess an identity document issued by its competent authorities specific to the exercise of a service activity, (f) the application of specific contractual arrangements between the provider and the recipient which prevent or restrict service provision by the self-employed; (g) an obligation on the provider to possess an identity document issued by its competent authority specific to the exercise of service activities; (h) requirements, except for those necessary for health and safety at work, which affect the use of equipment and material which are an integral part of the service provided; (i) restrictions on the freedom to provide services referred to in Article 19(1).

312. Pursuant to Article 16(3), the Member State to which the provider moves shall not be prevented from imposing requirements with regard to the provision of a service activity, where they are justified for reasons of public policy, public security, public health or the protection of the environment and in accordance with paragraph 1. Nor shall that Member State be prevented from applying, in accordance with Union law, its rules on employment conditions, including those laid down in collective agreements. Pursuant to Article 17, Article 16 shall not apply to.

313. Article 17 contains a number of additional derogations for certain sectors (post, electricity, gas, water, waste, etc.) and pursuant to Article 18 Member States may by way of derogation from Article 16, and in exceptional circumstances only, in respect of a provider established in another Member State, take measures relating to the safety of services.

314. Articles 19–21 contain right for recipients of services, including the right to assistance and the right not to be discriminated.

IV. Quality of Services

315. Chapter V (Articles 22–27) on quality of services comprises provisions on information by service providers to recipients (Article 22), liability insurance and guarantees, (Article 23), commercial communication by regulated professions (Article 24), multidisciplinary activities (Article 25), policy on quality of services (Article 26) and settlement of dispute (Article 27).

V. Information by Services Provider

316. Article 22 relates to information to be given by service providers to recipients. It reads:

1. Member States shall ensure that providers make the following information available to the recipient:
   a. the name of the provider, his legal status and form, the geographic address at which he is established and details enabling him to be contacted rapidly and communicated with directly and, as the case may be, by electronic means;
   b. where the provider is registered in a trade or other similar public register, the name of that register and the provider's registration number, or equivalent means of identification in that register;
   c. where the activity is subject to an authorisation scheme, the particulars of the relevant competent authority or the single point of contact;
   d. where the provider exercises an activity which is subject to VAT, the identification number referred to in Article 22(1) of Sixth Council Directive 77/388/EEC of 17 May 1977 on the harmonisation of the laws of the Member States relating to turnover taxes – Common system of value added tax: uniform basis of assessment;
   e. in the case of the regulated professions, any professional body or similar institution with which the provider is registered, the professional title and the Member State in which that title has been granted;
   f. the general conditions and clauses, if any, used by the provider;
   g. the existence of contractual clauses, if any, used by the provider concerning the law applicable to the contract and/or the competent courts;
   h. the existence of an after-sales guarantee, if any, not imposed by law;
   i. the price of the service, where a price is pre-determined by the provider for a given type of service;
   j. the main features of the service, if not already apparent from the context;
   k. the insurance or guarantees referred to in Article 23(1), and in particular the contact details of the insurer or guarantor and the territorial coverage.
2. Member States shall ensure that the information referred to in paragraph 1, according to the provider's preference:
   a. is supplied by the provider on his own initiative;

    b.   is easily accessible to the recipient at the place where the service is provided or the contract concluded;

    c.   can be easily accessed by the recipient electronically by means of an address supplied by the provider;

    d.   appears in any information documents supplied to the recipient by the provider which set out a detailed description of the service he provides.

3.   Member States shall ensure that, at the recipient's request, providers supply the following additional information:

    a.   where the price is not pre-determined by the provider for a given type of service, the price of the service or, if an exact price cannot be given, the method for calculating the price so that it can be checked by the recipient, or a sufficiently detailed estimate;

    b.   as regards the regulated professions, a reference to the professional rules applicable in the Member State of establishment and how to access them;

    c.   information on their multidisciplinary activities and partnerships which are directly linked to the service in question and on the measures taken to avoid conflicts of interest. That information shall be included in any information document in which providers give a detailed description of their services;

    d.   any codes of conduct to which the provider is subject and the address at which these codes may be consulted by electronic means, specifying the language version available;

    e.   where a provider is subject to a code of conduct, or member of a trade association or professional body which provides for recourse to a non-judicial means of dispute settlement, information in this respect. The provider shall specify how to access detailed information on the characteristics of, and conditions for, the use of non-judicial means of dispute settlement.

4.   Member States shall ensure that the information which a provider must supply in accordance with this Chapter is made available or communicated in a clear and unambiguous manner, and in good time before conclusion of the contract or, where there is no written contract, before the service is provided.

5.   The information requirements laid down in this Chapter are in addition to requirements already provided for in Community law and do not prevent Member States from imposing additional information requirements applicable to providers established in their territory.

6.   The Commission may, in accordance with the procedure referred to in Article 40(2), specify the content of the information provided for in paragraphs 1 and 3 of this Article according to the specific nature of certain activities and may specify the practical means of implementing paragraph 2 of this Article.

With regard to paragraph 5 it can be observed that these information obligations apply to all service providers irrespective of whether the recipients are consumers or traders. Where the recipients are consumers the information obligations of consumer law, such as the Consumer Rights Directive 2011/83 and the Unfair Commercial Practices Directive 2005/29 have to bet taken into account.

VI. Commercial Communications

317. Article 24 on commercial communications reads:

1. Member States shall remove all total prohibitions on commercial communications by the regulated professions.
2. Member States shall ensure that commercial communications by the regulated professions comply with professional rules, in conformity with Community law, which relate, in particular, to the independence, dignity and integrity of the profession, as well as to professional secrecy, in a manner consistent with the specific nature of each profession. Professional rules on commercial communications shall be non-discriminatory, justified by an overriding reason relating to the public interest and proportionate.

In *Société fiduciaire nationale d'expertise comptable*[418] the CJEU ruled that Article 24(1) must be interpreted as precluding national legislation (such as the French law in issue) which totally prohibits the members of a regulated profession, such as the profession of qualified accountant, from engaging in canvassing.

---

418. Judgment of 5 April 2011, *Société fiduciaire nationale d'expertise comptable*, C-119/09, EU:C:2011:728.

Part II. The Common Policies

Chapter 1. Competition Policy

§1. Introduction

I. Origin and Objectives

318. The competition rules of the TFEU[419] already existed in the EEC treaty that entered into force in 1958.[420] The numbering has changed twice. Articles 85 and 86 EEC (competition rules for undertakings) e.g., became Articles 81 and 82 EC and are now Articles 101 and 102 TFEU. Articles 87 and 88 EEC (on State aid) became Articles 92 and 93 EC and are now Articles 107 and 108 TFEU. Finally, Article 90 EEC (on State enterprises and services of general economic interest) became Article 86 EC and is now Article 106 TFEU. In substance these articles have not changed, except for the replacement of the notion of 'common market' by that of 'internal market', which, as discussed in the preceding Part I, covers more or less the same reality.

319. Competition policy in the EU has a double objective: maintaining a sufficient degree of competition in the market (effective competition) and integrating the national markets of the Member States into one single European market. In that sense, the competition rules supplement the rules on free movement discussed in Part I. Competition policy applies first and foremost to businesses ('undertakings') which shall not raise barriers to trade between Member States and comply with the prohibitions laid down in Article 101 (anticompetitive agreements), Article 102 TFEU (abuse of a dominant position) and merger control. Second, EU competition policy applies to Member States, in order to prevent them from distorting competition in the market by interventions with regard to pubic undertakings and undertakings to which they have granted special or exclusive rights (Article 106 TFEU) or by granting State aid (Articles 107 and 108 TFEU). These different rules will be examined in the subsequent sections of this chapter.

---

419. Consolidated version of the Treaty on the Functioning of the European Union, *OJ* C 326, 26 October 2012, pp. 47–390.
420. Treaty establishing the European Economic Community, signed in Rome on 25 March 1957.

II. General Overview

320. EU competition rules can be divided in five branches:

(1) Antitrust: prohibition of restrictive agreements and abuse of a dominant position (*see* §§ 4–6 and § 8).
(2) State monopolies and application of antitrust rules to the Member States: Article 106 TFEU on special or exclusive rights conferred by Member States and the obligation of Member States, under the principle of loyal cooperation, to abstain from facilitating restrictive practices by undertakings (*see* § 7).
(3) Liberalization of certain sectors (*see* § 9).
(4) Merger control: prior examination by the Commission of concentrations (or mergers) with a European dimension, with a view to prohibiting those that and significantly impede effective competition in the internal market (*see* § 10).
(5) State Aid: prohibition of and control of aid granted by the Member States that distort competition by favouring certain undertakings (*see* § 11). The EU Competition rules[421] can be found in the Articles 101–109 of the TFEU. The main *antitrust rules* are Articles 101 and 102 TFEU. They contain respectively (i) a prohibition of agreements and concerted practices between undertakings and of decisions of associations of undertakings which may affect trade between the Member States and which have as their object or effect the prevention, restriction or distortion of competition within the internal market and (ii) a prohibition of unilateral behaviour of dominant undertakings in the form of an abuse of such a position.

321. Article 103 TFEU gives the power to the Council, on the basis of proposals from the Commission and after consultation of the Parliament, to enact regulations or directives to give effect to the principles set out in Articles 101 and 102.

322. Council Regulation 1/2003,[422] contains the rules on the respective powers of the Commission and the national competition authorities (NCAs) in applying Articles 101 and 102. Since the entry into force of that Regulation, Articles 101 and 102 TFEU are entirely directly applicable by the NCAs and the national courts.

323. Articles 104 and 105 contain a transitory regime which enables the authorities in the Member States and the Commission to rule on infringements of Articles 101 and 102 before the entry into force of specific implementing provisions pursuant to Article 103. Such regulations, in particular Regulation 1/2003 (and earlier Regulation 17/62), have been issued. Articles 104 and 105 have therefore become irrelevant.

---

421. In addition to European Competition rules, national competition rules may apply depending on the circumstances.
422. Council Regulation (EC) No 1/2003 of 16 December 2002 on the implementation of the rules on competition laid down in Arts 81 and 82 of the Treaty, OJ 2003, L 1/1.

324. The next important area of EU competition law is merger or 'concentration' control. Such control existed from the outset for steel and coal pursuant to the now expired Treaty establishing the ECSC.[423] Rules on concentration (or merger) control were introduced for all sectors of the economy by Regulation in 1990. Presently merger rules can be found in Regulation 139/20004 on the control of concentrations between undertakings.[424]

325. The rules on *State aid* are contained in the Articles 107–109 TFEU. These rules prohibit in principle Member States to grant aid to undertakings which distorts or is likely to distort competition in the internal market. These provisions have been further implemented by regulations and some other instruments that will be discussed hereinafter.

326. Article 106 contains special provisions on State monopolies and on the duties of Member States concerning State enterprises and enterprises to which they have granted special or exclusive rights.

327. In addition to these Treaty provisions, sector-specific legislation applies to transport, energy, postal services and telecommunications. Indeed, these services have not always been as open to competition but were previously provided by national organizations with exclusive rights to provide a given service.

328. The European Commission has established *international cooperation* on competition policy in many ways. This was necessary since, with the increasing globalization, more and more companies, mergers and cartels are international. As a consequence hereof, the activities of companies based outside the EU may affect competition within the EU. The EU has thus not only established bilateral agreements on competition (with countries or regions outside the EU),[425] but has also made multilateral cooperation efforts and is for example involved in the International Competition Network (ICN),[426] the OECD[427] and the WTO.[428]

329. One of the most important multilateral agreements is the EEA agreement which entered into force in 1994.[429] The EEA agreement contains rules on competition which are very close to the EU competition rules.

---

423. *See* Art. 66 of the ECSC Treaty, available online at http://eur-lex.europa.eu/legal-content/FR/TXT /PDF/?uri=CELEX:11951K/TXT&from=EN, last accessed on 10 August 2016.
424. Council Regulation (EC) No 139/2004 of 20 January 2004 on the control of concentrations between undertakings ('the EC Merger Regulation'), *OJ* 2004, L 24/1.
425. Further information including a list of general agreements containing competition provisions or dedicated agreements concluded between the EU and third countries is available at http://ec.euro pa.eu/competition/international/bilateral/index.html, last accessed on 10 August 2016.
426. Further information is available at www.internationalcompetitionnetwork.org, last accessed on 10 August 2016.
427. Further information is available at www.oecd.org/competition, last accessed on 10 August 2016.
428. Further information is available at www.wto.org/english/tratop_e/comp_e/comp_e.htm, last acces sed on 10 August 2016.
429. Decision of the Council and the Commission of 13 December 1993 on the conclusion of the Agreement on the European Economic Area between the European Communities, their Member States

§2. KEY CONCEPTS

I. Undertaking

330. The EU Competition rules apply to undertakings. The concept is thus used to define the scope of the application of EU competition rules. Its purpose is also to identify to which entity a prohibition is attributable. The concept of 'undertaking' is not defined in the Treaty.

331. The Court of Justice has given the following definition of this notion: 'the concept of an undertaking encompasses every entity engaged in an economic activity regardless of the legal status of the entity and the way in which it is financed'.[430]

332. An economic activity is a very broad concept and consists in offering goods or services in the market.[431] Several consequences may be drawn from that definition. The concept of undertaking includes private as well as public undertakings (undertakings governed by the State). Liberal professions and their firms are also undertakings.[432]

333. The Court of Justice has identified entities that fall outside the scope of the competition rules, because they do not exercise an economic activity in the market. There are two main categories: social security bodies and bodies that exercise State power. However, these categories are not defined once and for all and the Court had to decide on borderline cases.

334. In the area of social security, there is a line of cases which culminated in the *AOK-Bundesverband* case[433] in 2004. In this judgment, the Court refers to the milestones of its former case law.[434]

335. In *AOK-Bundesverband*, the Court ruled out the qualification of undertaking and found that sickness funds in the German statutory health insurance scheme, like the bodies at issue in *Poucet and Pistre*, are involved in the management of the

---

and the Republic of Austria, the Republic of Finland, the Republic of Iceland, the Principality of Liechtenstein, the Kingdom of Norway, the Kingdom of Sweden and the Swiss Confederation* (94/1/ECSC, EC); *OJ* 1994, L1/1 (*The EEA agreement has not been ratified by the Swiss Confederation).

430. Judgment of 23 April 1991, *Klaus Höfner and Fritz Elser v. Macrotron GmbH*, C-41/90, EU:C:1991:161, para. 21.

431. Judgment of 11 July 2006, *Fenin*, C-205/03 P, EU:C:2006:453, and judgment of 4 March 2003, *Fenin*, T-319/99, EU:T:2003:50.

432. *See* for example judgment of 18 June 1998, *Commission v. Italy*, C-35/96, EU:C:1998:303 for customs agents; judgment 19 February 1999, *Wouters v. Algemene Raad van de Nederlandse orde van Advocaten*, C-309/99, EU:C:2009:609 for registered members of the bar.

433. Judgment of 16 March 2004, in *AOK-Bundesverband and Others*, Joined cases C-264/01, C-306/01, C-354/01, C-355/01, EU:C:2004:150.

434. Judgment of 17 February 1993, in *Poucet and Pistre*, Joined Cases C-159/91 and C-160/91, EU:C:1993:63, paras 15 and 18, Judgment of 22 January 2002, *Cisal v. INAIL*, C-218/00, EU:C:2002:36, Judgment 21 September 1999, *Albany International*, C-67/96, EU:C:1999:430.

social security system. In this regard, they fulfil an exclusively social function, which is founded on the principle of national solidarity and is entirely non-profit-making. The sickness funds are compelled by law to offer to their members essentially identical obligatory benefits which do not depend on the amount of the contributions. The funds therefore have no possibility of influence over those benefits. The sickness funds are therefore not in competition with one another or with private institutions as regards grant of the obligatory statutory benefits in respect of treatment or medicinal products which constitutes their main function. However, the Court adds, the possibility remains that, besides their functions of an exclusively social nature, engage in obligations which have a purpose that is not social, but economic.

336. This judgment also stresses that the notion of undertaking is a functional one. An entity can be an undertaking for only one of its activities and not for the other.

337. As to entities vested with public powers, the Court of Justice ruled that the focus should be on the nature of the activities so that an entity may well be considered as an undertaking subject to competition rules for one part of its activities while the remaining activities fall outside their scope.[435]

338. The Court of Justice decided that employees in an employment relationship which do not bear financial risk associated with the business do not qualify as undertakings subject to competition rules.[436] However, this does not prevent individual employees to be caught under national competition rules for example because they represented their company in the framework of a cartel.[437]

339. In addition, the Court ruled that collective agreements concluded between trade unions and employers relating to the conditions of employment and working conditions are excluded from the scope of Article 101(1) TFEU.[438]

340. Reference is often made to the concept of the 'single economic unit' which may be defined as 'an unitary organization of personal, tangible and intangible elements which pursues a specific economic aim on a long-term basis and can contribute to the commission of an infringement'.[439]

---

435. Judgment of 25 October 2001, *Ambulanz Glockner*, C-475/99, EU:C:2001:577. *See also* judgment of 26 March 2009, *SELEX Sistemi integrati*, C-113/07, EU:C:2009:191 and judgment of 1 July 2008, *Motosyklestiki Omospandia Ellados NPID v. Elliniko Dimosio*, C-49/07, EU:C:2008:376.
436. Judgment of 16 September 1999, *Criminal Proceedings Against Becu*, C-22/98, EU:C:1999:419.
437. Sanctions against individual may be applied for cartel infringements (or only for bid-rigging) notably in the following jurisdictions: Austria (bid-rigging), Belgium, the Czech Republic, Denmark, France, Germany (bid-rigging), Greece, Hungary (bid-rigging), Ireland, Italy, Poland, Romania, Slovenia, the UK.
438. Judgment of 21 September 1999, *Albany International BV v. Stichting Bedrijfspensioenfonds Textielindustrie*, C-67/96, EU:C:1999:430.
439. Judgment of 10 March 1992 in *Shell International Chemical Company v. Commission*, T-11/89, EU:T:1992:33.

341. The jurisprudence relying on the concept of 'single economic unit' has been used to involve and fine a parent company where a subsidiary that does enjoy any economic independence has committed an infringement of competition law.[440] The Court of Justice established that the core of this 'parental liability' lies in the analysis of whether the parent company has decisive influence over the policy and direct conduct of a subsidiary and it admitted that there is a rebuttable presumption that the parent company is exercising control over a subsidiary if it holds a 100% shareholding in a subsidiary.[441]

II. Effect on Trade Between Member States

342. The notion of 'effect on trade between Member States' was defined by EU Courts and later outlined in the Commission Notice containing the Guidelines on the effect on trade.[442] It serves as a jurisdictional threshold: Articles 101 and 102 TFEU only apply where trade between Member States is affected. Often conduct would be prohibited by Article 101 or 102 TFEU if it affected adversely trade between Member States. Where it only affects competition on the market of a particular Member States it can only be prohibited by the domestic competition rules of that Member State. Today all Member States have national competition rules that mirror more or less Articles 101 and 1021 TFEU, without requiring an effect on trade between Member States.

343. Normally an effect on trade between Member States will be easily established. It is not necessary to prove an actual effect on trade between Member States. It is sufficient to show that there might potentially be such an effect. Moreover, even if all the parties to an agreement are located in one Member State and the anticompetitive conduct is thus confined to the territory of one State, the behaviour is capable of having repercussions on trade between Member States.

344. On the other hand, there is also a quantitative threshold: trade between Member States must be affected to an *appreciable* extent which can be appraised in particular by reference to the position and the importance of the relevant undertakings on the market for the products concerned. The European Commission provides guidance regarding situation where, in principle, it will come to the conclusion that agreements are not capable of appreciably affecting trade between Member States when the following cumulative conditions are met: (a) the aggregate market share of the parties on any relevant market within the Community affected by the agreement does not exceed 5%, and (b) in the case of horizontal agreements, the aggregate annual Community turnover of the undertakings concerned in the products covered by the agreement does not exceed EUR 40 million.[443]

---

440. Judgment of 10 September 2009, *Akzo Nobel v. Commission*, C-97/08, EU:C:2009:536.
441. Judgment of 8 May 2013, *Eni SpA v. Commission*, C-508/11, EU:C:2013:289.
442. Commission Notice – Guidelines on the effect on trade concept contained in Arts 81 and 82 of the Treaty, *OJ* 2004, C 101/81.
443. *See* para. 52 of the Commission's Notice on the effect on trade.

345. Similarly, the European merger control rules only apply to mergers having a 'European dimension', i.e., where the turnover of the undertakings concerned are exceeded. Where a merger does not reach the EU thresholds, it will possibly have to be notified in one or more Member States. Most Member States have merger rules that resemble those of the EU but with lower thresholds. In any event where the thresholds of the EU merger regulation are reached only, the Commission has the power to veto the merger.

III. Relevant Market

346. In order to establish the existence of an anticompetitive behaviour, the relevant market must be defined.

347. One of the most important sources of information concerning the concept of the relevant market is the Commission's Notice on the definition of the relevant market for the purposes of Community competition law.[444]

348. The purpose of market definition is to identify in a systematic way the competitive constraints that the undertakings involved face. The objective of defining a market in both its product and geographic dimension is to identify those actual competitors of the undertakings involved that are capable of constraining those undertakings' behaviour and of preventing them from behaving independently of effective competitive pressure.

349. The relevant product market comprises all those products and/or services which are regarded as interchangeable or substitutable by the consumer, by reason of the products' characteristics, their prices and their intended use. On the basis of these criteria, the CJEU decided e.g., in United Brands[445] that there is a separate market for bananas and that there is not just one fruit market.

350. The relevant product market is essentially defined by looking at demand-side substitutability. Exceptionally supply-side substitutability will also be taken into account.

351. The assessment of demand substitution entails a determination of the range of products which are viewed as substitutes by the consumer. Conceptually, this approach means that, starting from the type of products that the undertakings involved sell and the area in which they sell them, additional products and areas will be included in, or excluded from, the market definition depending on whether competition from these other products and areas affect or restrain sufficiently the pricing of the parties' products in the short term. To this effect, the Commission normally applies the so-called Small but significant and non-transitory increase in price

---

444. Commission notice on the definition of the relevant market for the purposes of Community competition law, *OJ* 1997, C 372/5.
445. Judgment of 14 February 1978, *United Brands*, 27/76, EU:C:1978:22.

(SNNIP) test: the question to be answered is whether the parties' customers would switch to readily available substitutes or to suppliers located elsewhere in response to a hypothetical small (in the range 5% to 10%) but permanent relative price increase in the products and areas being considered. If substitution were enough to make the price increase unprofitable because of the resulting loss of sales, additional substitutes and areas are included in the relevant market. This would be done until the set of products and geographical areas is such that small, permanent increases in relative prices would be profitable.

352. Supply-side substitutability may also be taken into account when defining markets in those situations in which its effects are equivalent to those of demand substitution in terms of effectiveness and immediacy. This means that suppliers are able to switch production to the relevant products and market them in the short term without incurring significant additional costs or risks in response to small and permanent changes in relative prices. A practical example of the approach to supply-side substitutability when defining product markets is to be found in the case of paper. Paper is usually supplied in a range of different qualities, from standard writing paper to high quality papers to be used, for instance, to publish art books. From a demand point of view, different qualities of paper cannot be used for any given use, i.e., an art book or a high quality publication cannot be based on lower quality papers. However, paper plants are prepared to manufacture the different qualities, and production can be adjusted with negligible costs and in a short time-frame. By contrast when supply-side substitutability would entail the need to adjust significantly existing tangible and intangible assets, additional investments, strategic decisions or time delays, it will not be considered at the stage of market definition.

353. A relevant geographic market is defined as comprising the area in which the undertakings concerned are involved in the supply and demand of products or services, in which the conditions of competition are sufficiently homogeneous and which can be distinguished from neighbouring areas because the conditions of competition are appreciably different in those area'. In the already mentioned *United Brands*[446] case, e.g., the CJEU identified separate geographic market within the EU, such as Ireland or South Germany.

§3. Competent Bodies

354. Three European institutions are mainly involved in the application of EU competition policy: the Council, the European Commission and the European Courts.

355. The Council (of Ministers) has adopted several important pieces of competition legislation such as Regulation No 1/2003/EC implementing Articles 101 and 102 TFEU as well as the Merger Regulation (Regulation 139/2004 on the Control of Concentrations between undertakings).

---

446. *United Brands*, footnote 27.

356. The European Commission has an extremely important role. Not only is it charged with the enforcement of the EU competition rules (in the area of antitrust in cooperation with the NCAs), but it also has important delegated powers (and even legislative powers under Article 106(3)). There are e.g., a series of block exemption regulations in which the Commission has exempted certain categories of agreements from the prohibition of Article 101(1) TFEU under Article 101(3) TFEU. The Commission has exclusive powers in declaring aid granted by Member States or concentrations with a Union dimension compatible or incompatible with the internal market.

357. Within the European Commission, the Directorate specifically responsible for Competition Policy is Directorate General for Competition (European Commission) (DG COMP). DG COMP has one Director General,[447] one Chief Economist[448] and three Deputy Directors General: one for mergers,[449] one for antitrust[450] and one responsible for State aid.[451] DG COMP is further divided into nine administrative units, from A to H, each having their own responsibilities (A. Policy and strategy, B. Energy and Environment, C. Information, Communication and Media, D. Financial Services, E. Basis Industries, Manufacturing and Agriculture, F. Markets, Transports, Post and other services, G. Cartels, H. State Aid and R. Registry and Resources).

358. The website of the DG COMP is an invaluable source of information and legislation concerning Competition Policy.[452]

359. Decisions of the Commission can be appealed before the 'GC' by the undertakings concerned and/or other interested parties. A decision of the GC may be appealed – on points of law only – before the European Court of Justice ('CJEU'). A reference for preliminary rulings may also be addressed by national courts regarding the interpretation of EU law to the CJEU pursuant to Article 267. Many landmark judgments of the CJEU in the area of competition law have been rendered on preliminary reference.

360. The EP is only involved in competition legislation through the consultation procedure, despite regular calls for the ordinary legislative procedure to be extended to competition law. Its main role is therefore the scrutiny of the executive, i.e., the Commissioner responsible for competition is heard several times a year before Parliament's Committee on Economic and Monetary Affairs (ECON) to discuss the approach taken to and discuss individual decisions.[453]

---

447. Currently J. Laitenberger.
448. Currently M. Motta.
449. Currently C. Esteva Mosso.
450. Currently C. Madero Villarejo.
451. Currently Laitenberger acting.
452. http://ec.europa.eu/comm/competition/index_en.html, last accessed on 16 August 2016.
453. *See* www.europarl.europa.eu/, last accessed on 20 August 2016.

361. Other bodies including the Economic and Social Committee and the Committee of the Regions receive an annual report on competition policy from the European Commission.

362. Since Regulation (EC) 1/2003,[454] the 'Modernisation Regulation', came into force, Articles 101 and 102 TFEU can also be enforced by the NCAs and the national courts.

363. In order to ensure cooperation and the uniform application of the EC competition rules, the European Competition Network (ECN) has been founded in 2004. The ECN is based on Council Regulation 1/2003.

364. Through this network, the European Commission and the NCAs cooperate by informing each other of new cases and envisaged enforcement decisions, coordinating investigations where necessary, helping each other with investigations, exchanging evidence and other information, and discussing various issues of common interest. The objective of the ECN is to build an effective legal frame work in order to enforce competition law against companies which engage in cross-border activities that harm competition.[455]

365. National courts have an important role to apply the directly effective provisions of Articles 101, 102, 106 and 108(3) TFEU, meaning that they can establish violations of the prohibitions of restrictive agreements and abuse of a dominant position. In the area of State aid, national Courts can find that State aid is illegal if it has not been notified, without being exempt from notification, or where it has been notified but the Commission has not yet taken a decision, but they cannot declare State aid incompatible with the common market. This is an exclusive competence for the European Commission. This distinction and its consequences is further discussed below.

§4. Article 101 TFEU: Restrictive Agreements in General

I. Introduction

366. Article 101(1) TFEU prohibits 'all agreements between undertakings, decisions by associations of undertakings and concerted practices which may affect trade between Member States and which have as their object or effect the prevention, restriction or distortion of competition within the common market'.

---

454. Council Regulation (EC) No 1/2003 of 16 December 2002 on the implementation of the rules on competition laid down in Arts 81 and 82 of the Treaty, *OJ* 2006, L 1/1.
455. *See* http://ec.europa.eu/comm/competition/ecn/more_details.html, last accessed on 16 August 2016.

367. An agreement which falls under Article 101(1) TFEU is prohibited (an order to cease and a penalty can be imposed) and is void (Article 101(2) TFEU), unless the prohibition of Article 101(1) TFEU is declared inapplicable on the basis of Article 101(3) TFEU (exemption).

368. Many concepts of the definition in Article 101(1) TFEU require further explanation, different aspects of the prohibition will be discussed in more detail.

II. Agreements, Decisions and Concerted Practices

369. 'Agreement' is a very broad concept and requires only the consent of two economically independent undertakings. The concept of 'agreement' in Article 101 TFEU does not only comprise formal (written) legally binding agreements, but also informal or oral agreements, and even simple understandings, the constitution of an association of undertakings, etc.[456] The form of the agreement irrelevant. The meeting of the minds of two or more persons is sufficient.

370. As an exception, agreements between undertakings that form an economic unit – such as an agreement between a parent company and its subsidiary, where the subsidiary does not enjoy any real autonomy in determining its behaviour on the market – do not fall within the scope of Article 101 TFEU.[457]

371. Although unilateral conduct by an undertaking that is not dominant is not caught at all, conduct that might at first sight appear to be unilateral may be held to fall within the scope of Article 101 TFEU. Such characterization of an apparently unilateral action as an agreement is particularly likely to occur in the sphere of relations between a manufacturer and its distributors. Indeed, in such situation, the admission to the selective distribution network rests upon the tacit or express mutual acceptance of the parties to the network that admission of new parties is subject to adherence to the distribution policy of the producer.[458] The European Courts have drawn some limits to the possibility for the Commission to base an infringement of Article 101(1) on a tacit agreement between supplier and distributor.[459]

372. The concept of 'decisions by an association of undertakings' refers to decisions taken by organs of associations with legal personality or de facto associations. 'Decisions' is a broad concept and may include recommendations made by an association to its members, even if the recommendation is not binding, but it is generally followed by the members.[460]

---

456. For the purpose of this Chapter, 'agreements' shall refer to agreements, decisions or concerted practices unless provided otherwise.
457. Judgment of 24 October 1996, *Viho*, C-73/95P, EU:C:1996:405.
458. Judgment of 25 October 1983, *AEG Telefunken v. Commission*, C-107/82, EU:C:1983:293.
459. Judgment of 26 October 2000, T-41/16, *Bayer v. Commission*; Judgment of 6 January 2004, C-2/01, *Bayer*, EU:C:2004; and *see* R. Whish & D. Bailey, pp. 112–113.
460. Judgment of 7 October 1972, *Vereeniging van Cementhandelaren v. Commission*, 8/72, EU:C:1972:84; Judgment of 24 January 1987, *Verband der Sachversicherer*, 45/85, EU:C:1987:34.

373. The fact that a professional body has a public law status does not prevent the application of Article 101 TFEU. Indeed, the legal framework within which such agreements are made and such decisions are taken and the classification given to that framework by the various national legal systems are irrelevant as far as the applicability of the European rules on competition, and in particular Article 101 TFEU are concerned.[461]

374. The Court defined a concerted practice in the '*Dyestuffs*' case[462] as 'a form of coordination between undertakings which, without having reached the stage where an agreement properly so-called has been concluded, knowingly substitutes practical cooperation between them for the risks of competition'. By its nature, a concerted practice does not have all the elements of a contract, but may, *inter alia,* arise out of coordination which becomes apparent from the behaviour of the participants.

375. Although parallel behaviour cannot in itself be equated with a concerted practice, it can constitute a strong indication of the existence of such a practice if it leads to conditions of competition which do not correspond to the normal conditions of the market.

376. A more recent example of a concerted practice is the so-called *Lombard Club* case which concerned a banking cartel broken up by the European Commission in 2002. The Commission found that eight Austrian banks met monthly to organize widespread price fixing across Austria. The cartel and concerted practices covered the entire Austrian territory with a view to fixing deposit, lending and other rates to the detriment of businesses and consumers in Austria. During inspections, the Commission found hundreds of documents: minutes of meetings, memoranda, records of telephone conversations, correspondence, etc. which uncovered a network of committees covering the whole of Austria and all banking products and services. This evidence led to the cartel and concerted practice decision of the Commission. The parties appealed the decision of the Commission before the GC which rejected the appeal and confirmed the Commission decision.[463]

III. Horizontal and Vertical Agreements

377. Originally there could be some doubts about whether Article 101 TFEU applies not only to agreements between competitors (like 'horizontal' agreements

---

461. Judgment of 18 June 1998, *Commission v. Italy*, C-35/96, EU:C:1998:303. *See also* for example Judgment of 19 February 2002, *Wouters v. Algemene Raad van de Nederlandse Orde van Advocaten*, C-309/99, EU:C:2009:698.
462. Judgment of 14 July 1972, *ICI v. Commission*, 48/69, EU:C:1972:70, paras 64–67.
463. Judgment of 14 December 2006, *Raiffeisen Zentralbank Österreich AG and Others v. Commission* (Club Lombard), Joined Cases T-259/02 to T-264/02 and T-271/02, EU:T:2006:396.

between producers), but also to agreements between non-competitors, such as vertical agreements, like distribution agreements between a producer and a distributor. As early as in its *Consten* and *Grundig* case[464] the Court of Justice applied Article 101 to vertical agreements.

IV. Restrictions by Object or Effect

378. Under Article 101(1), the Commission, the NCA or the national court will assess whether an agreement, decision or concerted practice has as its object or effect the prevention, restriction or distortion of competition within the common market.

379. For practical guidance, Article 101(1) contains a list with examples of restrictive agreements. This list is however not exhaustive and many other kinds of behaviour may be caught under Article 101(1). The list enumerates the following restrictions:

(a) directly or indirectly fixing purchase or selling prices or any other trading conditions;
(b) limiting or controlling production, markets, technical development, or investment;
(c) sharing markets or sources of supply;
(d) applying dissimilar conditions to equivalent transactions with other trading parties, thereby placing them at a competitive disadvantage;
(e) making the conclusion of contracts subject to acceptance by the other parties of supplementary obligations which, by their nature or according to commercial usage, have no connection with the subject of such contracts.

380. It is settled case law[465] that the expression 'object or effect', refers to an alternative nature of the requirement as indicated by the conjunction 'or'. The types of behaviour falling within the scope of Article 101(1) are therefore divided in two categories, i.e., (i) restrictions by object and (ii) restrictions by effect. The first step is to look at the wording of the terms of the agreement in context[466] and at its objectives. Once it appears that the object of the agreement is to prevent, restrict or distort competition within the internal market, there is no need to take account of its actual effects,[467] because there is a presumption based on the serious nature of the restriction and on experience showing that restrictions of competition by object are likely to produce negative effects on the market.

---

464. Judgment of 13 July 1966, *Consten and Grundig v. Commission*, Joined cases 56/64 and 58/64, EU:C:1966:41.
465. Judgment of 30 June 1966, in *Société Technique Minière (L.T.M.) v. Maschinenbau Ulm GmbH (M.B.U.)*, C-56/65, EU:C:1966:38.
466. Judgment of 28 March 1983, *Compagnie Royale Asturienne des Mines SA and Rheinzink GmbH v. Commission*, 29/83 and 30/83, EU:C:1984:130.
467. Judgment of 21 September 2006, *Nederlandse Federatieve Vereniging voor de Groothandel op Elektrotechnisch Gebied v. Commission*, C-105/04 P, EU:C:2006:592, para. 125.

381. The prohibition applies even where the parties to an agreement acted without any subjective intention of restricting competition or even if they did not have the restriction of competition as its sole aim they also pursued other legitimate objectives.[468]

382. Typical restrictions by object include agreements between competitors (including secret cartels) leading to price fixing, output limitation, market sharing/client allocation as well as situations described as 'hardcore restrictions' in Commission block exemption regulations.[469] More detailed guidance is provided by the Commission in a 2015 staff working document accompanying the De Minimis Notice.[470]

383. However, if the above-mentioned analysis does not reveal the effect on competition to be sufficiently deleterious, one needs to consider the actual or potential consequences (or 'effects') of the agreement to establish whether competition has in fact been prevented or restricted or distorted to an appreciable extent.

384. The difference between restrictions 'by object' or 'by effect' is not merely conceptual and involves significant consequences on the burden of proof for the Commission and the undertaking subject to an investigation.

385. The principle is that in any national or Union proceedings for the application of Articles 101 and 102 TFEU, the burden of proving an infringement of Article 101(1) or of Article 102 TFEU shall rest on the party or the authority alleging the infringement. The undertaking or association of undertakings claiming the benefit of Article 101(3) of the Treaty shall bear the burden of proving that the conditions to benefit from the exemption are met.[471]

386. In case an agreement has as its object the restriction of competition, the case law of the Court of Justice clearly establishes that it is not necessary to prove

---

468. Judgment of 6 April 2006, *General Motors v. Commission*, C-551/03 P, EU:C:2006:229, paras 64–66 and cited case law.

469. For supply and distribution agreements between non-competitors, *see* in particular Art. 4 of Commission Regulation (EU) No 330/2010 of 20 April 2010 on the application of Art. 101(3) of the Treaty on the Functioning of the European Union to categories of vertical agreements and concerted practices (*OJ* 2010, L 102/1) and for licensing agreements between non-competitors, *see* in particular Art. 4(2) of Commission Regulation (EU) No 316/2014 of 21 March 2014 on the application of Art. 101(3) of the Treaty on the Functioning of the European Union to categories of technology transfer agreements (*OJ* 2014, L 93/17). For agreements between competitors, *see* in particular Art. 5 of Commission Regulation (EU) No 1217/2010 of 14 December 2010 on the application of Art. 101(3) of the Treaty on the Functioning of the European Union to certain categories of research and development agreements (*OJ* 2010, L 335/36), and Art. 4 of Commission Regulation (EU) No 1218/2010 of 14 December 2010 on the application of Art. 101(3) of the Treaty on the Functioning of the European Union to certain categories of specialisation agreements (*OJ* 2010, L 335/43) as well as Art. 4(1) of Regulation (EU) No 316/2014.

470. *See* the Commission's Guidance on restrictions 'by object' for the purpose of defining which agreements may benefit from the De Minimis Notice, available online at http://ec.europa.eu/competitio n/antitrust/legislation/de_minimis_notice_annex_en.pdf, last accessed on 25 August 2016.

471. Article 2 of Regulation 1/2003.

that the agreement will have an anticompetitive effect. In contrast, where the agreement does not have an anticompetitive object, the Commission will have to prove that there will be a restrictive effect. This effect will be more difficult to prove and often require more time and resources (data, economic analysis, etc.).

387. The determination of the types of restrictions which constitute restrictions by object is controversial. While the Commission had taken a rather broad approach, in *Cartes Bancaires*[472] the Court of Justice rejected the idea and ruled that it should be interpreted restrictively. The Court emphasized that the *concept of restriction of competition 'by object' can be applied only to certain types of coordination between undertakings which reveal a sufficient degree of harm to competition that it may be found that there is no need to examine their effects*. The Court thus clarified that there is a limit to the expansion of the category of restrictions by object.

V. *De Minimis*

388. A first step in examining an agreement under Article 101 TFEU is the question whether it is *'de minimis'*, i.e., of minor importance, such as not to restrict competition significantly. The Court of Justice has indeed, from the beginning, built in a threshold for the application of Article 101 TFEU in the *Völk and Vervaecke* case: this article only applies to agreements that restrict competition to an appreciable extent.[473] Later the Commission quantified what does not constitute an appreciable restriction of competition, on the basis of market share thresholds. The current rules of the Commission are contained in the De Minimis Notice of 2014.[474]

389. Pursuant to the De Minimis Notice, agreements between undertakings which affect trade between Member States do not appreciably restrict competition within the meaning of Article 101(1):

(i) if the aggregate market share held by the parties to the agreement does not exceed 10% on any of the relevant markets affected by the agreement, where the agreement is made between undertakings which are actual or potential competitors on any of these markets (agreements between competitors); or

(ii) if the market share held by each of the parties to the agreement does not exceed 15% on any of the relevant markets affected by the agreement, where the agreement is made between undertakings which are not actual or potential competitors on any of these markets (agreements between non-competitors).

---

472. Judgment of 11 September 2014, *Groupement des cartes bancaires (CB) v. European Commission*, C-67/13 P, EU:C:2014:2204.
473. Judgment of 9 July 1969, *Franz Völk v. S.P.R.L. Ets J. Vervaecke*, 5/69, EU:C:1969:35.
474. *OJ* 2014, C-291/1 replacing a Commission Notice of 2001.

390. In case it is difficult to classify the agreement as an agreement between competitors or non-competitors, the 10% threshold is applicable.[475]

391. However, apart from the above rules, there is a special rule in markets where the cumulative effect of several vertical agreements may lead to the foreclosure of the market. The notice indicates that such a situation is unlikely to occur if less than 30% of the relevant market is covered by parallel (networks of) agreements having similar effects. In case there is a foreclosure effect, the above market share thresholds ((i) and (ii)) are reduced to 5%, both for agreements between competitors and for agreements between non-competitors. According to the Notice, individual suppliers or distributors with a market share not exceeding 5% are in general not considered to contribute significantly to a cumulative foreclosure effect.[476]

392. For all of the above thresholds ((i), (ii) and the 5% rule), if an agreement exceeds the thresholds with not more than two percentage points during two successive calendar years, the Commission will not consider these agreements to be restrictive of competition.[477]

393. Paragraph 13 of the De Minimis Notice contains a list of hardcore restrictions such as price frying or market allocation between competitors or restrictions blacklisted in a block exemption regulation. These restrictions are excluded from its benefit.

VI. Ancillary Restraints

394. In EU competition law, the concept of ancillary restraints covers any alleged restriction of competition which is directly related and necessary to the implementation of a main non-restrictive transaction and proportionate to it. If an agreement in its main parts, for instance a distribution agreement or a joint venture, does not have as its object or effect the restriction of competition, then restrictions, which are directly related to and necessary for the implementation of that transaction, also fall outside Article 101(1). These related restrictions are called ancillary restraints. A restriction is directly related to the main transaction if it is subordinate to the implementation of that transaction and is inseparably linked to it; the restriction must be objectively necessary for the implementation of the main transaction and be proportionate to it. The ancillary restraints test applies in all cases where the main transaction is not restrictive of competition.[478]

395. If on the basis of objective factors, it can be concluded that without the restriction the main non-restrictive transaction would be difficult or impossible to

---

475. De Minimis Notice, para. 9.
476. *Ibid.*, para. 10.
477. *Ibid.*, para. 11.
478. Guidelines on the application of Art. 101(3) TFEU, para. 29.

implement, the restriction may be regarded as objectively necessary for its implementation and proportionate to it. If, for example, the main object of a franchise agreement does not restrict competition, then restrictions, which are necessary for the proper functioning of the agreement, such as obligations aimed at protecting the uniformity and reputation of the franchise system, also fall outside Article 101(1).[479]

396. The application of the ancillary restraint concept must be distinguished from the exemptions under Article 101(3), for agreements that generate certain economic benefits that outweigh their restrictive effects (*see* next paragraph). The application of the ancillary restraint concept does not involve any weighing of procompetitive and anticompetitive effects.[480]

VII. Exemptions

397. An agreement, concerted practice or decision that falls within the scope of Article 101(1) will not always be automatically prohibited and void. Article 101(3) provides that Article 101(1) may be declared inapplicable in case of four cumulative conditions. The agreement must:

(1) contribute to improving the production or distribution of goods or to promoting technical or economic progress;
(2) allow consumers a fair share of the resulting benefit;
(3) only impose restrictions which are not indispensable to the attainment of these objectives;
(4) not allow the undertakings the possibility of eliminating competition in respect of a substantial part of the products in question.

Basically, only those agreements which confer sufficient benefits to outweigh the anticompetitive effects are exempted.

398. Before the entry into force of Regulation 1/2003, parties had to notify an agreement within the meaning of Article 101(1) TFEU, not benefitting from a block exemption, to the Commission, in order to benefit from an individual exemption. The Commission enjoyed an exclusive power to apply Article 101(3) (*see* Regulation 17/62). Since the entry into force of Regulation 1/2003 on 1 May 2004, parties have to self-assess their agreement and not only the Commission, but also the national courts and national authorities can find that a practice that is caught by Article 101(1) TFEU fulfils or not the conditions of Article 101(3) TFEU and decide that it is therefore legal (i.e., 'exempted').

---

479. *Ibid.*, para. 31.
480. *Ibid.*, para. 30.

399. In order to facilitate the decentralized application of Article 101 and to enhance legal certainty to a certain extent,[481] the European Commission issued Guidelines on the application of Article 101(3) TFEU.[482] Those guidelines aim at providing detailed indication to undertakings but also to national courts and competition authorities on how to apply the four conditions of Article 101(3) in individual cases.

400. Next to the individual exemption available pursuant Article 101(3) TFEU, the Commission may also adopt 'group' or 'block' exemptions, declaring Article 101(1) inapplicable to certain categories agreements, decisions and concerted practices, provided that the conditions laid down in the Block Exemption are fulfilled.[483] A group exemption also binds national judges and competition authorities.

401. The Commission has currently adopted general block exemptions for technology transfer agreements, vertical agreements, research and development agreements, and specialization agreements.

402. Furthermore, there are sectorial block exemptions for the distribution of motor cars, for certain agreements in the field of insurance, for the maritime sector, for the air transport sector and for road and inland waterways.

403. Regulation 1/2013 introduced a decentralized enforcement of the EU rules. This means that the NCAs and the national courts can now also fully apply Articles 101 and 102. The Commission now shares the competence to rule whether or not the exemption criteria have been satisfied with the NCAs and the national courts, although the Commission has a right of first refusal (Article 11(6) Regulation 1/2003), which it will e.g., exercise with regard to important cross-EU cases.

§5. Article 101 TFEU: Different Categories of Restrictive Agreements

I. Introduction: Guidance

404. Agreements entered between two or more undertakings may be divided in two categories, i.e., (i) vertical agreements that are concluded between undertakings active at a different level of the supply chain, such as agreements between a producer and its distributors, and (ii) horizontal agreements, i.e., agreements concluded

---

481. Paragraph 6 of the Guidelines on the application of Art. 101(3) TFEU contains a reminder that while the Commission intends to provide guidance, it makes sure to keep a margin of discretion and explains that 'the standards set forth in the present guidelines must be applied in light of the circumstances specific to each case. This excludes a mechanical application. Each case must be assessed on its own facts and the guidelines must be applied reasonably and flexibly.'
482. Communication from the Commission containing the Guidelines on the application of Art. 81(3) of the Treaty, *OJ* 2004, C 101/97.
483. The Commission is entitled to adopt block exemption regulations pursuant to Art. 103 TFEU via a delegation of powers by the Council.

between undertakings active at the same level of the supply chain, such as agreements between producers. The following sections are drafted according to this division and follow the framework established by the European Commission.[484]

II. Vertical Agreements

A. The Vertical Agreements Block Exemption Regulation: General

405. A vertical agreement is defined under the Vertical Agreements Block Exemption Regulation (hereafter 'VABER')[485] as an agreement entered into between two or more undertakings, operating for the purposes of the agreement at a different level of the production or distribution chain (e.g., producer/manufacturer and distributor) and relating to the conditions under which the parties may purchase, sell or resell certain goods or services.[486]The VABER succeeds to earlier group exemption regulations for vertical agreements (since 1967).

406. Vertical agreements are not by themselves restrictive of competition. Under settled case law of the Court of Justice, an exclusive distribution agreement falls within the scope of Article 101(1) TFEU, but it can be exempted under Article 101(3), provided it does not confer on the exclusive distributor an absolute territorial protection (protection against parallel imports form distributors for other territories).[487] A selective distribution system[488] that is based on qualitative criteria that are applied without discrimination is not even caught by Article 101(1) TFEU.[489] Selective distribution based on quantitative criteria can however benefit from the VABER if the conditions of the regulation are fulfilled.

407. In principle, the VABER only applies to vertical agreements between non-competitors. However, it also applies to vertical agreements between competing undertakings where they enter into non-reciprocal vertical agreement and (a) the supplier is a manufacturer and a distributor of goods, while the buyer is a distributor and not a competing undertaking at the manufacturing level; or (b) the supplier

---

484. *See* http://ec.europa.eu/competition/antitrust/legislation/legislation.html, last accessed on 1 September 2016.
485. Commission Regulation 330/2010 of 20 April 2010 on the application of Art. 101(3) of the Treaty on the Functioning of the European Union to categories of vertical agreements and concerted practices, *OJ* 2010, L 102/7. The Commission also published guidelines explaining the principles for the assessment of vertical agreements under Art. 101 TFEU: Commission notice – Guidelines on Vertical Restraints, *OJ* 2010, C 130/7, (hereafter the 'Guidelines on Vertical Restraints').
486. Article 1(a) of Commission Regulation 330/2010.
487. Judgment of 13 July 1966, *Consten and Grundig v. Commission*, Joined cases 56/64 and 58/64, EU:C:1966:41.
488. Defined in Art. 1(e) VABER: *'selective distribution system' means 'a distribution system where the supplier undertakes to sell the contract goods or services, either directly or indirectly, only to distributors selected on the basis of specified criteria and where these distributors undertake not to sell such goods or services to unauthorised distributors within the territory reserved by the supplier to operate that system.'*
489. Judgment of 25 October 1977, *Metro v. Commission*, 26/76, EU:C:1977:167.

is a provider of services at several levels of trade, while the buyer provides its goods or services at the retail level and is not a competing undertaking at the level of trade where it purchases the contract services.[490]

408. The VABER applies from 1 June 2010 until 31 May 2022. The exemption applies to all vertical agreements including to agreements concerning motor vehicles.

409. While vertical agreements concerning motor vehicles used to be subject to a specific block exemption regulation,[491] the Commission decided in 2010 to progressively align the regime for cars on the general VABER. However, Regulation 461/2010 still contains specific rules for sale or resale of spare parts for motor vehicles or repair and maintenance services for motor vehicles.[492]

410. Vertical agreements containing ancillary provisions on the assignment or use of IPR are also covered by the VABER.[493]

411. To benefit from the exemption of the VABER, (i) the agreement shall not contain hardcore restrictions (including resale price maintenance, certain forms of territory or customer allocation, restriction on passive sales, etc.)[494] and (ii) the market share held by *the supplier* and the *buyer* must not exceed 30% of the respective relevant markets on which they sell/buy the contract goods or services.

412. Where under preceding regulations only the market share of the supplier was taken into account, Regulation 330/2010 introduced a buyer's market share threshold because buyers as well can leverage their market power to set up place

---

490. Article 2(4) of Regulation 330/2010.
491. *See* Commission Regulation 1400/2002 of 31 July 2002 on the application of Art. 81(3) of the Treaty to categories of vertical agreements and concerted practices in the motor vehicle sector, *OJ* L 203, 1.8.2002, pp. 30–41 which applied until 31 May 2013.
492. *See* Regulation 461/2010 of 27 May 2010 on the application of Art. 101(3) of the Treaty on the Functioning of the European Union to categories of vertical agreements and concerted practices in the motor vehicle sector, *OJ* 2010, L 129/52 and the Commission Notice containing Supplementary guidelines on vertical restraints in agreements for the sale and repair of motor vehicles and for the distribution of spare parts for motor vehicles, *OJ* C138, 28.5.2010, p. 16. The exemption is excluded for: (i) the restriction of the sales of spare parts by members of a selective distribution system to independent repairers; (ii) the agreement between a supplier of spare parts and a manufacturer of to restrict the supplier's ability to sell those goods to authorized or independent distributors/repairers or to end users; (iii) the agreement between a manufacturer which uses components for the initial assembly of motor vehicles and the supplier of such components to restrict the supplier's ability to place its trade mark/ logo effectively and in an easily visible manner on the components supplied or on spare parts.
493. Article 2(3) of Regulation 330/2010.
494. Article 4 of the VABER.

vertical restraints which are detrimental to consumers. According to the Commission, this supplementary threshold is in favour of SMEs[495] because they are the most likely to be harmed by such vertical restraints when they are acting as competitor of the buyer or as a supplier.[496]

413. The VABER also excludes certain clauses from the exemption, such as non-compete obligations which are for an infinite period of time or exceed five years, post-termination non-compete obligations of more than one year, and obligations concerning the prohibition of sale of specific competing brands in a selective distribution system.[497] The occurrence of such a clause in the agreement does however not prevent the application of the exemption to the rest of the agreement.

414. Further details are provided in the Commission's Guidelines on Vertical Restraints[498] which (i) describe vertical agreements generally falling outside Article 101(1) TFEU,[499] (ii) explain the application of the exemption;[500] outline the principles concerning the withdrawal and the non-application of the VABER;[501] address market definition and market share calculation issues;[502] and provide an overview of the general framework of analysis and the enforcement policy of the Commission in individual cases concerning certain vertical agreements featuring single branding, exclusive distribution, exclusive customer allocation, selective distribution, franchising, exclusive supply, upfront access payments, category management agreements, tying and resale price restrictions.[503]

415. Finally, the VABER does not apply to vertical agreements the subject matter of which falls within the scope of any other block exemption regulation, unless otherwise provided for in such a regulation.[504] Concretely, this means, e.g., that the VABER does not apply to vertical agreements covered by other block exemptions regarding technology transfer agreements,[505] specialization agreements,[506] and research and development agreements.[507]

---

495. Small and medium-sized enterprises.
496. *See* the FAQ on vertical agreements issued by the Commission on 20 April 2010 and available at http://europa.eu/rapid/press-release_MEMO-10-138_en.htm, last accessed on 1 September 2016.
497. Article 5 of the VABER.
498. Commission notice – Guidelines on Vertical Restraints, *OJ* C 130, 19.5.2010, p. 1.
499. Section II of the Guidelines on Vertical Restraints.
500. Section III of the Guidelines on Vertical Restraints.
501. Section IV of the Guidelines on Vertical Restraints.
502. Section V of the Guidelines on Vertical Restraints.
503. Section VI of the Guidelines on Vertical Restraints.
504. Article 2(5) of the VABER and Guidelines on Vertical Restraints, para. 46.
505. *See* hereafter, paras 322 et seq.
506. *See* III, paras 328–329.
507. *See* hereafter, paras 330 et seq.

B. The VABER: Black Listed Hardcore Restrictions

416. The VABER provides that certain restrictions cannot be included in a vertical agreement if the parties want the agreement to benefit from the block exemption. There is no severability rule which is applicable to these restrictions, meaning that if an agreement contains one of these 'hardcore restrictions' then the whole agreement will not benefit from the block exemption. The Commission has given some guidance as to the interpretation of these hardcore restrictions.[508] Hardcore restrictions listed are discussed below.

1. Resale Price Maintenance

417. Clauses which have as their direct or indirect object the establishment of a fixed or minimum resale price or a fixed or minimum price level to be observed by the buyer are black listed.[509]

418. Resale price maintenance is a broad concept and can be achieved through direct (the establishment of a resale price) or indirect means (e.g., fixing the maximum level of discount).

419. In contrast, an undertaking is allowed in principle to impose a maximum sale price or to recommend a certain price but only if no pressure is exercised to ensure compliance (by way of a stick or a carrot).

2. Resale Restrictions

420. Also the following restriction prevents the benefit of the block exemption for all the agreement: the restriction of the territory into which (territorial restriction) or of the customers to whom (customer restriction), a buyer party to the agreement, without prejudice to a restriction on its place of establishment, may sell the contract goods or services, *except*:

(1) the restriction of active sales into the exclusive territory or to an exclusive customer group reserved to the supplier or allocated by the supplier to another buyer, where such a restriction does not limit sales by the customers of the buyer;

(2) the restriction of sales to end users by a buyer operating at the wholesale level of trade;

(3) the restriction of sales by the members of a selective distribution system to unauthorized distributors within the territory reserved by the supplier to operate that system; and

---

508. Article 4 of the VABER and Guidelines on Vertical Restraints, paras 47 et seq.
509. Article 4(a) VABER and para. 48 of the Guidelines on vertical restraints.

(4) the restriction of the buyer's ability to sell components, supplied for the purposes of incorporation, to customers who would use them to manufacture the same type of goods as those produced by the supplier.[510]

421. Resale restrictions can be achieved through *direct* obligations (e.g., the obligation not to sell to certain customers or to customers in certain territories, or the obligation to refer orders from these customers to other distributors) or *indirect* measures aimed at inducing the distributor not to sell to such customers (such as refusal or reduction of bonuses or discounts, reduction of supplied volumes, or a threat of contract termination).

422. However, obligations on the reseller relating to the display of the supplier's brand name are not classified as hardcore. As Article 4(b) of the VABER only concerns restrictions of sales by the buyer or its customers; this implies that restrictions of the supplier's sales are not a hardcore restriction, subject to certain conditions regarding sales of spare parts.[511] In addition, a restriction on the buyer's place of establishment will not deprive an agreement from the benefit of the VABER if it is agreed that the buyer will restrict its distribution outlet(s) and warehouse(s) to a particular address, place or territory.

423. Regarding the first exception (restriction of active sales by an exclusive distributor), it can be noted that during the review of former Regulation 2790/1999, the Commission took into account the increasing share of online commerce. The result is translated into the distinction of active (i.e., actively approaching individual customers)[512] and passive (i.e., responding to unsolicited requests from individual customers)[513] sales.

424. Despite the fact that, as described above, a certain level of protection may be provided regarding a territory or a certain group of customers, the Commission takes the view that passive sales to such territories or customer groups shall never be prevented. In the specific context of online sale, the principle being that every

---

510. Article 4(b) VABER and paras 49–55 of the Guidelines on vertical restraints.
511. Paragraph 59 of the Guidelines on vertical restraints.
512. Paragraph 51 of the Guidelines on vertical restraints defines 'Active' sales *as actively approaching individual customers by for instance direct mail, including the sending of unsolicited e-mails, or visits; or actively approaching a specific customer group or customers in a specific territory through advertisement in media, on the internet or other promotions specifically targeted at that customer group or targeted at customers in that territory. Advertisement or promotion that is only attractive for the buyer if it (also) reaches a specific group of customers or customers in a specific territory, is considered active selling to that customer group or customers in that territory.*
513. Paragraph 51 of the Guidelines on vertical restraints defines 'passive' sales as *responding to unsolicited requests from individual customers including delivery of goods or services to such customers. General advertising or promotion that reaches customers in other distributors' (exclusive) territories or customer groups but which is a reasonable way to reach customers outside those territories or customer groups, for instance to reach customers in one's own territory, are considered passive selling. General advertising or promotion is considered a reasonable way to reach such customers if it would be attractive for the buyer to undertake these investments also if they would not reach customers in other distributors' (exclusive) territories or customer groups.*

distributor must be allowed to use the internet (e.g., a website) to sell products since it is a reasonable way to allow customers to reach the distributor.

425. The use of a website may have effects that extend beyond the distributor's own territory and customer group. However, the Commission takes the view that such effects result from the technology allowing easy access from everywhere. The same is true if a customer opts to be kept (automatically) informed by the distributor and it leads to a sale. In addition, displaying different language options on the website does not, of itself, change the passive character of such selling.

426. Based on the above-mentioned principle that passive sales shall be allowed, the Commission thus regards the following as examples of hardcore restrictions:

(a) an agreement that the (exclusive) distributor shall prevent customers located in another (exclusive) territory from viewing its website or shall automatically re-route its customers to the manufacturer's or other (exclusive) distributors' websites. This does not exclude an agreement that the distributor's website shall also offer a number of links to websites of other distributors and/or the supplier;
(b) an agreement that the (exclusive) distributor shall terminate consumers' transactions over the internet once their credit card data reveal an address that is not within the distributor's (exclusive) territory;
(c) an agreement that the distributor shall limit its proportion of overall sales made over the internet. This does not exclude the supplier requiring, without limiting the online sales of the distributor, that the buyer sells at least a certain absolute amount (in value or volume) of the products offline to ensure an efficient operation of its brick and mortar shop (physical point of sales), nor does it preclude the supplier from making sure that the online activity of the distributor remains consistent with the supplier's distribution model. This absolute amount of required offline sales can be the same for all buyers, or determined individually for each buyer on the basis of objective criteria, such as the buyer's size in the network or its geographic location;[514]
(d) an agreement that the distributor shall pay a higher price for products intended to be resold by the distributor online than for products intended to be resold offline. This does not exclude the supplier agreeing with the buyer a fixed fee (i.e., not a variable fee where the sum increases with the realized offline turnover as this would amount indirectly to dual pricing) to support the latter's offline or online sales efforts.

427. However, the Commission accepts that vertical agreement may legitimately contain limitations to active selling by online means. This applies to online advertisement specifically addressed to certain customers as a form of active selling to those customers such as territory-based banners on third-party websites. In general, the Commission considers that efforts to be found specifically in a certain territory or by a certain customer group is active selling into that territory or to that

---

514. Paragraphs 54 and 56 Guidelines vertical restraints.

customer group, e.g., paying a search engine or online advertisement provider to have advertisements displayed specifically to users in a particular territory is active selling into that territory.

428. In addition, especially in the context of selective distribution, the VABER allows the supplier to require quality standards for the use of the internet site to resell its goods, just as the supplier may require quality standards for a shop or for selling by catalogue or for advertising and promotion in general.

429. Furthermore, the supplier may require that its distributors have one or more brick and mortar shops or showrooms as a condition for becoming a member of its distribution system. However, this type of condition shall not be used to directly or indirectly limit the online sales by the distributors. Similarly, a supplier may require that, where the distributor's website is hosted by a third-party platform, customers do not visit the distributor's website through a site carrying the name or logo of the third-party platform.[515]

430. With regard to the use of third-party platforms by members of a selective distribution system, the Court of Justice confirmed in *Coty*[516] that a selective distribution system for luxury goods designed, primarily, to preserve the luxury image of those goods complies with Article 101 TFEU to the extent that resellers are chosen on the basis of objective criteria of a qualitative nature that are laid down uniformly for all potential resellers and applied in a non-discriminatory fashion and that the criteria laid down do not go beyond what is necessary. Second the Court accepted, in view of the fact that, notwithstanding the growing importance of third-party platforms, the distributor's own webshops still account for 90% of online sale, as compatible with Article 101(1) a clause which prohibits authorized distributors of luxury goods, from using, in a discernible manner, third-party platforms for the internet sale of the contract goods, on condition that the clause has the objective of preserving the luxury image of those goods, that it is laid down uniformly and not applied in a discriminatory fashion, and that it is proportionate in the light of the objective pursued, these being matters to be determined by the referring court. Such a prohibition does not constitute neither a customer (hardcore) restriction within the meaning of Article 5(b) of the VABER nor a restriction on passive sales (also a hardcore restriction) within the meaning of Article 5(c) of the VABER.

3. Hardcore Restriction in Case of Selective Distribution: Prohibition of Sales to End Users

431. The hardcore restriction set out in Article 4(c) of the Block Exemption Regulation excludes the restriction of active or passive sales to end users, whether professional end users or final consumers, by members of a selective distribution

---

515. Paragraph 54 of the Guidelines on vertical restraints.
516. Judgment of 6 December 2017, *Coty*, C-230/16, EU:C:2017:941.

network, without prejudice to the possibility of prohibiting a member of the network from operating out of an unauthorized place of establishment.[517]

432. Accordingly, dealers who are part of a selective distribution system cannot be restricted in the choice of users to whom they may sell, or purchasing agents acting on behalf of those users except to protect an exclusive distribution system operated elsewhere. Within a selective distribution system, the dealers should be free to sell, both actively and passively, to all end users, also with the help of the internet. Therefore, the Commission considers any obligations which dissuade appointed dealers from using the internet to reach a greater number and variety of customers by imposing criteria for online sales which are not overall equivalent to the criteria imposed for the sales from the brick and mortar shop as a hardcore restriction.

433. The criteria imposed for online sales must not necessarily be identical to those imposed for offline sales, but they should pursue the same objectives and achieve comparable results.

434. Within the territory where the supplier operates selective distribution, this system may not be combined with exclusive distribution as that would lead to a hardcore restriction of active or passive selling by the dealers under Article 4(c) of the Block Exemption Regulation, with the exception that restrictions can be imposed on the dealer's ability to determine the location of its business premises. Therefore, selected dealers may be prevented from operating their business from different premises or from opening a new outlet in a different location. For that purpose, the operation of a website cannot be considered as the same thing as opening a new outlet in a different location.

With regard to a prohibition on authorized distributor to sell via a third-party platform, see the *Coty* judgment mentioned in the preceding section.

4.   Hardcore Restriction in Case of Selective Distribution: Prohibition of Cross-
     Supplies

435. An agreement or concerted practice may not have as its direct or indirect object to prevent or restrict the active or passive selling of the contract products between the selected distributors.[518] Selective distributors must indeed remain free to purchase the contract products from other appointed distributors within the network, operating either at the same or at a different level of trade. Consequently, selective distribution cannot be combined with vertical restraints aimed at forcing distributors to purchase the contract products exclusively from a given source. It also means that within a selective distribution network, no restrictions can be imposed on appointed wholesalers as regards their sales of the product to appointed retailers.

---

517. Paragraphs 53–54 of the Guidelines on vertical restraints.
518. Article 4(d) VABER and para. 55 of the Guidelines on vertical restraints.

5.   Restrictions on the Sale of Components

436. The last hardcore resale restriction is the restriction, agreed between a supplier of components and a buyer who incorporates those components, of the supplier's ability to sell the components as spare parts to end users or to repairers or other service providers not entrusted by the buyer with the repair or servicing of its goods.[519] This hardcore restriction is the one that prevents or restricts end users, independent repairers and service providers from obtaining spare parts directly from the manufacturer of these spare parts.[520] Agreements between a manufacturer of spare parts and a buyer who incorporates these parts into his own products (original equipment manufacturer (OEM)), may not prevent or restrict sales by the manufacturer of these spare parts to end users, independent repairers or service providers.

437. Indirect restrictions may arise particularly when the supplier of the spare parts is restricted in supplying technical information and special equipment which are necessary for the use of spare parts by users, independent repairers or service providers. However, the agreement may place restrictions on the supply of the spare parts to the repairers or service providers entrusted by the OEM with the repair or servicing of its own goods. In other words, the OEM may require its own repair and service network to buy spare parts from it.[521]

C. *The VABER: Hardcore Restrictions That Are Permitted in Individual Cases*

438. The Commission considers that hardcore restrictions may be objectively necessary in exceptional cases for an agreement of a particular type or nature and therefore fall outside Article 101(1) TFEU. For example, a hardcore restriction may be objectively necessary to ensure that a public ban on selling dangerous substances to certain customers for reasons of safety or health is respected.[522] Where substantial investments by the distributor to start up and/or develop the new market are necessary, restrictions of passive sales by other distributors into such a territory or to such a customer group may be necessary for the distributor to recoup those investments during the first two years that the distributor is selling the contract goods. Similarly, in case of the genuine testing of a new product in a limited territory or with a limited customer group the distributors appointed to sell the new product on the test market or to participate in the first round(s) of the staggered introduction may be restricted in their active selling outside the test market or the market(s). Finally, undertakings may plead an efficiency defence under Article 101(3) in an individual case.

---

519. Article 4(e) VABER and para. 56 of the Guidelines on vertical restraints.
520. Paragraph 59 of the Guidelines on vertical restraints.
521. *Ibid.*
522. Paragraph 60 of the Guidelines on vertical restraints.

D. The VABER: Excluded Restrictions under the Block Exemption Regulation

439. The VABER excludes certain obligations from the benefit of the Block Exemption Regulation even though the market share threshold is not exceeded.[523] However, the Block Exemption Regulation continues to apply to the remaining part of the vertical agreement if that part is severable from the non-exempted obligations.

1. Non-compete Obligations

440. The first exclusion concerns non-compete obligations.[524] A non-compete obligation means: any direct or indirect obligation causing the buyer not to manufacture, purchase, sell or resell goods or services which compete with the contract goods or services, or any direct or indirect obligation on the buyer to purchase from the supplier or from another undertaking designated by the supplier more than 80% of the buyer's total purchases of the contract goods or services and their substitutes on the relevant market, calculated on the basis of the value or, where such is standard industry practice, the volume of its purchases in the preceding calendar year.[525]

441. Such non-compete obligations are not covered by the Block Exemption Regulation where the duration is indefinite or exceeds five years, including where a clause tacitly renews its duration beyond a period of five years.

442. As an exception, the five-year duration limit does not apply when the goods or services are resold by the buyer from premises and land owned by the supplier or leased by the supplier from third parties not connected with the buyer. In such cases the non-compete obligation may be of the same duration as the period of occupancy of the point of sale by the buyer. The reason for this exception is that it is normally unreasonable to expect a supplier to allow competing products to be sold from premises and land owned by the supplier without its permission. However, artificial ownership constructions, such as a transfer by the distributor of its proprietary rights over the land and premises to the supplier for only a limited period, intended to avoid the five-year limit cannot benefit from this exception.

---

523. Article 5 of the VABER.
524. Article 5(1)(a) of the VABER.
525. Article 1(d) VABER; for the purpose of the calculation of total purchases, where, in the first year after entering in the agreement, for the year preceding the conclusion of the contract no relevant purchasing data for the buyer are available, the buyer's best estimate of its annual total requirements may be used.

2. Post-term Non-compete Obligations

443. The second exclusion concerns post-term non-compete obligations on the buyer.[526] They are exempted provided the following conditions are met:

(a) the obligation relates to goods or services which compete with the contract goods or services;
(b) the obligation is limited to the premises and land from which the buyer has operated during the contract period;
(c) the obligation is indispensable to protect know-how transferred by the supplier to the buyer;
(d) the duration of the obligation is limited to a period of one year after termination of the agreement.

3. Sale of Competing Goods in a Selective Distribution System

444. The third exclusion concerns the sale of competing goods in a selective distribution system.[527] The VABER covers the combination of selective distribution with a non-compete obligation, obliging the dealers not to resell competing brands in general. However, if the supplier prevents its appointed dealers, either directly or indirectly, from buying products for resale from specific competing suppliers, such an obligation cannot enjoy the benefit of the Block Exemption Regulation. The objective of the exclusion of such an obligation is to avoid a situation whereby a number of suppliers using the same selective distribution outlets prevent one specific competitor or certain specific competitors from using these outlets to distribute their products which would result in the foreclosure of a competing supplier in similar way to collective boycott.

E. Agency Agreements

445. An agency agreement is an agreement where a person (the agent) is entrusted with the task to negotiate and/or conclude contracts on behalf of another person (the principal), either in the agent's own name (commission agency contract) or in the name of the principal (agency contract in the strict sense).

446. A genuine agent (*see* hereafter) is treated under European competition law as if he were part of the same economic unit as his principal. The Commission considers that in the case of 'genuine' agency agreements, the obligations imposed on the agent as to the contracts negotiated and/or concluded on behalf of the principal do not fall within the scope of application of Article 101(1) TFEU.[528]

---

526. Article 5(1)(b) and Art. 5(3) VABER.
527. Article 5(1)(c) of the VABER and para. 69 of the Guidelines on Vertical Restraints.
528. *See* paras 12–21 of the Guidelines on Vertical Restraints.

447. The determining factor in assessing the genuine nature of an agency agreement is the financial or commercial risk borne by the agent in relation to the activities for which he has been appointed by the principal. In respect of those criteria, it is not material for the assessment whether the agent acts for one or several principals.

Further guidance is provided at paragraphs 13–20 of the Guidelines on Vertical Restraint.

F. Franchising

448. Franchise agreements are defined in paragraph 189 of the guidelines. A franchise agreement is an agreement whereby one party (the franchisor) grants the other party (the franchisee) the right to sell a good or a service by providing the franchisee with IPR and commercial and technical assistance. The franchisor is in general paid a franchise fee by the franchisee.[529]

449. Franchise agreements usually contain licences of IPR relating in particular to trade marks or signs and know-how for the use and distribution of goods or services.

450. The CJEU ruled for the first time on the compatibility of franchise agreements with Article 101 TFEU in the *Pronuptia* case:[530] franchise agreements do not in themselves interfere with competition and the compatibility of such agreements with Article 101(1) TFEU has to be assessed on a case-per-case basis. The Court continued that the provisions of franchise agreements which are strictly necessary for the functioning of the system of franchises – such as provisions which protect the know-how and assistance provided by the franchisor or which establish the control strictly necessary for maintaining the identity or reputation of the network identified by the franchisor's business name or symbol – do not constitute restrictions of competition. Conversely, provisions which, for example, share markets between the franchisor and the franchisees or between the franchisees will constitute restrictions of competition.

451. Article 2(3) VABER[531] expressly recognizes the applicability of the regulation to (business format) franchise agreements by providing that the exemption applies to vertical agreements containing provisions which relate to the assignment to the buyer or use by the buyer of IPR, provided that those provisions do not constitute the primary object of such agreements and are directly related to the use, sale or resale of goods or services by the buyer or its customers. The exemption applies on condition that, in relation to the contract goods or services, those provisions do

---

529. Paragraphs 199–201 of the Guidelines on vertical restraints.
530. Judgment of 28 January 1986, *Pronuptia de Paris GmbH v. Pronuptia de Paris Irmgard Schillgallis*, Case 161/84, EU:C:1986:41.
531. *See* above, paras 286 et seq.

not contain restrictions of competition having the same object as vertical restraints which are not exempted under this Regulation.

III. Horizontal Agreements: General Principles

452. Horizontal cooperation agreements are agreements between undertakings that operate at the same level of the supply chain, such as producers, who are possibly direct competitors. Where such agreements aim at certain forms of cooperation they may generate economic benefits; meaning that where they are restrictive of competition (in particular where they are concluded between competitors), they may generate economic benefits qualifying them for an exemption under Article 101(3) TFEU.

In order to provide guidance to stakeholders, the Commission has issued three Block Exemption Regulations ('BERs') regarding technology transfer (*see* section V), specialization (*see* section VI) and research & development (*see* section VII) as well as Horizontal Guidelines (*see* section IV).

IV. The Horizontal Guidelines

453. The objective of the Horizontal Guidelines is to provide an analytical framework based on legal and economic criteria such as market power and structure, for the most common types of horizontal cooperation agreements and the context in which they occur, for the assessment under Article 101 TFEU. The horizontal guidelines provide for general guidance on the assessment of cooperation agreements under Article 101 TFEU[532] and also detailed guidance on the assessment of six types of specific agreements: information exchange, R&D agreements, production agreements, purchasing agreement, agreements on commercialization, and standardization agreements. These guidelines complement existing BERs on R&D and Specialisation agreements. Cooperation can take the form of a joint venture, a joint company. A first important point of attention is to distinguish whether one is dealing with a full-function joint venture or a mere cooperative joint venture (e.g., cooperation limited to the stage of production, where the joint venture does not sell the goods in the market). The importance of the distinction lies in the fact that in case of a full-function joint venture, the Merger Regulation[533] will apply and requires under certain condition a merger filing, while Article 101 TFEU will only apply to the so-called cooperative aspects of such a joint venture. Cooperative joint ventures (joint ventures that are not full function) have to be exclusively assessed in the light of Article 101 TFEU.

---

532. The Horizontal Guidelines do not apply to the extent that sector specific rules apply as is the case for certain agreements with regard to agriculture, transport or insurance. *See* para. 18 of the Horizontal Guidelines.

533. *See* § 9 hereafter on Merger control. The existence of sufficient means for the JV to behave to a certain extent independently from its parents on the market is an important criterion.

454. Next the Commission gives an outline of the basic principles for the assessment of horizontal cooperation agreements under Article 101 TFEU.[534] In some cases, it will already be clear that the agreement has as its object the restriction of competition and will infringe Article 101(1) TFEU.[535] In many cases though, horizontal cooperation agreements do not have as their object the restriction of competition and therefore the effects of the agreement have to be analysed.[536] Whether an agreement has anticompetitive effects will depend on the economic context. The nature and content of the agreement,[537] the combined market power of the parties and the structure of the market[538] have to be taken into account.

455. First of all, the nature of the agreement relates to factors such as the area and objective of the cooperation, the competitive relationship between the parties and the extent to which they combine their activities. These factors will indicate the likelihood of the parties coordinating their behaviour in the market.

456. Second, the market power and the market structure also have to be considered. The position of the parties in the markets affected by the cooperation is indeed important. If parties to an agreement have only an insignificant market share, it is unlikely that the cooperation will have restrictive effects. The market concentration, i.e., the position and the number of competitors, also have to be taken into account. Other factors to be considered are the stability of the market shares over time, entry barriers or the nature of the products.

A. *Information Exchange*

457. A first form of horizontal cooperation discussed by the Commission is information exchange. Information exchange is a common feature of many competitive markets. It may solve problems of information asymmetries and improve the functioning of markets or help companies enhance their internal efficiency through benchmarking against each other's best practices. For consumers, it may reduce their search costs and improve choice. However, information exchange between competitors may also lead to restrictions of competition in particular in situations where it is liable to enable undertakings to be aware of market strategies of their competitors.

458. The Commission aims at providing guidance on situations where it is likely to consider that information exchange is prohibited under Article 101 TFEU based on an analysis including the characteristics of the market in which it takes place

---

534. *See* section 1.2 of the Horizontal Guidelines.
535. *See* paras 32–38 of the Horizontal Guidelines.
536. *See* paras 26–31 of the Horizontal Guidelines.
537. *See* paras 32–38 of the Horizontal Guidelines.
538. *See* paras 39–47 of the Horizontal Guidelines.

(such as concentration, transparency, stability, symmetry, complexity etc.) as well as on the type of information exchanged.[539]

459. According to the Commission, information exchange can only be addressed under Article 101 TFEU if it establishes or is part of an agreement, a concerted practice or a decision by an association of undertakings.[540]

460. Article 101 TFEU does not deprive companies of the right to adapt themselves intelligently to the existing or anticipated conduct of their competitors. However, it precludes any direct or indirect contact between competitors, the object or effect of which is to reduce strategic uncertainty in the market thereby facilitating collusion.[541]

461. Regarding the market characteristics, the Commission considers that collusive outcomes are more likely in transparent markets and that the lower the pre-existing level of transparency in the market, the more value an information exchange may have in achieving a collusive outcome. This pre-existing degree of transparency, *inter alia*, depends on the number of market participants and the nature of transactions, which can range from public transactions to confidential bilateral negotiations between buyers and sellers.[542] Collusive outcomes are also more likely where the demand and supply conditions are relatively stable or in symmetric market structures.[543]

462. As to the type of information exchanged, the prohibition covers information of strategic nature, such as prices (e.g., actual prices, discounts, increases, reductions or rebates), customer lists, production costs, quantities, turnovers, sales, capacities, qualities, marketing plans, risks, investments, technologies and R&D programmes and their results.

463. Market coverage is also an important factor since an information exchange is more likely to have restrictive effects on competition if the companies involved in the exchange have to cover a sufficiently large part of the relevant market.[544] The concept of 'a sufficiently large part of the market' will depend on the specific facts of each case and the type of information exchange in question.

464. Other important factors include the level of aggregation of data (e.g., including data of at least three companies versus individualized data), the age of data (historic or not), the frequency of the exchange, the public or confidential nature of the information or of the exchange itself.[545]

---

539. *See* section 2 of the Horizontal Guidelines.
540. Paragraph 60 of the Horizontal Guidelines. *See also* section B.
541. Paragraph 61 of the Horizontal Guidelines.
542. Paragraph 78 of the Horizontal Guidelines.
543. Paragraphs 81–82 of the Horizontal Guidelines.
544. Paragraphs 87 of the Horizontal Guidelines.
545. Paragraphs 89–94 of the Horizontal Guidelines.

465. The Commission also provides examples of assessment of information exchange.[546]

B. *Production Agreements*

466. The Commission notes that production may be carried out by only one party or by two or more parties or that companies can produce jointly by way of a joint venture, that is to say, a jointly controlled company operating one or several production facilities or by looser forms of cooperation in production such as sub-contracting agreements where one party (the 'contractor') entrusts to another party (the 'subcontractor') the production of a good. There are different types of subcontracting agreements: horizontal subcontracting agreements concluded between companies operating in the same product market irrespective of whether they are actual or potential competitors and vertical subcontracting agreements are concluded between companies operating at different levels of the market.[547] Horizontal subcontracting agreements comprise unilateral[548] and reciprocal specialization agreements[549] as well as subcontracting agreements with a view to expanding production.[550]

467. The Commission indicates that the Horizontal Guidelines apply to all forms of joint production agreements and horizontal subcontracting agreements. It also underlines that subject to certain conditions, joint production agreements as well as unilateral and reciprocal specialization agreements may benefit from the Specialisation BER.[551] It also excludes vertical subcontracting agreements from the scope of the Horizontal Guidelines and specifies that those should be analysed under the VABER and its guidelines or by the 1978 Subcontracting Notice.[552]

---

546. Paragraphs 105–110 of the Horizontal Guidelines.
547. *See* section 4 of the Horizontal Guidelines.
548. Paragraph 152 of the Horizontal Guidelines define unilateral specialization agreements as agreements between two parties which are active on the same product market or markets, by virtue of which one party agrees to fully or partly cease production of certain products or to refrain from producing those products and to purchase them from the other party, which agrees to produce and supply the products.
549. Paragraph 152 of the Horizontal Guidelines define reciprocal specialization agreements as agreements between two or more parties which are active on the same products market or markets, by virtue of which two or more parties agree, on a reciprocal basis, to fully or partly cease or refrain from producing certain but different products and to purchase those products from the other parties, which agree to produce and supply them.
550. Paragraph 152 of the Horizontal Guidelines define subcontracting agreements with a view to expanding production as agreements where the contractor entrusts the subcontractor with the production of a good, while the contractor does not at the same time cease or limit its own production of the good.
551. *See* hereafter section VI.
552. *See* the Commission notice of 18 December 1978 concerning its assessment of certain subcontracting agreements in relation to Art. 85(1) of the EEC Treaty, *OJ* 1979, C 1/2, which provide guidance on the analysis under Art. 101 TFEU of the restriction that the contractor may impose on the

468. According to the Commission, the main competition concerns regarding production agreements include direct limitation of competition between the parties, coordination and anticompetitive foreclosure. In the context of production agreements, price fixing, limiting output or sharing markets or customers are considered as restrictions by object except where (i) the parties agree on the output directly concerned by the production agreement (e.g., the capacity and production volume of a joint venture or the agreed amount of outsourced products), provided that the other parameters of competition are not eliminated; or (ii) a production agreement that also provides for the joint distribution of the jointly manufactured products envisages the joint setting of the sales prices for those products, and only those products, provided that that restriction is necessary for producing jointly, meaning that the parties would not otherwise have an incentive to enter into the production agreement in the first place.[553]

469. The Commission also indicates that below a combined market share of 20%, parties are unlikely to enjoy market power.

470. Further indications regarding the conditions to apply Article 101(3) TFEU[554] as well as examples of analysis applied to certain production agreements are provided in the Horizontal Guidelines.[555]

C. *Purchasing Agreements*

471. Agreements concerning the joint purchase of products can be carried out by a jointly controlled company, by a company in which many other companies hold non-controlling stakes, by a contractual arrangement or by even looser forms of cooperation (collectively referred to as 'joint purchasing arrangements').[556]

472. Those arrangements usually aim at the creation of buying power which can lead to lower prices or better quality products or services for consumers. However, they may also lead to restrictive effects on competition on the purchasing and/or downstream selling market or markets, such as increased prices, reduced output, product quality or variety, or innovation, market allocation, or anticompetitive foreclosure of other possible purchasers.

---

use by the subcontractor of technology or equipment provided by the contractor to what is necessary for the purpose of the subcontracting agreement to protect the economic value of such technology or equipment.
553. Paragraph 160 of the Horizontal Guidelines.
554. Paragraphs 183–186 of the Horizontal Guidelines.
555. Paragraphs 187–193 of the Horizontal Guidelines.
556. *See* section 5 of the Horizontal Guidelines.

473. Negative competitive effects of joint purchasing arrangements may materialize on two markets: (i) the relevant purchasing market or markets; and (ii) the selling market or markets downstream where the parties to the joint purchasing arrangement are active as sellers.[557]

474. A two-step analysis is necessary where joint purchasing arrangements involve both horizontal and vertical agreements. First, the horizontal agreements between the companies have to be assessed according to the principles described in the Horizontal Guidelines. Second, if that assessment leads to the conclusion that the joint purchasing arrangement does not give rise to competition concerns, a further assessment will be necessary to examine the relevant vertical agreements under the VABER and the Block Exemption Regulation on Vertical Restraints and the Vertical Guidelines.[558]

475. The Commission indicates that it is unlikely that market power exists if the parties to the joint purchasing arrangement have a combined market share not exceeding 15% on the purchasing market or markets as well as a combined market share not exceeding 15% on the selling market or markets. Above that threshold, the likely impact of the agreement must be assessed.

476. Further indication regarding the conditions to apply Article 101(3) TFEU[559] as well as examples of analysis applied to certain production agreements are provided in the Horizontal Guidelines.[560]

D. *Commercialization Agreements*

477. Commercialization agreements involve cooperation between competitors in the selling, distribution or promotion of their substitute products. Depending on the commercialization functions which are covered by the cooperation, their scope ranges from joint selling agreements that may lead to a joint determination of all commercial aspects related to the sale of the product, including price to more limited agreements that only address one specific commercialization function, such as distribution.[561] after-sales service or advertising.[562]

---

557. *See* paras 197–199 of the Horizontal Guidelines and note that if the parties are, in addition, competitors on one or more selling markets, those markets are also relevant for the assessment.
558. For example, that is the case for an 'alliance', that is to say an association of undertakings formed by a group of retailers for the joint purchasing of products.
559. Paragraphs 217–220 of the Horizontal Guidelines.
560. Paragraphs 221–224 of the Horizontal Guidelines.
561. The VABER and the Vertical Guidelines generally cover distribution agreements unless the parties to the agreement are actual or potential competitors except for certain non-reciprocal vertical agreements between competitors. *See* para. 226 of the Horizontal Guidelines and above, para. 287.
562. *See* section 6 of the Horizontal Guidelines.

478. The Commission takes the view if the parties combined market share does not exceed 15%, it is likely that the agreement is pro-competitive.[563] Above that threshold, the likely impact of the agreement must be assessed.

479. According to the Commission, the main competition concerns regarding agreements on commercialization include price fixing, output limitation, market and customer allocation as well as exchanges of strategic information relating to aspects within or outside the scope of the cooperation or to commonality of costs.[564]

480. Further indications regarding the conditions to apply Article 101(3) TFEU[565] as well as examples of analysis applied to certain production agreements are provided in the Horizontal Guidelines.[566]

E. Standardization Agreements

481. Standardization agreements have as their objective the definition of technical or quality requirements with which current or future products, production processes, services or methods may comply.[567] They cover various issues, such as standardization of different grades or sizes of a particular product or technical specifications in product or services markets where compatibility and interoperability with other products or systems is essential as well as agreements setting out standards on the environmental performance of products or production processes. The terms of access to a particular quality mark or for approval by a regulatory body can also be regarded as a standard.[568] However, the preparation and production of technical standards as part of the execution of public powers are not covered by the Horizontal Guidelines.[569]

482. Standardization agreements usually produce significant positive economic effects, notably by promoting economic interpenetration in the internal market and encouraging the development of new and improved products or markets and improved supply conditions.

483. The Commission provides guidance on market definition[570] and outlines the main competition concerns, namely reduction in price competition, foreclosure of innovative technologies and exclusion of, or discrimination against, certain companies by prevention of effective access to the standard.[571]

---

563. Paragraphs 240–241 of the Horizontal Guidelines.
564. Paragraphs 230–233 of the Horizontal Guidelines.
565. Paragraphs 246–251 of the Horizontal Guidelines.
566. Paragraphs 252–256 of the Horizontal Guidelines.
567. *See* section 7 of the Horizontal Guidelines.
568. Paragraph 257 of the Horizontal Guidelines.
569. Paragraph 258 of the Horizontal Guidelines.
570. *See* section 7.2 of the Horizontal Guidelines.
571. *See* section 7.3.1 and especially paras 263–264 of the Horizontal Guidelines.

484. The Commission describes the framework to analyse restrictions potentially falling in the 'by object' or in the 'by effect' categories.[572]

485. The Commission also outlines the conditions under which it is possible for standardization agreements to benefit from an exemption under Article 101(3) TFEU due to an overall pro-competitive impact of an agreement.[573]

Finally, the Commission provides examples of analysis of standardization agreements under competition rules.[574]

V. Technology Transfer Block Exemption Regulation

486. The Technology Transfer Block Exemption Regulation ('TTBER')[575] exempts agreements concerning the licensing of technology rights, i.e., patents, utility modes, design rights, topographies of semiconductor products, supplementary protection certificates ('SPC') for medicinal products or other products for which such SPC may be obtained, plant breeder's certificates and software copyrights.[576]

487. The TTBER does not apply to agreements which fall within the scope of block exemption regulations regarding specialization or R&D agreements.

488. The Commission also issued guidelines providing further details regarding the application of the TTBER as well as guidance in situations where the TTBER is not applicable.[577]

489. The block exemption only applies subject to a combined market share threshold of 20% on the relevant market(s) for competing undertakings and 30% for non-competitors.[578] The TTBER provides guidance on how to compute market shares and on consequences of market shares exceeding the thresholds.[579]

490. The exemption shall apply for as long as the licensed technology rights have not expired, lapsed or been declared invalid or, in the case of know-how, for

---

572. *See* sections 7.32. and 7.3.3 of the Horizontal Guidelines.
573. *See* section 7.4 of the Horizontal Guidelines.
574. *See* section 7.5 of the Horizontal Guidelines.
575. Commission Regulation (EU) No 316/2014 of 21 March 2014 on the application of Art. 101(3) of the Treaty on the Functioning of the European Union to categories of technology transfer agreements, *OJ* 2014, L 93.
576. Article 1 of the TTBER. It also includes know-how and applications for or applications for registration of those rights.
577. Communication from the Commission – Guidelines on the application of Art. 101 of the Treaty on the Functioning of the European Union to technology transfer agreements, *OJ* 2014, C89/3, the 'TTBER Guidelines'. Those guidelines replaced Commission Notice – Guidelines on the application of Art. 81 of the EC Treaty to technology transfer agreements, *OJ* 2004, C 101/2.
578. Article 3 of the TTBER. *See also* Art. 4(3) of the TTBER regarding situations where undertakings party to the agreement are not competing undertakings at the time of the conclusion of the agreement but become competing undertakings afterwards.
579. Article 8 of the TTBER.

as long as the know-how remains secret or for the duration of the agreement if it becomes publicly known as a result of action by the licensee.

491. The exemption shall also apply to provisions, in technology transfer agreements, which relate to the purchase of products by the licensee or which relate to the licensing or assignment of other IPR or know-how to the licensee, if, and to the extent that, those provisions are directly related to the production or sale of the contract products.

492. In order to benefit from the exemption, agreements shall not contain hardcore restrictions. Where the undertakings party to the agreement are competitors, these restrictions include: (i) the restriction of a party's ability to determine its prices when selling products to third parties; (ii) the limitation of output, except limitations on the output of contract products imposed on the licensee in a non-reciprocal agreement or imposed on only one of the licensees in a reciprocal agreement; (iii) the restriction of the licensee's ability to exploit its own technology rights or the restriction of the ability of any of the parties to the agreement to carry out research and development, unless such latter restriction is indispensable to prevent the disclosure of the licensed know-how to third parties; and (iv) the allocation of markets or customers. Where the udnertakings party to the agreement are not competitors, the black list is somewhat different (*see* Article 4(2)).

493. There are four exceptions where it is possible to allocate markets or customers to a certain extent, namely: (a) the obligation on the licensor and/or the licensee, in a non-reciprocal agreement, not to produce with the licensed technology rights within the exclusive territory reserved for the other party and/or not to sell actively and/or passively into the exclusive territory or to the exclusive customer group reserved for the other party, (b) the restriction, in a non-reciprocal agreement, of active sales by the licensee into the exclusive territory or to the exclusive customer group allocated by the licensor to another licensee provided the latter was not a competing undertaking of the licensor at the time of the conclusion of its own licence, (c) the obligation on the licensee to produce the contract products only for its own use provided that the licensee is not restricted in selling the contract products actively and passively as spare parts for its own products, and (d) the obligation on the licensee, in a non-reciprocal agreement, to produce the contract products only for a particular customer, where the licence was granted in order to create an alternative source of supply for that customer.[580]

494. The exemption shall not apply to the following obligations: (i) any direct or indirect obligation on the licensee to grant an exclusive licence or to assign rights, in whole or in part, to the licensor or to a third party designated by the licensor in respect of its own improvements to, or its own new applications of, the licensed technology; (ii) any direct or indirect obligation on a party not to challenge the validity of IPR which the other party holds in the Union, without prejudice to the

---

580. Article 4(1) of the TTBER. *See also* section 3.4.2 of the TTBER Guidelines; for agreements between non-competitors, *see* the different exceptions in Art. 4(2) TTBER.

possibility, in the case of an exclusive licence, of providing for termination of the technology transfer agreement in the event that the licensee challenges the validity of any of the licensed technology rights.[581]

495. Where the undertakings party to the agreement are not competing undertakings, the exemption provided shall not apply to any direct or indirect obligation limiting the licensee's ability to exploit its own technology rights or limiting the ability of any of the parties to the agreement to carry out research and development, unless such latter restriction is indispensable to prevent the disclosure of the licensed know-how to third parties.[582]

496. The Commission may withdraw[583] the benefit of this Regulation in a particular case where it finds that an exempted technology transfer agreement nevertheless has effects which are incompatible with Article 101(3) TFEU and in particular where: (i) access of third parties' technologies to the market is restricted, for instance by the cumulative effect of parallel networks of similar restrictive agreements prohibiting licensees from using third parties' technologies; and (ii) access of potential licensees to the market is restricted, for instance by the cumulative effect of parallel networks of similar restrictive agreements prohibiting licensors from licensing to other licensees or because the only technology owner licensing out relevant technology rights concludes an exclusive licence with a licensee who is already active on the product market on the basis of substitutable technology rights.[584]

497. A NCA may also decide to withdraw the exemption if a technology transfer agreement has effects which are incompatible with Article 101(3) in the territory of a Member State, or in a part thereof, which has all the characteristics of a distinct geographic market, in respect of that territory, under the same circumstances as provided for the Commission.[585]

498. Licensing agreements also fall outside the block exemption, where the market share thresholds are exceeded or the agreement involves more than two parties. It does not mean that they are under a presumption of illegality; they are simply subject to individual assessment for which the TTBER guidelines provides a framework of analysis.

499. For example, the Commission takes the view that outside the area of the above-mentioned hardcore restrictions, Article 101 TFEU is unlikely to be infringed where there are four or more independently controlled technologies in addition to

---

581. Article 5(1) of the TTBER. *See also* section 3.5 of the TTBER Guidelines.
582. Article 5(2) of the TTBER.
583. Article 29(1) of Regulation 1/2003. *See also* section 3.6 of the TTBER Guidelines.
584. Article 6(1) of the TTBER.
585. Article 6(2) of the TTBER.

the technologies controlled by the parties to the agreement that may be substitutable for the licensed technology at a comparable cost to the user.[586]

500. The Commission describes how various factors including (a) the nature of the agreement;[587] (b) the market position of the parties;[588] (c) the market position of competitors;[589] (d) the market position of buyers on the relevant markets;[590] (e) entry barriers;[591] and (f) maturity of the market[592] may affect its analysis in individual cases.

501. The Commission also provides guidance on various types of restraints that are commonly included in licence agreements and how they are assessed outside the safe harbour of the TTBER. Those include royalty obligations, sales restrictions, output restrictions, field of use restrictions, captive use restrictions, tying and bundling, and non-compete obligations.

502. Finally, the Commission deals with settlement agreements in the context of technology disputes[593] and with technology pools.[594]

VI. Specialization Agreements

503. The Specialisation Agreements Block Exemption Regulation applies to:

1. unilateral specialisation agreements, i.e. agreements between two parties which are active on the same product market by virtue of which one party agrees to fully or partly cease production of certain products or to refrain from producing those products and to purchase them from the other party, who agrees to produce and supply those products;

2. reciprocal specialisation agreements, i.e. agreements between two or more parties which are active on the same product market, by virtue of which two or more parties on a reciprocal basis agree to fully or partly cease or refrain from producing certain but different products and to purchase these products from the other parties, who agree to produce and supply them;

---

586. *See* para. 157 of the TTBER Guidelines including further explanation on the assessment of substitutability.
587. Paragraph 161 of the TTBER Guidelines.
588. Paragraph 162 of the TTBER Guidelines.
589. Paragraph 163 of the TTBER Guidelines.
590. Paragraph 164 of the TTBER Guidelines.
591. Paragraphs 165–166 of the TTBER Guidelines.
592. Paragraph 167 of the TTBER Guidelines.
593. *See* section 4.3 of the TTBER Guidelines and Judgment of 8 September 2016, in *Lundbeck v. Commission*, T-472/13, EU:T:2016:449, confirming the approach of the Commission considering certain pay-for-delay settlement as an infringement of Art. 101 TFEU.
594. *See* section 4.4 of the TTBER Guidelines.

3. joint production agreements, i.e. agreements by virtue of which two or more parties agree to produce certain products jointly.[595]

504. The exemption shall apply on condition that the combined market share of the parties does not exceed 20% on any relevant market. In addition, the agreement shall not contain the following hardcore restrictions: (a) the fixing of prices when selling the products to third parties with the exception of the fixing of prices charged to immediate customers in the context of joint distribution; (b) the allocation of markets or customers; and (c) the limitation of output or sales with the exception. There are two exceptions to the prohibition of the limitation of output or sales: (i) provisions on the agreed number of products in the context of unilateral or reciprocal specialization agreements or the setting of the capacity and production volume in the context of a joint production agreement, and (ii) the setting of sales targets in the context of joint distribution.

505. The conditions of the exemption are also further detailed in the Horizontal Guidelines.[596]

VII. Research & Development Agreements

506. For the purpose of the Research & Development Block Exemption Regulation (R&D BER),[597] research & development is defined as the acquisition of know-how relating to products, technologies or processes and the carrying out of theoretical analysis, systematic study or experimentation, including experimental production, technical testing of products or processes, the establishment of the necessary facilities and the obtaining of IPR for the results.

507. The R&D BER aims at facilitating the cooperation between undertakings at the stages of funding, research and exploitation of results under R&D agreements.

508. The following agreements fall within the scope of the R&D BER (Article 1(1)(a)):

i. joint research and development of contract products or contract technologies and joint exploitation of the results of that research and development;

---

595. Commission Regulation No 1218/2010 of 14 December 2010 on the application of Art. 101(3) of the Treaty to categories of specialisation agreements, *OJ* 2010, L 335/43. It is complemented by the Communication from the Commission – Guidelines on the applicability of Art. 101 of the Treaty on the Functioning of the European Union to horizontal cooperation agreements, *OJ* 2011, C 11/, 14.1.2011, p. 1, the 'Horizontal Guidelines'.
596. *See* paras 5, 152–153, 169–170, 190 of the Horizontal Guidelines.
597. Commission Regulation No 1217/2010 of 14 December 2010 on the application of Art. 101(3) of the Treaty on the functioning of the European Union to categories of research and development agreements, *OJ* 2010, L 335/ 36, the 'R&D Block Exemption Regulation' or 'R&D BER'. It is complemented by the Horizontal Guidelines.

ii. joint exploitation of the results of research and development of contract products or contract technologies jointly carried out pursuant to a prior agreement between the same parties;

iii. joint research and development of contract products or contract technologies excluding joint exploitation of the results;

iv. paid-for research (R&D that is carried out by one party and financed by a financing party) and development of contract products or contract technologies and joint exploitation of the results of that research and development;

v. joint exploitation of the results of paid-for research and development of contract products or contract technologies pursuant to a prior agreement between the same parties;

vi. paid-for research and development of contract products or contract technologies excluding joint exploitation of the results.[598]

509. The exemption under the R&D BER is subject to (i) a market share threshold, of 25%,[599] (ii) the absence of certain hardcore restrictions and (iii) does not cover certain other restrictions.[600]

510. The exemption applies also agreements containing IPRs assignment or licensing provisions to one or more of the parties or to an entity the parties establish to carry out the joint research and development, paid-for research and development or joint exploitation, provided that those provisions do not constitute the primary object of such agreements, but are directly related to and necessary for their implementation.

511. For agreements between non-competitors, the exemption applies for the duration of the research and development. Where the results are jointly exploited, the exemption shall continue to apply for seven years from the time the contract products or contract technologies are first put on the market within the internal market.

512. For agreements between competitors, the exemption applies for the same duration only if, at the time the research and development agreement is entered into: (a) in the case of research and development agreements referred in paragraph 509 as (i), (ii) or (iii) of Article 1(1)(a) the combined market share of the parties to a research and development agreement does not exceed 25% on the relevant product and technology markets; or (b) in the case of research and agreements referred in paragraph 509as (iv), (v) or (vi), the combined market share of the financing party and all the parties with which the financing party has entered into research and

---

598. Article 1, (b) of the R&D BER provides definitions of the concepts used in the categories of covered agreements.
599. *See* details below.
600. *See* Arts 4 and 5 of the R&D BER.

development agreements with regard to the same contract products or contract technologies, does not exceed 25% on the relevant product and technology markets.

513. After the end of the above-mentioned period, the exemption shall continue to apply as long as the combined market share of the parties does not exceed 25% on the relevant product and technology markets.[601]

514. The benefit of the exemption under the R&D BER is lost if an agreement contains one of the following hardcore restriction:

(a) the restriction of the freedom of the parties to carry out research and development independently or in cooperation with third parties in a field unconnected with that to which the research and development agreement relates or, after the completion of the joint research and development or the paid-for research and development, in the field to which it relates or in a connected field;

(b) the limitation of output or sales, with the exception of:
   (1) the setting of production targets where the joint exploitation of the results includes the joint production of the contract products;
   (2) the setting of sales targets where the joint exploitation of the results includes the joint distribution of the contract products or the joint licensing of the contract technologies;
   (3) practices constituting specialization in the context of exploitation; and
   (4) the restriction of the freedom of the parties to manufacture, sell, assign or license products, technologies or processes which compete with the contract products or contract technologies during the period for which the parties have agreed to jointly exploit the results;

(c) the fixing of prices when selling the contract product or licensing the contract technologies to third parties, with the exception of the fixing of prices charged to immediate customers or the fixing of licence fees charged to immediate licensees where the joint exploitation of the results includes the joint distribution of the contract products or the joint licensing of the contract technologies;

(d) the restriction of the territory in which, or of the customers to whom, the parties may passively sell the contract products or license the contract technologies, with the exception of the requirement to exclusively license the results to another party;

(e) the requirement not to make any, or to limit, active sales of the contract products or contract technologies in territories or to customers which have not been exclusively allocated to one of the parties by way of specialization in the context of exploitation;

(f) the requirement to refuse to meet demand from customers in the parties' respective territories, or from customers otherwise allocated between the parties by way of specialization in the context of exploitation, who would market the contract products in other territories within the internal market;

---

601. The calculation of market shares is further explained at Art. 7 of the R&D BER for the purpose of the application of the thresholds laid down at Art. 4 of the R&D BER.

(g) the requirement to make it difficult for users or resellers to obtain the contract products from other resellers within the internal market. The exemption does not apply to the following obligations (excluded restrictions) contained in R&D agreements (Article 6):

(a) the obligation not to challenge after completion of the research and development the validity of IPR which the parties hold in the internal market and which are relevant to the research and development or, after the expiry of the research and development agreement, the validity of IPR which the parties hold in the internal market and which protect the results of the research and development, without prejudice to the possibility to provide for termination of the research and development agreement in the event of one of the parties challenging the validity of such IPR;

(b) the obligation not to grant licences to third parties to manufacture the contract products or to apply the contract technologies unless the agreement provides for the exploitation of the results of the joint research and development or paid-for research and development by at least one of the parties and such exploitation takes place in the internal market vis-à-vis third parties.

515. The conditions of the exemption are also further detailed in the Horizontal Guidelines.[602]

VIII. Cartels

516. A cartel is a group of similar, independent companies which, instead of competing against each other, secretly join and aim at altering parameters of competition (i.e., price, quantity, territory/client allocation) to their benefit and to the detriment of consumers.[603] There are many forms of cartel agreements: horizontal price fixing, collusive tendering, exchange of information, allocation of markets output limitation etc.

517. Cartels are so-called hardcore infringements of competition rules because they are the most damaging and serious form of infringement of Article 101(1) TFUE. The European Courts and the Commission regard them as practices having as their object the restriction of competition.[604]

518. Instead of competing, cartel members rely on each other's agreed course of action, which reduces their incentives to provide new or better products and services at competitive prices. Therefore, their clients (consumers or other businesses) end up paying more for less quality.

---

602. *See* paras 8, 13, 14,18, 86, 100 and especially 111–149 of the Horizontal Guidelines.

603. *See* the definition provided by the European Commission in the Commission notice on immunity from fines and reduction of fines in cartel cases, *OJ* 2006, C 298/17, para. 1, as amended by Communication from the Commission – Amendments to the Commission Notice on Immunity from fines and reduction of fines in cartel cases, *OJ* 2015, C 256/1.

604. *See* above §§ 271 et seq.

519. Not only undertakings involved in the cartels but also 'facilitators' to the organization of the cartel may breach competition rules. The Court of Justice confirmed the liability under Article 101 TFEU of a consultancy firm, although it was not active on the market impacted by the cartel, but which had concluded a service agreement with the cartelists under which it organized and actively participated to meetings, supplied sales data to the participants, monitored the implementation of the agreements, offered to act as a moderator in case of disagreements between them and encouraged them to find compromises.[605]

520. Since 2005, an entire Directorate composed of four units (Directorate G) in the Competition Directorate General has been involved exclusively in helping the Commission to detect and punish cartels.

521. The present Commissioner for competition, Margrethe Vestager recently underlined in commenting the decision in the truck producer's cartel that 'The fight against cartels will remain one of our main priorities. We work to ensure that people and companies in Europe are not faced with prices illegally agreed between supposed competitors or even denied innovative products.'[606]

522. Since cartels are secret and hard to find, the Commission mainly relies on three sources to uncover them: (i) publicly available information (news, media, information published by industry associations, etc.), (ii) information exchanged via the ECN (i.e., from another NCA in Europe or elsewhere if cooperation agreements allow it.) and (iii) under the Leniency policy. The Leniency policy was set up in 1996 to create an incentive for cartelists to self-report and give evidence to the Commission in exchange for either total immunity from fines or a reduction of fines which the Commission would otherwise have imposed on them.[607] A revised Leniency notice was published in 2006 to clarify the information that applicants need to provide, establish a procedure to protect corporate statements and to introduce a so-called marker system allowing an applicant to have more time to collect and submit information to support its application while keeping the rank obtained on the day of first contact with the Commission.[608]

523. A settlement notice was also issued by the Commission in June 2008.[609] Under the settlement procedure, the Commission enjoys discretion to select a cartel

605. *See* judgment of 22 October 2015, in *AC-Treuhand AG v. European Commission*, C-194/04, EU:C:2015:717.
606. *See* the press release issued by Commissioner Vestager regarding the truck producer's cartel, 19 July 2016 STATEMENT/16/2585.
607. Commission Notice on the non-imposition or reduction of fines in cartel cases, *OJ* 1996, C 207/4.
608. Commission's Notice on immunity from fines and reduction of fines in cartel cases, *OJ* 2006, C 298/17. This notice replaced Commission notice on immunity from fines and reduction of fines in cartel cases, *OJ* C 45, 19.2.2002, pp. 3–5 and Commission Notice on the non-imposition or reduction of fines in cartel cases, *OJ* C 207, 18.7.1996, pp. 4–6.
609. Commission Notice on the conduct of settlement procedures in view of the adoption of Decisions pursuant to Art. 7 and Art. 23 of Council Regulation (EC) No 1/2003 in cartel cases, *OJ* 2008, C 167/1.

case and offer the involved undertakings to settle by shortening the otherwise applicable procedure in exchange for an addition discount on the amount of the of maximum 10%.

524. Statistics produced by the European Commission indicate that between 2012–2016 an average of six cartel decision are issued per year and that there is a significant increase in the level of fine, three of the highest fines ever included in a cartel decision of the Commission since 1969 were imposed in 2016 reaching more than 1 billion for a single undertaking in the Truck cartel. The total amount of cartel fines imposed from 1969 until 2018 (before review by the European Courts) amounts to nearly EUR 25 billion. The chart below provides an overview of the highest cartel fines imposed per investigation.[610]

Year	Case Name	Amount in EUR
2016/2017	Truck	2,926,499,00
2012	TV and computer monitor tubes	1,409,588,000
++2013/2016++	Euro interest rates derivatives (EIRD)**	1,310,039,000
2008	Carglass	1,185,500,000
2014	Automotive bearings	953,306,000
2007	Elevators and escalators	832,422,250
2001	Vitamins	790,515,000
2013/2015	Yen interest rate derivatives (YIRD)	684,679,000
2007/2012	Gas insulated switchgear (including re-adoption)	675,445,000
2009	E.ON/GDF collusion	640,000,000

§6. ARTICLE 102 TFEU/ABUSE OF A DOMINANT POSITION

I. Introduction

525. While Article 101 TFEU prohibits collusion between businesses (restrictive practices between undertakings and decisions by associations of undertakings), Article 102 TFEU relates to unilateral practices by dominant undertakings, generally by one dominant undertaking (single dominance), exceptionally by a group of undertakings holding a collective dominant position. In essence practices that are acceptable if they are applied by undertakings without a dominant position, such as fidelity schemes or unequal treatment of clients, may constitute a form of abuse,

---

610. Available on http://ec.europa.eu/competition/cartels/statistics/statistics.pdf, last accessed on 9 January 2017. Please note that this chart was last updated on 7 December 2016, and that the amounts adjusted for changes following judgments of the Courts (General Court and European Court of Justice) and / or amendment decisions.

prohibited under Article 102 TFEU if they are applied by dominant undertakings, i.e., undertakings that hold a dominant position.

526. Pursuant to Article 102 TFEU any abuse by one or more undertakings of a dominant position within the internal market or in a substantial part of it shall be prohibited as incompatible with the internal market in so far as it may affect trade between Member States.

Such abuse may, in particular, consist in:

(a) directly or indirectly imposing unfair purchase or selling prices or other unfair trading conditions;
(b) limiting production, markets or technical development to the prejudice of consumers;
(c) applying dissimilar conditions to equivalent transactions with other trading parties, thereby placing them at a competitive disadvantage;
(d) making the conclusion of contracts subject to acceptance by the other parties of supplementary obligations which, by their nature or according to commercial usage, have no connection with the subject of such contracts.

These are only examples. The decision practice of the Commission and the case law of the EU Courts show other examples, such as refusal to deal or to give access to essential facilities, abuse of buying power or predation.

527. For the application of Article 102, it is essential to define the relevant market(s): dominance does not exist *in abstracto* but on a given market. Over the years, the Commission has defined the notion of dominance (e.g., a market share of more than 50% will normally indicate the existence of dominance, but, especially where market shares are high (between 40% and about 60%) but not very high, other factors (such as financial resources, the existence of barriers to entry or the degree of concentration on the market) will be taken into account as well. In a Notice of 1997,[611] the Commission has given guidance for the definition of relevant markets.

528. Over the years several forms of abuse (of which Article 102 itself gives a few examples) have been better defined in Commission decisions. The Commission has been criticized for taking a too formalistic approach and for looking too much at the protection of competitors rather than looking at the competitive process. Hence its Guidance on Article 102 published in 2009.[612]

---

611. Commission Notice on the definition of relevant market for the purposes of Community Competition law, *OJ* 1997, C 372/5.
612. Communication from the Commission- Guidance on the Commission's enforcement priorities in applying Art. 82 EC to abusive exclusionary conduct by dominant undertakings, *OJ* 2009, C 45/7.(hereafter: Guidance on Art. 102).

529. The importance of Article 102 TFEU has undoubtedly increased over the years. New markets have emerged on which often a successful first mover has rapidly acquired a dominant position (even without acquiring competitors). Microsoft, Intel, Google, are good examples.

First, the notion of dominance will be discussed: indices of dominance and definition of relevant markets, next the most important forms of abuse will be discussed

II. Dominant Position: Notion and Indices

530. According to settled case law, dominance is a position of economic strength enjoyed by an undertaking which enables it to prevent effective competition being maintained on the relevant market by affording it the power to behave to an appreciable extent independently of its competitors, its customers and ultimately of the consumers.[613]

531. In general, a dominant position derives from a combination of several factors which, taken separately, are not necessarily determinative.[614]

532. In its Guidance on Article 102, based on the EU courts' case law, the Commission gives its view on the factors to be taken into account and their respective weight. Market shares provide a useful first indication for the Commission of the market structure and of the relative importance of the various undertakings active on the market. The Commission considers that low market shares are generally a good proxy for the absence of substantial market power. The Commission's experience suggests that dominance is not likely if the undertaking's market share is below 40% in the relevant market. However, there may be specific cases below that threshold where competitors are not in a position to constrain effectively the conduct of a dominant undertaking, for example where they face serious capacity limitations.

533. It should however be noted that in *Akzo*,[615] the Court of Justice has set a *presumption of dominance* where an undertaking has a *market share of 50% or more*. Experience, thus the Commission, suggests that the higher the market share and the longer the period of time over which it is held, the more likely it is that it constitutes an important preliminary indication of the existence of a dominant position and, in certain circumstances, of possible serious effects of abusive conduct, justifying an intervention by the Commission under Article 102. The Commission attaches a lot of importance to barriers to expansion or entry. Barriers to expansion or entry can take various forms. They may be legal barriers, such as tariffs or quotas, or they may take the form of advantages specifically enjoyed by the dominant undertaking, such as economies of scale and scope, privileged access to essential

---

613. Judgment of 14 February 1978, *United Brands*, 27/76, EU:C:1978:22, para. 65 and Judgment of 24 May 1979, *Hoffman-La Roche*, 85/76, EU:C:1979:36, paras 38–39.
614. *United Brands*, para. 61.
615. Judgment of 3 July 1991, *Akzo*, C-62/86, EU:C:1991:280.

inputs or natural resources, important technologies or an established distribution and sales network. They may also include costs and other impediments, for instance resulting from network effects, faced by customers in switching to a new supplier. The dominant undertaking's own conduct may also create barriers to entry, for example where it has made significant investments which entrants or competitors would have to match or where it has concluded long-term contracts with its customers that have appreciable foreclosing effects. Persistently high market shares may be indicative of the existence of barriers to entry and expansion.

III. A Substantial Part of the Internal Market

534. Article 102 TFEU also requires an abuse of a dominant position within the internal market or 'in a substantial part of it'. Where an abuse of a dominant position only affects competition on a non-substantial part of the internal market national competition law may apply, but Article 102 will not apply (let alone that in addition it is required that the abuse affects trade between Member States). It results from the case law and decision practice that the territory of one, even smaller Member State, like Belgium, or even part of a lager Member State, e.g., South Germany[616] may suffice. Even an important port or airport can represent a substantial part of the internal market.[617]

IV. Forms of Abuse

535. Abuse is an objective concept and does not require a fault or negligence on the side of the dominant undertaking. The motivation for taking a certain action will however not always be irrelevant and – as an example – where prices cover average variable costs but are below average total costs, this will only constitute an abuse if they are determined as part of a plan to eliminate a competitor.[618]

536. A distinction can be made between exploitative abuses and exclusionary abuses. Exploitative abuses are acts of exploitation of suppliers or customers, such as excessive pricing or applying unequal conditions without justification. However discrimination of a client or refusal to supply a client who is a competitor, can constitute a form of exclusionary abuse, in that it is aimed at or having as an effect the exclusion of a competitor of the market. Clear examples of exclusionary abuse are fidelity rebates, granted to customers, but with a view to eliminate a competitor, or refusals to supply essential facilities, likewise aimed at or possibly leading to the elimination of a competitor from the market or frustrating its market entrance.

---

616. Judgment of 16 December 1975, *Suiker Unie,* 40 et seq./73, EU:C:1975:174.
617. *See,* e.g., Judgment of 10 December 1991, *Merci,* C-179/90, EU:C:1991:464 (the port of Genova); Judgment of 29 March 2001, *Portugal v. Commission,* C-163/99, EU:C:2001:289 (Portuguese airports).
618. Judgment of 3 July 1991, *Akzo Chemie,* C-62/86, EU:C:1991:286.

537. In its Guidance Paper on Article 102 TFEU, the Commission suggests a framework for the continued rigorous enforcement of Article 102 TFEU, building on the economic analysis carried out in cases, and setting out one possible methodology for the assessment of some of the most common abusive practices. The Commission focuses on exclusionary practices and does not touch upon exploitative abuses. The exclusionary abuses mentioned by the Commission are the following: exclusive dealing (exclusive purchasing, conditional rebates), tying and bundling, predation and refusals to supply and margin squeeze. These different forms of abuse will shortly be discussed in the next paragraphs.

538. A first from of exclusive dealing is the imposition of an *exclusive purchasing obligation* on a customer, requiring him to purchase exclusively or to a large extent only from the dominant undertaking. Certain other obligations, such as stocking requirements, which appear to fall short of requiring exclusive purchasing, may in practice lead to the same effect.

539. A second form of exclusive dealing is the granting of *conditional rebates*. While straightforward volume discounts are fine, conditional rebates or fidelity rebates when granted by a dominant undertaking may have a foreclosure effect to the detriment of smaller competitors. Conditional rebates are rebates granted to customers to reward them for a particular form of purchasing behaviour. The usual nature of a conditional rebate is that the customer is given a rebate if its purchases over a defined reference period exceed a certain threshold, the rebate being granted either on all purchases (retroactive rebates) or only on those made in excess of those required to achieve the threshold (incremental rebates).[619]

540. A dominant undertaking may try to foreclose its competitors by *tying* or *bundling*. Tying is the broader concept where a customer of a certain good is forced (contractually) or induced by the supplier of that good to buy another good from him, that he may not want to (or which he may purchase from another source). Bundling is the practice of offering several (not necessarily related) goods as one package. The Commission will normally take action under Article 102 where an undertaking is dominant in the tying market and where, in addition, the following conditions are fulfilled: (i) the tying and tied products are distinct products, and (ii) the tying practice is likely to lead to anticompetitive foreclosure. A first example where the Commission was successful in qualifying tying as an abuse of a dominant position (because its decision was confirmed by the EU courts) was *Hilti*:[620] the users of Hilti's patented nail cartridges were obliged to acquire nails from Hilti as well. A well-known more recent example is *Microsoft*:[621] Microsoft had tied its Media Player to Windows.

---

619. Judgment of 17 September 2007, *Microsoft*, T-201/04, EU:T:2007: 289, paras 917, 921 and 922.
620. Judgment of 12 December 1991, in *Hilti*, T-30/89, EU:T:1990:70.
621. Judgment of 17 September 2007, *Microsoft*, T-201/04, EU:T:2007:289.

541. Predation is the conduct whereby a dominant undertaking deliberately incurs losses or foregoes profits in the short term (referred to hereafter as 'sacrifice'), so as to foreclose or be likely to foreclose one or more of its actual or potential competitors with a view to strengthening or maintaining its market power, thereby causing consumer harm. Specifically prices charged by a dominant undertaking will be considered being predatory where they are below average avoidable costs (AAC) (which generally coincides with the average variable cost). However, the concept of sacrifice does not only include pricing below AAC. In order to show a predatory strategy, the Commission may also investigate whether the allegedly predatory conduct led in the short term to net revenues lower than could have been expected from a reasonable alternative conduct.[622]

542. Refusals to supply. Dominance does not lead to an obligation to conclude contracts or to supply any prospective client. However a refusal to deal may constitute an abuse (in a situation where an undertaking without a dominant position would be free to decide to deal or not). Typically competition problems arise when the dominant undertaking competes on the 'downstream' market with the buyer whom it refuses to supply. The term 'downstream market' is used to refer to the market for which the refused input is needed in order to manufacture a product or provide a service.

543. The concept of refusal to supply covers a broad range of practices, such as a refusal to supply products to existing or new customers.[623] refusal to license IPR,[624] including when the licence is necessary to provide interface information,[625] or refusal to grant access to an essential facility or a network.[626]Where one undertaking controls a certain facility (such as an airport, a port, a pipeline, an energy distribution network, etc.) which is necessary for a competitor in order to be able to compete in a downstream or neighbouring market, this facility will be said to be 'essential'. In these cases, the undertaking having control over such an 'essential facility' has the obligation, in case it uses this facility for itself, to make it available on non-discriminatory terms to non-competitors. However, in case an undertaking refuses access to a certain facility and there are no technical, legal or even economic obstacles capable of making it impossible or even unreasonably difficult to exercise a certain economic activity, than this refusal will not constitute an infringement of Article 82.[627]

---

622. Guidance on Art. 102; paras 64 et seq.
623. Judgment of 6 March 1974, *Commercial Solvents*, 6/73 and 7/73, EU:C:1974:18.
624. Judgment of 6 April 1995, *Magill*, C-241/91 P and C-242/91 P, EU:1995:9; Judgment of 29 April 2004, *IMS Health*, C-418/01, EU:C:2004:257.
625. *Microsoft*, T-201/04.
626. *See* Commission Decision 94/19/EC of 21 December 1993 in Case IV/34.689 *Sea Containers v. Stena Sealink – Interim Measures*, OJ 1994, L 15/8 and Commission Decision 92/213/EEC of 26 February 1992 in Case IV/33.544 *British Midland v. Aer Lingus*, OJ 1992, L 96/34.
627. Judgment of 26 November 1998, *Oscar Bronner*, C-7/97, EU:C:1998:569.

544. Margin squeeze. A dominant undertaking may charge a price for the product on the upstream market which, compared to the price it charges on the downstream market, does not allow even an equally efficient competitor to trade profitably in the downstream market on a lasting basis (a so-called margin squeeze).

545. Forms of abuse not discussed by the Commission in its Guidance include *excessive pricing* and *unfair trading conditions, including price discrimination.* A definition of excessive pricing was given in the *United Brands* case, where the Court of Justice stated that an excessive price is a price which has no reasonable relation to the economic value of the product supplied.[628] According to the Court of Justice, the questions to be asked are therefore whether the difference between the costs actually incurred and the price actually charged is excessive and whether a price has been imposed which is either unfair in itself or when compared to other competing products.[629]

§7. Articles 101 and 102 TFEU and the Member States

I. Introduction

546. Articles 101 and 102 TFEU are addressed to undertakings. Only undertakings can violate the prohibition of restrictive practices (Article 101) and that of abuse of a dominant position (Article 102). The notion of undertakings is wide and encompasses public undertakings. But where the State acts within its imperium and not as an entrepreneur the competition rules do not apply as such to it.

547. However Articles 101 and 102 TFEU may apply indirectly to the Member States. On the one hand, there is the specific provision in Article 106(1), an obligation on Member States to abstain from distorting competition in their relations with public undertakings and undertakings to which they have granted special or exclusive rights. On the other hand, the Court of Justice has developed case law to the effect that under the duty of sincere cooperation, now enshrined in Article 4(3) TEU, Member States have to abstain from complicity with violations of Articles 101 and 102 by undertakings, be they public or private. Reference can also be made to the section on State aid hereafter (§ 11): Member States shall not distort competition by granting certain forms of aid to undertakings. Under the principle of sincere cooperation, Member States are bound to abstain from other forms of distortion of competition than by granting aid to undertakings, but the application of this principle implies an underlying restrictive practices by one or more undertakings.

---

628. Judgment of 14 February 1978, *United Brands*, 17/76, EU:C:1978:22.
629. *United Brands,* para. 252.

II. Article 106 TFEU

548. Article 106 TFEU contains three quite different provisions. The first paragraph contains an obligation on Member States, the second one contains an exception to the application of the competition rules to services of general economic interest and the last paragraph grants special powers to the Commission to implement and to enforce Article 106(1).

549. Article 106(1) provides that public undertakings and undertakings to which Member States have granted special or exclusive rights have to comply with the rules contained in the Treaty and especially the competition rules. It reads:

> In the case of public undertakings and undertakings to which Member States grant special or exclusive rights, Member States shall neither enact nor maintain in force any measure contrary to the rules contained in this Treaty, in particular to those rules provided for in Article 18 and Articles 101 to 109.

A. *Special or Exclusive Eights*

550. Special or exclusive rights granted by a Member State enables the Member State to influence the behaviour of the undertakings concerned. Special rights put undertakings in a market position which they would not have had without those rights (e.g., a licence, such as that for a telecom operator that has not been granted according to objective and non-discriminatory criteria). Exclusive rights usually concern legal (de jure[630] or de facto) monopolies.

B. *Public Undertaking*

551. The concept of a public undertaking is not defined in the Treaty. A definition appears in the Transparency Directive,[631] i.e. the directive on transparency in financials flows between Member States and public undertakings; which *inter alia* helps the Commission to detect the existence of State aid. The definition is:

> any undertaking over which the public authorities may exercise directly or indirectly a dominant influence by virtue of their ownership of it, their financial participation therein, or the rules which govern it.
>
> A dominant influence on the part of the public authorities shall be presumed when these authorities, directly or indirectly in relation to an undertaking:
>
> (a) hold the major part of the undertaking's subscribed capital; or

---

630. *See*, e.g., local monopolies for the artificial insemination of cattle: Judgment of 5 October 1994, *La Crespelle*, C-323/93, EU:C:1994:368.

631. Commission Directive 80/723/EEC of 25 June 1980 on the transparency of financial relations between Member States and public undertakings, *OJ* 1980, L 195/35.

(b) control the majority of the votes attaching to shares issued by the undertakings; or

(c) can appoint more than half of the members of the undertaking's administrative, managerial or supervisory body.

The CJEU has endorsed this definition given by the Commission.[632]

C. Measures That Are Contrary to Article 106(1)

552. First Article 106(1) can be triggered in combination with Article 102 TFEU. As was said above, a dominant position will not per se infringe Article 102 TFEU. A Member State will only breach Articles 106(1) and 102 TFEU in case the undertaking – merely by exercising the exclusive right granted to it – cannot avoid abusing its dominant position or where an exclusive right granted to an undertaking is liable to create a situation in which that undertaking is led to infringe Article 102 TFEU or will inevitably be led to do this,[633] or where a legal monopoly is extended beyond what is necessary to guarantee the exercise of a service of general economic interest (*see* hereafter Article 106(2)).[634]

553. The combination of Article 106(1) and Article 101 is less likely, because it implies at least two undertakings to which the Member State has conferred special rights. However Article 106(1) does not only refer to the competition rules. It rather states that Member States shall neither enact nor maintain in force any measure contrary to the rules contained in this Treaty, *in particular* to those rules provided for in Article 18 and Articles 101–109.

554. The Commission has sometimes applied Article 106(1) – on the basis of the special enforcement powers it has under Article 106(3), *see* hereafter – in combination with the Treaty provisions on the internal market: the freedom of establishment and the freedom to provide services.[635]

555. The second paragraph of Article 106 contains a limited exception to the rule in paragraph 1 and to the application of the competition rules, including those on State aid in Articles 107 and 108 for undertakings which are either entrusted with services of general interest or which have the character of a revenue-producing

---

632. Judgment of 6 July 1982, *France, Italy and the U.K. v. Commission*, 188 to 190/80, EU:C:1982:257, paras 24–27.
633. *See*, e.g., Judgment of 23 April 1991, *Höfner* & Elser, C-41/90, EU:C:1991:61; Judgment of 18 June 1991, *ERT v. Dimotiki*, C-260/89, EU:C:1991:254.
634. Judgment of 19 March 1993, *Corbeau*, C-320/91, EU:C:1993:198.
635. *See*, e.g., Judgment of 8 July 1999, *Vlaamse Televisiemaatschappij*, T-266/97, EU:C:1999:144.VTM.

monopoly. These public or private undertakings will only be subject to the competition rules, '*in so far as the application of such rules does not obstruct the performance of the particular tasks assigned to them. The development of trade must not be affected to such an extent as would be contrary to the interests of the Community*'.

556. Very often, but not always, the CJEU has rejected claims that restrictions of competition were justified in the light of Article 106(2). The restriction indeed has to be necessary to attain the objective pursued. In the absence of the restriction, the performance of the tasks assigned should be obstructed.

557. Article 106(3) reads: 'The Commission shall ensure the application of the provisions of this Article and shall, where necessary, address appropriate directives or decisions to Member States.'

558. Pursuant to this provision, the Commission can either act individually by taking a decision against a Member State or issue general rules in the form of a Directive. The Commission used the latter possibility to adopt the so-called Transparency Directive[636] as well as for the first generation of EU legislation in the field of telecommunications. The latter initiative was unsuccessfully challenged by a few Member States, claiming that this provision does not confer on the Commission any legislative power.[637] Although the Court upheld the directive, the Commission never used the instrument again thereafter.

559. In that Article 106(3) also refers to decisions it goes further than the general enforcement power of the Commission, since it gives the Commission, the power to adopt a decision finding a violation by a Member State of its obligations under Article 106(1), whereas under the general Treaty provisions the Commission, which is responsible for the supervision of compliance with EU law by the Member States, can only obtain a condemnation of a Member State for failure to fulfil its Treaty obligations by requesting for a judgment by the Court (after a lengthy procedure).

III. Application of Articles 101 and 102 TFEU to the Member States: Article 3(4) TEU

560. Article4(3) TEU requires Member States to take all appropriate measures to ensure fulfilment of the obligations arising out of the EC Treaty or resulting from action taken by the institutions of the Union. Moreover, Member States have to abstain from any measure which could jeopardize the attainment of the objectives of the Treaties.

---

636. Directive 80/723, *OJ* (1980) L 195/35, replaced by Directive 2006/111, *OJ* 2006, L 318/17.
637. Judgment of 19 March 1990, *France v. Commission*, C-202/88, EU:C:1990:120; Judgment of 17 November 1992, *Spain e.a. v. Commission*, C-271/90 et seq., EU:C:1992:440.

The question arising in the context of Article 4(3) TEU is when and to what extent measures by public bodies be caught by the European Competition rules.

561. The existing case law mainly concerns Article 4(3) TEU in relationship with Article 101 TFEU.

Building on earlier case law[638] and refining it, in *Van Eycke* case,[639] the CJEU held that Articles 101 and 102 TFEU:

> require the Member States not to introduce or maintain in force measures, even of a legislative nature, which may render ineffective the competition rules applicable to undertakings. Such would be the case … if a Member State were to require or favour the adoption of agreements, decisions or concerted practices contrary to Article 85 (now Art. 101 TFEU) or to reinforce their effects, or to deprive its own legislation of its official character by delegating to private traders responsibility for taking decisions affecting the economic sphere.

562. The ruling in *Van Eycke* contains two prohibitions.

First, Member States may not take measures requiring or favouring the adoption of practices contrary to Article 101 TFEU or reinforcing their effects. *Second*, they shall also abstain from delegating to private bodies (such as associations of undertakings) the power to take decisions affecting the economic sphere.

Examples of the first prohibition are the so-called *Nouvelles Frontières* case: French legislation making tariffs agreed upon between airlines (in violation of Article 101 TFEU) obligatory for all market participants (here tour operators selling tickets) and *Vereniging van Vlaamse Reisbureaus*,[640] where a legal provision in Belgium extended the effect of an anticompetitive agreement between associations of tour operators and travel agencies.

563. The second prohibition was found to be infringed in *Commission v. Italy*,[641] where the professional association of customs agents in Italy was entrusted by the State with fixing the tariffs for the services of their members.

However where the State does not approve or confirm a measure taken by undertakings but adopts itself a measure that restricts competition, it does not act in violation of the principle of sincere cooperation, because there is no underlying corporate conduct, even though undertakings, or their association, have petitioned the State to take the measure, but have not taken themselves restrictive measures in the market. The case law of the Court of Justice gives several examples of this, e.g., the fixing of lawyers' fees in Italy.[642]

---

638. The first case was Judgment of 16 November 1977, *INNO v. ATAB*, 13/77, EU:C:1977:185.
639. Judgment of 21 September 1988, *Van Eycke v. ASPA*, 267//86, EU:C:1988:427.
640. Judgment of 1 October 1987, *Vereniging van Vlaamse Reisbureaus v. Sociale Dienst*, 311/85, EU:C:1987:418.
641. Judgment of 18 June 1998, *Commission v. Italy*, C-35/96, EU:C:1998:303.
642. Judgment of 19 February 1999; *Arduino*, C-35/99; Judgment of 5 December 2006, *Cipolla*, C-94/04, EU:C:2006:758.

564. There is however a thin line between a State measure reinforcing the effects of a restrictive practice of undertakings on the one hand and agreements or decision taken at the level of the undertakings belonging to a given sector. Where decisions are formally taken by the State, even though they are prepared and inspired by the undertakings concerned, they will not be caught by Article 101 in conjunction with Article 4(3) TEU. In *Reiff*,[643] the CJEU ruled that these Treaty provisions do not oppose to a German law provision that tariffs for the long-distance transport of goods by road are to be fixed by tariff boards and are to be made compulsory for all economic agents, after approval by the public authorities, if the members of those boards, although chosen by the public authorities on a proposal from the relevant trade sectors, are not representatives of the latter called on to negotiate and conclude an agreement on prices but are independent experts called on to fix the tariffs on the basis of considerations of public interest and if the public authorities do not abandon their prerogatives but in particular ensure that the boards fix the tariffs by reference to considerations of public interest and, if necessary, substitute their decision for that of the boards. The Court ruled in the same sense in two judgments of the same day, concerning the insurance sector: *Ohra*[644] and *Meng*.[645]

§8. ANTITRUST ENFORCEMENT

I. The Treaty Provision

565. Article 101(1) TFEU contains a prohibition of restrictive agreements. An agreement contrary to Article 101(1) TFEU is automatically void pursuant to Article 101(2) TFEU. The nullity sanction only affects those clauses of an agreement which infringe Article 81(1). The validity of the rest of the agreement (or other acts based on the agreement) will depend on national law.[646]

566. This nullity sanction does not however affect concerted practices because these are, per definition, not based on an act which could be declared void.

The nullity sanction is not specifically foreseen for abuses of a dominant position prohibited under Article 102 TFEU. In some cases, however, an agreement entered between a dominant undertaking and its counterpart may constitute an abuse of a dominant position (e.g., an exclusive purchase agreement) where it may be null and void.

567. A prohibition of a conduct under either Article 101 or 102 TFEU will normally be the result of a public enforcement of procedures.

---

643. Judgment of 17 November 1993, *Reiff*, EU: C-185/91, EU:C:1993:886.
644. Judgment of 17 November 1993, *Ohra*, C-245/91, EU:C:1993:887.
645. Judgment of 17 November 1993, *Meng*, C-2/91, EU:C:1993:885.
646. Judgment of 14 December 1983, *Société de Vente de Ciments et Bétons de l'Est SA v. Kerpen & Kerpen GmbH und Co. KG.*, C-319/82, EU:C:1983:374.

The European Commission together with NCAs of the ECN are responsible for public enforcement. Private enforcement, i.e., initiated by private claimants, is dealt with before national courts of the Member States.[647]

568. The Treaty provides for the possibility to supplement the Treaty rules on competition (Articles 101–106) with secondary legislation adopted on the basis of Article 103(2) TFEU which provides that 'the appropriate regulations or directives to give effect to the principles set out in Articles 101 and 102 shall be designed in particular (a) to ensure compliance with the prohibitions laid down in Article 101(1) and in Article 102 TFEU by making provision for fines and periodic penalty payments; (b) to lay down detailed rules for the application of Article 101(3) TFEU, taking into account the need to ensure effective supervision on the one hand, and to simplify administration to the greatest possible extent on the other; [...] (e) to determine the relationship between national laws and the provisions contained in this Section or adopted pursuant to this Article'.

II. Secondary Legislation

569. The first general Regulation adopted based on Article 103 TFEU was Regulation 17/62.[648] It contained a system of pubic enforcement including the possibility for the Commission to conduct dawn raids, impose fines and periodic penalty payments.[649] The main feature of this system was the possibility for the Commission to grant 'negative clearance' certifying that, based on the facts in its possession, there are no grounds under Article 101(1) TFEU for action on its part in respect of an agreement, decision or practice.[650] Under Regulation 17/62, the Commission had the exclusive power to declare Article 101(1) TFEU inapplicable pursuant to Article 101(3) TFEU.

Today this system of public enforcement is to be found in Regulation 1/2003.[651] (which is discussed in more detail in the next section III).

It is supplemented by Implementing Regulation 773/2004 which lays down rules concerning the initiation of proceedings by the Commission as well as the handling of complaints and the hearing of the parties concerned.[652]

In addition, the Commission has issued notices and best practices including on proceedings,[653] the right to be heard.[654] Other legal sources may also have an impact

---

647. Private enforcement may also take the form of arbitration proceedings.
648. Regulation No 17 implementing Arts 85 and 86 of the Treaty, *OJ* 1962, 204.
649. Article 3 of Regulation 17/62.
650. Articles 2 and 4 of Regulation 17/62.
651. Council Regulation (EC) No 1/2003 of 16 December 2002 on the implementation of the rules on competition laid down in Arts 81 and 82 of the Treaty, *OJ* 2003, L 1/1.
652. Commission Regulation (EC) No 773/2004 of 7 April 2004 relating to the conduct of proceedings by the Commission pursuant to Arts 81 and 82 of the EC Treaty, *OJ* 2004, L 123/18.
653. Best Practices in proceedings concerning Arts 101 and 102 TFEU, *OJ* C 308, 20.10.2011, pp. 6–32.
654. Terms of Reference of the Hearing Officer, *OJ* 2011, L 275/29.

on competition proceedings including Regulation 1049/2001 regarding public access to EP, Council and Commission documents[655] and the Charter of fundamental tights of the EU.[656]

570. More recently, based on case law of the CJEU, Directive 2014/104/EU (discussed in section IV) has enlarged the private enforcement of EU competition law (*see* Article 101(2) TFEU) by imposing on Member States the obligation to foresee the possibility for victims to claim damages related to infringements of competition rules.[657]

III. Public Enforcement

A. *Cooperation Between the European Commission and NCAs*

571. Both the European Commission and NCAs[658] are competent to apply Articles 101 and 102 TFEU. NCAs must apply Articles 101 and 102 TFEU where they apply national competition law to agreements and practices which may affect trade between Member States. To create a level playing field for agreements within the internal market, the application of national competition laws to such agreements within the meaning of Article 101(1) TFEU may not lead to their prohibition if they are not also prohibited under European competition law. However, Member States are not precluded from adopting and applying on their territory stricter national competition laws which prohibit or impose sanctions on unilateral conduct engaged in by undertakings.[659]

572. Regulation 1/2003 provides for close cooperation between the Commission and the NCAs. The pillars of this cooperation include a mechanism to (i) exchange information (solely for the purpose of applying competition rules) and (ii) a mechanism designed to settle jurisdictional issues under which: (a) the initiation by the Commission of proceedings for the adoption of a decision shall relieve the NCAs of their competence, (b) each NCA shall inform the Commission in writing before or without delay after commencing the first formal investigative measure, and (c) each NCA shall submit a draft decision to the Commission before its adoption. That information may also be made available to the other NCAs.

---

655. Regulation (EC) No 1049/2001 of the European Parliament and of the Council of 30 May 2001 regarding public access to European Parliament, Council and Commission documents, *OJ* 2001, L 145/43.
656. Charter of fundamental rights of the European Union.
657. Directive 2014/104/EU of the European Parliament and of the Council of 26 November 2014 on certain rules governing actions for damages under national law for infringements of the competition law provisions of the Member States and of the European Union, *OJ* 2014, L 349/1.
658. Note that note that in some EU Member States (e.g., Finland, Ireland and Sweden), not only administrative bodies but national courts may also act as public enforcers. The designations of NCAs is subject to Art. 35 of Modernisation Regulation 1/2003.
659. Article 3 Regulation 1/2003. These stricter national laws may include provisions which in its absence of a dominant position prohibit or impose sanctions on abusive behaviour towards economically dependent undertakings.

573. In addition, for the sake of efficiency, where NCAs of two or more Member States have received a complaint or are acting on their own initiative against the same practice, the fact that one authority is dealing with the case shall be sufficient grounds for the others to suspend the proceedings before them or to reject the complaint. Likewise, the Commission may reject a complaint because a competition authority of a Member State is dealing with the case.[660]

The following section focuses mainly on enforcement by the European Commission. The rules applicable to enforcement by NCAs are available on their respective website.[661]

B. Enforcement by the European Commission

1. Start of an Infringement Procedure

574. An investigation for possible infringements may originate from a complaint, a leniency application, information from another competition authority or may be ex officio.[662,663]

a. Complaints

575. Complaints may be lodged to the European Commission by natural or legal persons who can show a legitimate interest as well as by Member States.[664] On the one hand, undertakings directly affected by a practice which they suspect restricts competition and who are able to provide specific information may lodge a formal complaint subject to certain requirements (e.g., use of 'C' form and including certain information),[665] on the other hand, it is possible to provide market information or such as a name and an address as well as an identification of the firms and products concerned and description of the practice observed. Further guidance is provided in the Commission's notice on the handling of complaints.[666]

---

660. Articles 11–13 Regulation 1/2003.
661. *See* the section on the European Competition Network (ECN) on the website of DG Competition, available at http://ec.europa.eu/competition/ecn/competition_authorities.html, last accessed on 11 January 2017.
662. For more details on enforcement of competition rules by the European Commission, *see* C.S. Kerse & N. Khan, *EU Antitrust Procedure* (6th ed., 2012); L. Ortiz Blanco, *EU Competition Procedure* (3rd ed., 2013).
663. Article 7 Regulation 1/2003.
664. Article 7(2) Regulation 1/2003.
665. The 'C' form is attached as an annex to Commission Regulation (EC) No 773/2004 of 7 April 2004 relating to the conduct of proceedings by the Commission pursuant to Arts 81 and 82 of the EC Treaty, *OJ* L 123, 27.4.2004, pp. 18–24.
666. Commission Notice on the handling of complaints by the Commission under Arts 81 and 82 of the EC Treaty, *OJ* 2004, C 101/65.

b. Leniency Applications

576. Leniency applications are specific to cartels and are excluded for other types of competition law infringements. In 1996, the Leniency policy was set up to create an incentive for cartelists to self-report and give evidence to the Commission in exchange for either total immunity from fines or a reduction of fines which the Commission would otherwise have imposed on them.[667]

The current rules applicable to leniency application are outlined in the 2006 Leniency Notice.[668]

Under the Leniency Policy, the Commission offers companies involved in a cartel – which self-report and hand over evidence – either total immunity from fines or a reduction of fines. This creates a deterrent effect on cartel formation and it destabilizes the operation of existing cartels by creating suspicion among cartel members.[669]

To obtain total immunity, an undertaking involved in a cartel must be the first to inform the Commission of an undetected cartel by providing sufficient information for the Commission to raid the premises of the other companies allegedly involved in the cartel. If the Commission already has enough information to launch a dawn-raid or if it has already conducted one, the company must provide evidence that enables the Commission to prove the cartel infringement.

As a leniency applicant, the undertaking is under an obligation to fully cooperate with the Commission throughout its procedure, provide it with all evidence in its possession, swiftly reply to requests for information and put immediately an end to its participation to the cartel. The leniency application and the cooperation with the Commission cannot be disclosed to any other company. The undertaking that coerced other undertakings to participate in the cartel may not benefit from immunity.

Assuming an applicant does not qualify for full immunity, it may nevertheless benefit from a reduction of fine if it provides evidence that represents 'significant added value' (i.e., it reinforces its ability to prove the infringement) to information already available to the Commission. Requirement to end its participation to the cartel and the non-disclosure of the leniency application also apply. The first company to meet these conditions is granted 30% to 50% reduction, the second 20% to 30% and subsequent companies up to 20%.

The Commission uses a so-called marker system allowing an applicant to have more time to collect and submit information to support its application, it also allows to determine the rank of each applicant based on the day of first contact with the Commission where a marker is accepted by the Commission.

---

667. Commission Notice on the non-imposition or reduction of fines in cartel cases, *OJ* 1996, C 207/4.
668. Commission's Notice on immunity from fines and reduction of fines in cartel cases, *OJ* 2006, C 298/17. This notice replaced Commission notice on immunity from fines and reduction of fines in cartel cases, *OJ* 2002, C 45/3 and Commission Notice on the non-imposition or reduction of fines in cartel cases, *OJ* 1996, C 207/4.
669. A leniency application submitted to the European Commission does not protect an undertaking regarding infringements of national competition rules of Member States.

Leniency application may contain corporate statements which benefit under the 2006 Leniency Notice from special protection against future disclosure.[670]

c. Ex Officio Investigation

577. The European Commission may initiate an investigation on its own initiative on the basis of systematic analysis of publicly available information (news, media, information published by industry associations, market information received from informal complainants).

2. Powers of Investigation

578. Regulation 1/2003 provides that the Commission is empowered to: (i) request information either to a defined set of undertakings,[671] or (ii) to all undertakings belonging to a whole sector of the economy (so-called sector inquiry) or regarding a certain type of agreement used across various sectors,[672] (iii) to take statements from any natural or legal person with their consent,[673] (iv) to conduct inspections at the premises of undertakings,[674] homes of directors, managers and other members of staff of the undertakings, transport means and land (so-called dawn raids).[675]

579. The Commission may also request information from other undertakings than the undertaking under scrutiny,[676] from governments and from competition authorities of other Member States.[677]

580. During dawn raids, the Commission can inspect with or without giving prior notice to the undertaking or association of undertakings. During those inspections, the Commission has the power to:

– take statements of any legal or natural person;
– enter any premises, land and means of transport of undertakings or associations of undertakings;
– examine books and records;
– take copies or extracts from books or records;
– seal business premises and books or records for a certain time.

---

670. *See* paras 31–35 of the 2006 Leniency Notice and the guidance on delivery oral statements at DG Competition, published on the website of the Commission on 8 October 2013, available at http:// ec.europa.eu/competition/cartels/leniency/oral_statements_procedure_en.pdf, last accessed on 11 January 2017.
671. Article 18 Regulation 1/2003.
672. Article 17 Regulation 1/2003.
673. Article 19 Regulation 1/2003.
674. Article 20 Regulation 1/2003.
675. Article 21 Regulation 1/2003.
676. Article 18 Regulation 1/2003.
677. Article 18(5) Regulation 1/2003.

581. The Commission can thus take all necessary measures in order to establish the existence of an infringement of the competition rules, provided those remain within the scope of the investigation.

3.   Interim Measures

582. In case of urgency, when there is a risk of serious and irreparable damage to competition, the Commission may, on its own initiative, and on the basis of a prima facie finding of infringement, order interim measures.[678]

The interim measures will be taken for a specific period of time and cannot exceed what is necessary given the situation.

4.   Statement of Objections and Hearing

583. Once the Commission has assembled all necessary information to consider behaviour or an agreement under Article 101 or 102 TFEU, it will send a statement of objections ('SO') to the undertakings concerned[679] and set a date for the parties to submit written observations.[680] The parties can also request to be heard and so can any other legal or natural person who shows a sufficient interest.[681] Together with the SO, the undertakings will receive access to the case file of the Commission containing information used by the Commission during the investigation and notably relied upon in the SO. It may also happen that, after the SO has been issued, new evidence is identified which the Commission intends to rely upon, then the undertakings under scrutiny shall have the opportunity to present their observations on these new aspects. If the new evidence justifies the issuance of additional objections or the intrinsic nature of the infringement with which an undertaking is charged is modified, the Commission shall notify this to the parties in a supplementary statement of objections ('SSO'). Before doing so, a State of Play meeting will normally be offered to the parties.[682]

Upon reception of the responses of the undertaking(s) concerned and after the hearing, the Commission will issue a decision. Regarding cartel infringement, the Commission may also invite the undertakings involved to enter into settlement discussion and later adopt a decision-making the settlement binding.[683]

---

678. Article 8 Regulation 1/2013.
679. *See* Article 10 Commission Regulation 773/2004.
680. Article 10 Regulation 773/2004.
681. Articles 12 and 13 Regulation 773/2004.
682. Section 3.1.7 of the Best Practices for the conduct of proceedings concerning Arts 101 and 102 TFEU.
683. *See* paras 335 et seq. on cartels.

5. Decision and Fines

584. In its decision, the Commission can only deal with objections in respect of which the parties have been able to comment.[684]

In case the Commission finds that there is an infringement of Article 101 or 102 TFEU, it may by decision require the undertakings concerned to put an end to the infringement. As such, the Commission can impose appropriate behavioural or structural remedies on the undertakings which are necessary to put an end to the infringement.[685]

585. Where the Commission intends to adopt a decision requiring that an infringement be brought to an end, the undertakings concerned can offer *commitments* in order to meet the concerns of the Commission. The Commission can then – by decision – make those commitments binding on the undertakings. This decision will be adopted for a certain period and will conclude that there are no longer any grounds for action by the Commission.[686]

586. The Commission can impose *fines* for procedural or substantive infringements. In fixing the amount of the fine, the Commission will take both the gravity and the duration of the infringement into account.

Where the undertakings, intentionally or negligently, supply incorrect, incomplete or misleading information or where they refuse to submit to investigations ordered by decision of the Commission, or where they break seal affixed by the Commission, the Commission may by decision impose a fine of maximum 1% of their total turnover of the preceding year on the company.[687]

The Commission may impose fines by decision on undertakings and associations of undertakings which, intentionally or negligently infringe Article 101 or 102 TFEU, contravene a decision ordering interim measures or fail to comply with a commitment which has been made binding by a decision of the Commission.

The amount of the fine for each undertaking or association of undertakings cannot exceed 10% of its total turnover of the preceding business year.

Where the infringement of an association is related to the activities of its members, the total fine can amount to up to 10% of the sum of the total turnover of each member active on the market affected by the infringement of the association.[688]

587. The Commission can also, by decision, impose *periodic penalty payments* of a maximum of 5% of the average daily turnover in the preceding business year per day and calculated from the date appointed by the decision in order to compel undertakings or associations of undertakings to end an infringement in accordance

---

684. Article 11 Regulation 773/2004.
685. Article 7 Regulation 1/2003.
686. Article 9 Regulation 1/2003.
687. Article 23(1) Regulation 1/2003.
688. Article 23(2) Regulation 1/2003.

with a Commission decision, to comply with an interim measures decision or a commitments decision, to supply correct and complete information requested by the Commission or to submit to an inspection ordered by decision.[689]

588. The Commission shall publish its decisions including the names of the parties and the main content of the decision, including any penalties imposed. In doing so, it shall also have regard to the legitimate interest of undertakings in the protection of their business secrets.[690]

589. The Court of Justice (now the GC and on appeal the Court of Justice) enjoys unlimited jurisdiction to review decisions whereby the Commission has fixed a fine or periodic penalty payment and it may cancel, reduce or increase the fine or periodic penalty payment imposed.[691]

590. The parties concerned may lodge an appeal with the GC within two months of the notification of the decision of the Commission or within two months of its publication on the Official Journal.[692]

591. Decisions of the Court of First Instance can be appealed before the European Court of justice, but only on points of law.

6.   Legal Protection

592. Regulation 1/2003 contains some provisions which guarantee legal protection.

a.   Professional Secrecy

593. The information which the Commission collect within the framework of investigations or inspections can only be used for the purpose for which it was acquired, i.e., a competition investigation. For example, it shall not be transmitted to a tax authority.

The Commission, the competition authorities of other Member States, their officials, servants and other persons working under their supervision cannot disclose information acquired or exchanged by them pursuant to the Modernisation Regulation.[693]

---

689. Article 24 Regulation 1/2003.
690. Article 30 Regulation 1/2003.
691. Article 31 Regulation 1/2003.
692. Article 263 TFEU.
693. Article 28 Regulation.

b. Legal Professional Privilege

594. An undertaking can refuse to disclose or produce written communications with its lawyer provided that (i) such communications are made for the purpose and in the interests of the client's (the undertaking's) rights of defence and (ii) provided that the lawyer is an independent lawyer, i.e., not bound to the undertaking in a relationship of employment.[694]

The legal professional privilege does not apply to communications between the undertaking and its in-house lawyer in the framework of an investigation conducted by the European Commission.

c. Protection Against Self-incrimination

595. The Commission may, in the course of a request for information, compel an undertaking to provide all necessary information concerning such facts as may be known to it and to disclose to it, even if the information may be used to establish the existence of anticompetitive conduct. However, the Commission may not compel an undertaking to provide it with answers which might involve an admission on its part of the existence of an infringement which it is incumbent upon the Commission to prove.[695] There is thus a limited protection against self-incrimination.

IV. Private Enforcement

596. 'Private enforcement' refers to the enforcement based on the fact that Articles 101 and 102 TFEU produce direct effects in relations between individuals and create rights and obligations which national courts must enforce. It also includes alternative avenues of redress including consensual dispute resolution.

A. The Case Law of the Court of Justice

597. It is the Court of Justice that has established the right to seek compensation for damages resulting from a breach of competition rules. In *Courage v. Crehan,*[696] the CJEU had to deal with a reference for a preliminary ruling from the Court of Appeal (England and Wales) (Civil division) notably regarding the question whether a party can obtain compensation for loss which he alleges to result from his being subject to a contractual clause contrary to Article 101 TFEU (ex- 85 TCE) and whether, therefore, Union law precludes a rule of national law which denies a person the right to rely on his own illegal actions to obtain damages. After reminding that the task of national courts is to apply the provisions of Community law in areas within their jurisdiction in order to ensure that those rules take full effect and must

---

694. Judgment of 18 May 1982, *AM&S*, C-155/79, EU:C:1982:157 and Judgment of 14 September 2010, *Akzo*, C-550/07 P, EU:C:2010:512.

695. Judgment of 18 October 1989, *Orkem*, C- 374/87, EU:C:1989:207.

696. Judgment of 20 September 2001, *Courage Ltd v. Bernard Crehan and Bernard Crehan v. Courage Ltd and Others*, C-453/99), EU:C:2001:465.

protect the rights which they confer on individuals, the Court stated that the full effectiveness of Article 101 TFEU and, in particular, the practical effect of the prohibition laid down in Article 101(1) TFEU would be put at risk if it were not open to any individual to claim damages for loss caused to him by a contract or by conduct liable to restrict or distort competition. The Court further added that the existence of such a right was strengthening the working of the Union competition rules and making a significant contribution to the maintenance of effective competition in the Union.

598. In *Manfredi,*[697] the Court of Justice had to deal with a reference for a preliminary ruling by an Italian judge regarding the question whether the limitation period for bringing actions for damages, and the amount of damages to be paid, both of which are fixed by national law, are compatible with Article 101 TFEU. The Court ruled that in the absence of Union rules governing the matter, it is for the domestic legal system of each Member State notably to prescribe the detailed procedural rules governing those actions, provided the provisions concerned are not less favourable than those governing actions for damages based on an infringement of national competition rules and that those national provisions do not render practically impossible or excessively difficult the exercise of the right to seek compensation for the harm caused by an agreement or practice prohibited under Article 101 TFEU.

599. In *Pfleiderer,*[698] the Court of Justice had to deal with a reference for a preliminary ruling a German judge regarding access to leniency documents. After re-stating the principles established in the case law mentioned above, the Court ruled that EU competition law must be interpreted as not precluding a person who has been adversely affected by an infringement of that law and is seeking to obtain damages from being granted access to documents relating to a leniency procedure involving the perpetrator of that infringement.

600. In *Otis,*[699] the Court of Justice stated again the principle established in the case law mentioned above that the full effectiveness of Article 101 TFEU and, in particular, the practical effect of the prohibition laid down in would be put at risk if it were not open to any person to claim damages for loss caused to him by a contract or conduct liable to restrict or distort competition.

601. In *Donau Chemie,*[700] upon a reference for a preliminary ruling from the Austrian Oberlandesgericht Wien regarding access to the judicial case file in competition case, the Court of Justice relied again upon the principles mentioned in the

---

697. Judgment of 13 July 2006, *Vincenzo Manfredi v. Lloyd Adriatico Assicurazioni SpA* (C-295/04), *Antonio Cannito v. Fondiaria Sai SpA* (C-296/04) and *Nicolò Tricarico* (C-297/04) and *Pasqualina Murgolo* (C-298/04) *v. Assitalia SpA*, C-295/04 to C-298/04, EU:C:2006:461.
698. Judgment of 14 June 2011, *Pfleiderer AG v. Bundeskartellamt*, C-360/09, EU:C:2011:389.
699. Judgment of 6 November 2012, *Europese Gemeenschap v. Otis NV and Others*, C-199/11), EU:C:2012:684.
700. Judgment of 6 June 2013, *Bundeswettbewerbsbehörde v. Donau Chemie AG and Others*, C-536/11, EU:C:2013:366.

case law above. The Court ruled that Union law, in particular the principle of effectiveness, precludes a provision of national law under which access to documents forming part of the file relating to national proceedings concerning the application of Article 101 TFEU – including access to documents made available under a leniency programme – by third parties who are not party to those proceedings with a view to bringing an action for damages against participants in an agreement or concerted practice is made subject solely to the consent of all the parties to those proceedings, without leaving any possibility for the national courts of weighing up the interests involved.

602. Finally, in *Kone*[701] in the framework of a reference for a preliminary ruling from the Austrian Oberster Gerichtshof, the Court of Justice re-stated the principles mentioned in the case law above and ruled that Article 101 TFEU must be interpreted as meaning that it precludes the interpretation and application of domestic legislation enacted by a Member State which categorically excludes, for legal reasons, any civil liability of undertakings belonging to a cartel for loss resulting from the fact that an undertaking not party to the cartel, having regard to the practices of the cartel, set its prices higher than would otherwise have been expected under competitive conditions.

603. This right to compensation described by the Court of Justice, the right to effective judicial protection[702] and the Charter of Fundamental Rights[703] require each Member State to ensure the effective exercise of the right of victims of infringements of the EU competition rules to claim damages.

B. *The Directive on Action for Damages*

604. The European Commission wanted to further develop private enforcement as it considered it as a compliment to public enforcement. Based on the identification of several difficulties including of procedural nature, for private claimants to seek relief by taking damages actions before the national courts, the Commission consulted with stakeholders on how to resolve those issues and published a Green Paper end 2005,[704] a White Paper in 2008[705] and organized several public consultations and hearings at the EP. This ultimately lead the Commission to submit a proposal for a directive which was adopted on 11 June 2013 as Directive 2014/104/EU

---

701. Judgment of the Court of 5 June 2014, *Kone AG and Others v. ÖBB-Infrastruktur AG*, C-557/12, EU:C:2014:1317.
702. Article 19(1) TFEU.
703. Article 47(1) of the Charter of Fundamental Rights.
704. Green Paper – Damages actions for breach of the EC antitrust rules, COM(2005) 672.
705. White Paper on Damages Actions for Breach of the EC antitrust rules, COM(2008) 165.

on certain rules governing actions for damages under national law for the infringement of the competition law of the Member States (the 'Directive'). Member States had to implement the Directive in national law by 27 December 2016.[706]

605. The Directive aims at removing practical obstacles to compensation for all victims of infringements of EU competition law and applies to all damages actions, whether individual or collective, which are available in the Member States. The Directive also clarifies the relationship between private and public enforcement of EU antitrust rules by the Commission and NCAs.

606. The headlines of the Directive are the following:

(1) *First*, it provides easier access to evidence by allowing parties to obtain a court order for the disclosure of those document that are in the hands of other parties or third parties to prove a claim or a defence to support their actions for damages. In addition, the disclosure of categories of evidence, described as precisely and narrowly as possible, will also be possible under the condition, monitored by national judges, that disclosure orders are proportionate and maintain a protection of confidential information.
(2) *Second*, A civil court must consider as full proof a Commission infringement decision and a final infringement decision of the competition authority of the same Member State. National courts of other Member States will at least have to consider a decision of a competition authority of another Member as prima facie evidence of the infringement.
(3) *Third*, the Directive sets clear rules for limitation period to provide victims with sufficient time to bring an action, i.e., at least five years to bring damages claims, starting from the moment when they had the possibility to discover that they suffered harm from an infringement. This period will be subject to suspension or interruption if a NCA starts infringement proceedings, to allow victims to decide to wait until the end of public proceedings. Victims will have at least one year to bring damages actions after a competition authority's infringement decision becomes final.
(4) *Fourth*, the Directive clarifies the legal consequences of 'passing on', i.e., the increased price that direct customers of an infringer apply to their own customer (indirect customers). The existence of 'passing on' allows the infringer to reduce compensation to direct customers by the amount they passed on to indirect customers. The Directive facilitates claims of indirect customers by establishing a rebuttable presumption (where certain conditions are met) that they suffered some level of overcharge harm, to be estimated by the judge.
(5) *Fifth*, the Directive clarifies that victims are entitled to full compensation for the harm suffered including compensation for actual loss, for loss of profit and payment of interest until compensation is paid.

---

706. The European Commission maintain a chart indicating where each Member State stands regarding the implementation of the directive in national law, available at http://ec.europa.eu/competition/antitrust/actionsdamages/directive_en.html, last accessed on 12 January 2016.

(6) *Sixth*, based on the finding that more than 90% of cartels cause a price increase, the Directive contains a rebuttable presumption that cartel infringements cause harm.
(7) *Seventh*, the Directive established the principle of joint and several liabilities among infringers so that any participant in an infringement will be responsible towards the victims for the whole harm caused by the infringement, with the possibility of obtaining a contribution from other infringers for their share of responsibility.

However, this will not apply to infringers which obtained immunity under a leniency programme to safeguard effectiveness of such programmes. Therefore, these immunity recipients will normally be obliged to compensate only their (direct and indirect) customers and other injured parties where full compensation cannot be obtained from other infringers.

§9. LIBERALIZATION OF SPECIFIC SECTORS

I. Introduction

607. Services in certain sectors have not always been open for competition but were traditionally offered by the Member States or by national organizations which had exclusive rights. Examples of such sectors are: transport, energy, postal services and telecommunications.

One of the principles of competition policy is the liberalization of these sectors to open them up for international competition. The consequence of the opening up of the market is the entry of new competitors and consequently better products and services for the consumers.

The approach of the Commission in liberalizing these traditional sectors has evolved over the years. Where in earlier years the Commission encouraged the establishment of competing facilities, it has rather promoted the use of the same facilities network by several undertakings in more recent years since the establishment of a new nationwide facilities network is often very expensive and ineffective.

The opening up of these sectors requires additional regulation, not only to ensure that these essential public services continue to be provided but also to ensure that the consumer is not adversely affected by the liberalization.

Hereafter, a brief overview is given of the legislation in the main sectors which are being liberalized by the European Commission.

II. Postal Services

608. The Commission adopted a first Directive in 1997 (97/67/EC[707]) in order
to accomplish the Single Market for postal services and open up the sector gradually to competition. This Directive was later amended by Directive 2002/39/EC[708]
which defined the further steps in the opening up of the postal services.

In 2006, the Commission put forward a proposal[709] to open postal markets of the
EU fully to competition by 2009, in line with the target date set out in Postal Directive 2002/39/EC.

III. Telecommunications

A. Introduction

609. The current rules governing the sector of telecommunications in the EU
were agreed in 2002. However, the telecommunications sector is a fast-developing
sector and the current rules now need to be revised, to ensure they continue to serve
the best interests of consumers and industry in today's marketplace.

The Commission's review proposals were adopted in November 2007 and are
intended to bring the EU rules up to date.

B. The Current Rules

610. The current framework is made up of a package of six Directives and one
Regulation. All these Directives entered into force on 25 July 2003. The EU Mem-
ber States were required to implement this legislation into their national regimes by
July 2003. The package that has been received in 2009[710] includes:

– Directive 2002/21/EC[711] or the 'Framework Directive' on a common regulatory
framework.

---

707. Directive 97/67/EC of the European Parliament and of the Council of 15 December 1997 on com-
     mon rules for the development of the internal market of Community postal services and the
     improvement of quality of service, *OJ* 1998, L 15/14.
708. Directive 2002/39/EC of the European Parliament and of the Council of 10 June 2002 amending
     Directive 97/67/EC with regard to the further opening to competition of Community postal ser-
     vices, *OJ* 2002, L 176/21.
709. Proposal for a directive of the European Parliament and of the Council amending Directive 97/67/
     EC concerning the full accomplishment of the internal market of community postal services –
     COM/2006/594 final.
710. For the consolidated version of the directives mentioned hereafter, *see eur lex.*
711. Directive 2002/21/EC of the European Parliament and of the Council of 7 March 2002 on a com-
     mon regulatory framework for electronic communications networks and services ('Framework
     Directive'), *OJ* 2002, L 108/33.

– Directive 2002/19/EC[712] or the 'Access Directive' on access and interconnection.
– Directive 2002/20/EC[713] or the 'Authorisation Directive' on the authorization of electronic communications networks and services.
– Directive 2002/22/EC[714] or the 'Universal Service Directive' on universal service and users' rights relating to electronic communications networks and services.
– Directive 2002/58/EC[715] or the 'Directive on privacy and electronic communications'.
– Directive 2002/77/EC[716] on competition in the markets for electronic communications services.
– Regulation 2000/2887/EC[717] on unbundled access to the local loop.

C. Review

611. As was said in the introduction a review of the EU rules on telecommunications is ongoing. There are still many obstacles in telecoms which have to be handled. The reforms are based on four key areas: more competition, better regulation, strengthening the internal market and protecting consumers better. The proposals will not be discussed in detail here because of their detailed nature.

The Commission expects the new framework to be in place from 2010 onwards.

IV. Energy

A. Electricity

612. In 1996, a first Directive (96/92/EC[718]) concerning common rules of the internal market in electricity was adopted. This Directive entered into force on 19 February 1997. As was said in preamble 5 of this Directive, the internal market in electricity needs to be established gradually, in order to enable the industry to adjust

---

712. Directive 2002/19/EC of the European Parliament and of the Council of 7 March 2002 on access to, and interconnection of, electronic communications networks and associated facilities ('Access Directive'), *OJ* 2002, L 108/7.
713. Directive 2002/20/EC of the European Parliament and of the Council of 7 March 2002 on the authorization of electronic communications networks and services ('Authorisation Directive'), *OJ* 2002 L 108/21.
714. Directive 2002/22/EC of the European Parliament and of the Council of 7 March 2002 on universal service and users' rights relating to electronic communications networks and services ('Universal Service Directive'), *OJ* 2002, L 108/51.
715. Directive 2002/58/EC of the European Parliament and of the Council of 12 July 2002 concerning the processing of personal data and the protection of privacy in the electronic communications sector ('Directive on privacy and electronic communications'), *OJ* 2002, L 201/37.
716. Commission Directive 2002/77/EC of 16 September 2002 on competition in the markets for electronic communications networks and services, *OJ* 2002, L 249/21.
717. Regulation (EC) No 2887/2000 of the European Parliament and of the Council of 18 December 2000 on unbundled access to the local loop, *OJ* 2000, L 336/4.
718. Directive 96/92/EC of the European Parliament and of the Council of 19 December 1996 concerning common rules for the internal market in electricity, *OJ* 1997, L 27/20.

in a flexible and ordered manner to its new environment and to take account of the different ways in which electricity systems are organized at present. Directive 96/92/EC established common rules for the generation, transmission and distribution of electricity.

613. Directive 96/92/EC was repealed by Directive 2003/54/EC.[719]

In September 2007, the Commission accepted a package of legislative proposals in the context of an Energy Action Plan. These proposals form the next step in the gradual establishment of the internal market for electricity and gas.

614. Presently Directive 2009/72 concerning common rules for the internal market in electricity applies.[720] The Directive establishes common rules for the generation, transmission, distribution and supply of electricity, together with consumer protection provisions, with a view to improving and integrating competitive electricity markets in the Community. It lays down the rules relating to the organization and functioning of the electricity sector, open access to the market, the criteria and procedures applicable to calls for tenders and the granting of authorizations and the operation of systems. It also lays down universal service obligations and the rights of electricity consumers and clarifies competition requirements.

B. Gas

615. In 1998, a first Directive (98/30/EC[721]) concerning common rules for the internal market in natural gas was adopted. This Directive had to be implemented by the Member States by August 2000. As was said in preamble 7 of this Directive, the internal market in natural gas needs to be established gradually, in order to enable the industry to adjust in a flexible and ordered manner to its new environment and in order to take account of the different market structures in the Member States. Directive 98/30/EC established common rules for the internal market of natural gas.

616. Directive 98/30/EC was repealed by Directive 2003/55/EC.[722] Currently Directive 2009/73 concerning common rules for the internal market in natural gas[723] applies. The Directive establishes common rules for the transmission, distribution, supply and storage of natural gas. It lays down the rules relating to the organization and functioning of the natural gas sector, access to the market, the criteria

---

719. Directive 2003/54/EC of the European Parliament and of the Council of 26 June 2003 concerning common rules for the internal market in electricity and repealing Directive 96/92/EC, *OJ* 2003, L 176/37.
720. *OJ* 2009, L 211/55.
721. Directive 98/30/EC of the European Parliament and of the Council of 22 June 1998 concerning common rules for the internal market in natural gas, *OJ* 1998, L 204/1.
722. Directive 2003/55/EC of the European Parliament and of the Council of 26 June 2003 concerning common rules for the internal market in natural gas and repealing Directive 98/30/EC, *OJ* L 176, 15.7.2003, pp. 57–78.
723. *OJ* 2009, L 211/94.

and procedures applicable to the granting of authorizations for transmission, distribution, supply and storage of natural gas and the operation of systems.

§10. CONCENTRATION CONTROL

I. Introduction

617. The rules on concentration control allow the Commission to intervene in major corporate mergers in order to safeguard effective competition in the internal market. It complements the application of Articles 101 and 102 TFEU. The EC Treaty did not contain rules on mergers. This created an enforcement gap. In the 1970s, the Commission used the prohibition of abuse of a dominant position to prevent a company that was already dominant from acquiring a competitor.[724] Not only was this a mere *ex post* control but Article 102 could only be applied where an already dominant undertaking acquired a competitor (and not where two non-dominant undertakings merge and acquire a dominant position as a result of the merger). After a long consultation process, Regulation EEC 4064/89[725] establishing a full-fledged *ex ante* control of concentrations was adopted. It was later replaced by Merger Regulation 139/2004 (the 'EU Merger Regulation').[726]

618. The system is based on the principle that all concentrations with a European dimension must be notified to the Commission (and more specifically to the 'DG COMP') and cannot be implemented prior to clearance. The Commission has the power to prohibit concentrations which are incompatible with the internal market, i.e., concentrations which would significantly impede effective competition in the internal market or in a substantial part of it in particular because they create or strengthen a dominant position.[727]

619. In addition, the Commission adopted Implementing Regulation 802/2004 including annexes containing the merger notification form (Form CO), the notification form for concentrations that are unlikely to raise competition concerns (Short Form CO), the form for reasoned submissions to initiate referral requests between the Commission and the NCAs (Form RS) and the form for submitting remedies (Form RM).[728]

---

724. Judgment of 21 February 1973, *Europemballage Corporation and Continental Can Company Inc. v. Commission of the European Communities,* C-6/72, EU:C:1973:22.
725. Council Regulation (EEC) No 4064/89 of 21 December 1989 on the control of concentrations between undertakings, *OJ* 1989, L 351/1.
726. Council Regulation (EC) 139/2004 of 20 January 2004, *OJ* 2004, L 24/1.
727. EU Merger Regulation, Art. 2(3).
728. Commission Regulation (EC) No 802/2004 of 21 April 2004 implementing Council Regulation (EC) No 139/2004 on the control of concentrations between undertakings, *OJ* 2004, L 133/1. The Implementing Regulation was amended in 2006, 2008 and twice in 2013. A consolidated version is available at http://data.europa.eu/eli/reg/2004/802/2014-01-01, last accessed on 10 January 2017.

620. To provide further guidance to stakeholders notably regarding jurisdictional issues (i.e., whether and to what extent their operations may be covered by European control of concentrations), the Commission published a consolidated jurisdictional notice[729] (hereafter 'the Consolidated Notice'). This Notice replaces the previous four jurisdictional Notices which were all adopted by the Commission in 1998 under the previous Merger Regulation (Council Regulation No 4064/89): the Notice on the concept of concentration,[730] the Notice on the concept of full-function joint ventures,[731] the Notice on the concept of undertakings concerned[732] and the Notice on calculation of turnover.[733]

621. Furthermore, the Commission issued Notices and Guidelines on the simplified procedure,[734] case referrals,[735] the role of the hearing officer,[736] access to file,[737] abandonment of concentration[738] as well as on substance including on the assessment of horizontal mergers,[739] non-horizontal merger,[740] relevant market,[741] the submission of remedies[742] and on ancillary restraints.[743]

622. Guidance can also be found in the best practices published by the Commission on merger proceedings, the disclosure of information in data rooms, the preparation of public versions of merger decisions, divestiture commitments and the submission of economic evidence.[744]

---

729. Commission consolidated jurisdictional notice under Council under Council Regulation (EC) No 139/2004 of 10 July 2007, *see* website DG Competition: http://ec.europa.eu/comm/competition/mergers/legislation/jn_en.pdf.
730. *OJ* 1998, C 66/5.
731. *OJ* 1998, C 66/1.
732. *OJ* 1998, C 66/14.
733. *OJ* 1998, C 66/25.
734. Commission Notice of 5 December 2013 on a simplified procedure for treatment of certain concentrations under Council Regulation (EC) No 139/2004, *OJ* 2013, C 366/5.
735. Commission Notice on Case Referral in respect of concentrations, *OJ* 2005, C 56/2.
736. Decision 2011/695/EU of the President of the European Commission of 13 October 2011 on the function and terms of reference of the hearing officer in certain competition proceedings, *OJ* 2011, L 275/29.
737. Commission Notice on the rules for access to the Commission file in cases pursuant to Arts 81 and 82 of the EC Treaty, Arts 53, 54 and 57 of the EEA Agreement and Council Regulation (EC) No 139/2004, *OJ* 2005, C 325/7, amendments published in *OJ* 2016, C 144/29.
738. The text of the DG Competition Information note on abandonment of concentrations is available at http://ec.europa.eu/competition/mergers/legislation/abandonment.pdf, last accessed on 10 January 2017.
739. Guidelines on the assessment of horizontal mergers under the Council Regulation on the control of concentrations between undertakings, *OJ* 2004, C 31/5.
740. Guidelines on the assessment of non-horizontal mergers under the Council Regulation on the control of concentrations between undertakings, *OJ* 2008, C 265/1.
741. Commission notice on the definition of the Relevant Market for the purposes of Community competition law, *OJ* 1997, C 372/5.
742. Commission Notice on remedies acceptable under the Council Regulation (EC) No 139/2004 and under Commission Regulation (EC) No 802/2004, *OJ* 2008, C 267/1.
743. Commission Notice on restrictions directly related and necessary to concentrations, *OJ* 2005, C 56/24.
744. Texts of the Best Practices are available on the website of the European Commission at http://ec.europa.eu/competition/mergers/legislation/legislation.html, last accessed on 10 January 2017.

623. The European Union Merger regulation (EUMR) provides that the Regulation applies to 'concentrations' which have a 'Union dimension' (in the Regulation 'Community dimension'). These concentrations are examined by the European Commission on the basis of the EUMR.[745]

The concept of 'concentration' refers to any operation resulting in a change of control on a lasting basis following a merger of two or more independent undertakings, parts of undertakings, acquisitions by one or more persons already controlling at least one undertaking, or by one or more undertakings, whether by purchase of securities or assets, by contract or by any other means, of direct or indirect control of the whole or parts of one or more other undertakings.

624. Concentrations which do not have a Union dimension can be subject to the national rules on competition. There are two exceptions to this division of the competence between the NCAs and the European Commission. First of all, Member State(s) may request the Commission to examine a concentration that does not have a Union dimension but which affects trade between Member States and threatens to significantly affect competition within the territory of the Member State(s) making the request.[746] Second, in certain circumstances, the Commission may refer a notified concentration to the competent authorities of the Member States.[747]

625. According to the EUMR, a concentration arises where a change of control on a lasting basis results from:

(1) the *merger* of two or more previously independent undertakings or parts of undertakings, or
(2) the *acquisition*, by one or more persons already controlling at least one undertaking, or by one or more undertakings, whether by purchase of securities or assets, by contract or by any other means, of direct or indirect control of the whole or parts of one or more undertakings.
(3) the creation of a *joint venture* performing on a lasting basis all the functions of an autonomous economic entity.

626. The Consolidated Notice however provides further some guidance on the notion of concentration. There are two categories of concentrations: a merger can arise if two previously independent undertakings merge or in case there is acquisition of control. The first category is quite straightforward. The concept of acquisition of control is more complicated. Article 3(2) EUMR provides that control shall be constituted:

by rights, contracts or any other means which, either separately or in combination and having regard to the considerations of fact or law involved, confer the possibility of exercising decisive influence on an undertaking, in particular by:

---

745. *See* Art. 1 EUMR and section C of the Consolidated Notice.
746. This is the so-called Dutch clause which is to be found in Art. 22 of the EU Merger Regulation.
747. The so-called German clause which is to be found in Art. 9 of the EU Merger Regulation.

a) ownership or the right to use all or part of the assets of the undertaking;
b) rights or contracts which confer decisive influence on the composition, voting or decisions of the organs of an undertaking.

627. The Consolidated Notice gives an overview of different forms of control. *Sole control* means that a specific shareholder has the power to determine the strategic decisions in an undertaking. Joint control however arises when there is a possibility of a deadlock situation resulting from the power of two or more parent companies to reject proposed strategic decisions.

628. *Joint control* (and sole control) can be established on a de jure or a de facto basis. The clearest form of joint control exists where there are only two parent companies which equally share the voting rights in a joint venture. Joint control may also exist where there is no equality between the parent companies in votes or in representation in decision-making bodies or where there are more than two parent companies. This will be the case where minority shareholders have the right to veto decisions – on the basis of a shareholders agreement, statutory rights or otherwise – which are essential for the strategic commercial behaviour of the joint venture.

629. A concentration will thus arise when two or more undertakings acquire joint control in another undertaking. This will be the case when a joint venture is created. However, not all joint venture will be concentrations. Only so-called full-function joint ventures, i.e., joint ventures performing on a lasting basis all the functions of an autonomous economic entity i.e., enjoying a certain level of autonomy on the conduct of business on the market, qualify as joint ventures. 'Limited function joint ventures' fall outside the scope of the EUMR. However, these joint ventures can still be subject to Article 101 TFEU in case they are used for cooperation between the parent companies.[748]

All full-function joint ventures with a Community dimension have to be notified to the European Commission.

II. Substantive Assessment

630. The Commission has to declare concentrations that would 'significantly impede effective competition in the internal market, or a substantial part of it, in particular as a result of the creation or strengthening of a dominant position' (SIEC-test) incompatible with the internal market. Where a concentration does not have such an effect, it has to declare it compatible with the internal market (Article 2).

When applying the SIEC-test, the Commission weighs the potential anticompetitive effects against the potential efficiencies of the merger.

This means that the Commission will look at possible anticompetitive effects resulting from a merger: (i) of two undertakings active in the same market absent any coordination with other competitors ('non-coordinated effects'), (ii) that would

---

748. *See* above para. 472.

enhance the risk of coordination between the merged entity and other firms ('coordinated effects'), or (iii) between firms active in vertically or closely related markets that would lead to the foreclosure of competitors ('vertical effects' and 'conglomerate effects', respectively).

In its assessment of efficiencies claimed by the parties to the concentration, the Commission will only consider them if they are verifiable, merger-specific and likely to be passed on to consumers.

The potential concerns identified by Commission may eventually be alleviated by a proposal made by the parties to the concentration to amend the transaction.

III. Union Dimension: The Thresholds

631. Once the European thresholds have been reached ('Union dimension'), the concentration will fall under the EUMR and the parties have to notify to the European Commission.[749]

A concentration has a Union dimension where:

- the combined aggregate worldwide turnover of all the undertakings concerned is more than EUR 5,000 million; and
- the aggregate Community-wide turnover of at least two of the undertakings concerned is more than EUR 250 million;

unless each of the undertakings concerned achieves more than two-thirds of its aggregate Community-wide turnover within one and the same Member State.

632. Since it often happened that concentrations falling short of one of the thresholds had to be notified to different NCAs, a second set of thresholds was introduced[750] in order to widen the scope of the EUMR and to reduce the number of multiple national filings. A concentration that does not meet the previous thresholds still has a European dimension where:

- the combined aggregate worldwide turnover of all the undertakings concerned is more than EUR 2,500 million;
- in each of at least three Member States, the combined aggregate turnover of all the undertakings concerned is more than EUR 100 million;
- in each of at least three Member States included for the purpose of point (b), the aggregate turnover of each of at least two of the undertakings concerned is more than EUR 25 million; and
- the aggregate Community-wide turnover of each of at least two of the undertakings concerned is more than EUR 100 million;

unless each of the undertakings concerned achieves more than two-thirds of its aggregate Union-wide turnover within one and the same Member State.

---

749. *See* Art. 1 EUMR and section B of the Consolidated Notice.
750. This was introduced by Regulation (EC) No 1310/97, *see* Art. 1(3) EUMR.

In case a concentration has a Union dimension, the Commission has exclusive jurisdiction and the Member States cannot apply national law to them. The EUMR has provided two exceptions to this principle[751] (*see* above).

633. For the calculation of turnover, it is necessary to compute the turnover of the undertakings involved to calculate whether the concentration has a community dimension and has to be notified to the European Commission. Detailed computation rules are included in Article 5 EUMR and section C (IV) of the Consolidated Notice.

634. The EUMR defines aggregate turnover in Article 5(1) as comprising the amounts derived by the undertakings concerned in the preceding financial year from the sale of products and the provision of services falling within the undertakings' ordinary activities after deduction of sales rebates and of VAT and other taxes directly related to turnover. The turnover to take into account is 'net' turnover, after deduction of sales rebates and certain taxes. The Commission's aim is to adjust turnover in such a way as to enable it to decide on the real economic strength of the undertaking. Sales rebates are all rebates or discounts which are granted by the undertakings to their customers and which have a direct influence on the amount of sales. As regards the deduction of taxes, the Merger Regulation refers to VAT and other taxes directly related to the turnover. An adjustment must always be made in case of permanent changes in the economic reality of the undertakings concerned (e.g., acquisitions or divestments) to identify the true resources being concentrated and to better reflect the economic situation of the undertakings concerned.

635. Article 5(4) EUMR thus provides that the aggregate turnover of an undertaking concerned shall be calculated by adding together the respective turnovers of the undertaking concerned; the subsidiaries and their subsidiaries of the undertaking concerned; the parent undertakings and their parents; and the sister undertakings of the undertakings concerned.

636. To determine whether a concentration has a 'Union' dimension, the geographical location of the turnover of the undertakings concerned has to be determined. The thresholds aim to identify cases which have sufficient turnover within the Union and within individual Member States. The second subparagraph of Article 5(1) provides that the location of turnover is determined by the location of the customer at the time of the transaction: 'Turnover, in the Union or in a Member State, shall comprise products sold and services provided to undertakings or consumers, in the Community or in that Member State as the case may be.'
The general rule is that turnover should be attributed to the place where the customer is located. This location is normally also the place where the characteristic action under the contract is to be performed, i.e., where the service/product is actually provided/delivered.[752]

---

751. *See* above para. 634.
752. *See also* section C (V) of the Consolidated Notice.

IV. No Concentration

637. Article 3(5) EUMR provides that a concentration will not be deemed to arise where:

(a) credit institutions or other financial institutions or insurance companies, hold on a temporary basis securities which they have acquired in an undertaking with a view to reselling them, provided that they do not exercise voting rights in respect of those securities with a view to determining the competitive behaviour of that undertaking;
(b) control is acquired according to the law of a Member State relating to liquidation, winding up, insolvency, cessation of payments, compositions or analogous proceedings;
(c) financial holding companies (referred to in Council Directive 78/660/EEC) acquire control, provided however that the voting rights in respect of the holding are exercised only to maintain the full value of those investments and not to determine directly or indirectly the competitive conduct of the controlled undertakings.

V. Procedure

A. Notification

638. Concentrations with a Union dimension as defined above must be notified to the European Commission (DG COMP) and prior to their implementation and following the conclusion of the agreement, the announcement of the public bid, or the acquisition of a controlling interest.

639. A draft agreement may also be notified, provided that the final version does not significantly differ from the draft agreement. The EUMR provides that a notification may also be made where the undertakings concerned demonstrate to the Commission a good faith intention to conclude an agreement. This means that in case the parties notify a draft agreement, the agreement has to be sufficiently concrete.

640. As a general rule, DG COMP finds it useful to have pre-notification contacts with the notifying parties, even in seemingly non-problematic cases. Therefore, DG COMP will always give notifying parties the opportunity, if they so request, to discuss an intended concentration informally and in confidence prior to the notification.[753]

641. A notification has to be made by the following parties:

---

753. *See* Best Practices on merger control proceedings. *See also* recital 10 of Implementing Regulation 802/2004.

– in case of a merger: all parties to the merger;
– in case of the acquisition of control: all parties acquiring control (so in the case of acquisition of sole control, only the party acquiring sole control).

642. Notification is made to DG COMP in a form CO for a normal procedure and in a Short Form CO in case of a simplified procedure.[754]

1. First Phase

643. The Commission is required to examine the notification as soon as they receive it and it has to take one of the following three decisions within twenty-five working days (extendable with ten working days in case the parties submit commitments) from the first working day following the notification:

– that the notified concentration does not fall within the scope of the EUMR.[755] In this case, the Commission has no jurisdiction, either because the agreement cannot be qualified as a concentration or because it does not have a Union dimension;
– that, although it falls within the scope of the EUMR, it does not raise any serious doubts as to its compatibility with the common market.[756] This is a so-called first phase clearance decision. Such a decision is deemed to cover all ancillary restrictions, i.e., restrictions directly related and necessary to the implementation of the concentration;[757]
– that the concentration notified falls within the scope of the EUMR and raises serious doubts as to its compatibility with the common market.[758]

In the latter case, the Commission will decide to initiate proceedings, the so-called phase II investigations. Such proceedings have to be closed by means of a decision, unless the undertakings concerned demonstrate to the satisfaction of the Commission that they have abandoned the concentration.

Article 10(6) provides that in case the Commission has not taken a decision within the required period of time, the concentration will be deemed to have been declared compatible with the common market.

During this first phase, undertakings can propose commitments in order to allow the Commission to clear the concentration. Where the Commission finds that, following modification by the undertakings concerned, a notified concentration no longer raises serious doubts, it will declare the concentration compatible with the common market.[759] The Commission can also attach itself conditions and obligations to its clearance decision in order to ensure that the undertakings concerned

---

754. These forms are annexed to the Implementing Regulation 802/2004.
755. Article 6(1)(a) EUMR.
756. Article 6(1)(b) EUMR.
757. *See* the Commission Notice on restrictions directly related and necessary to concentrations, *OJ* C 056, 5.3.2005, pp. 24–31.
758. Article 6(1)(c) EUMR.
759. Article 6(2) EUMR.

comply with the commitments they have entered into vis-à-vis the Commission with a view to rendering the concentration compatible with the common market.

Once the Commission has cleared a decision, it may only revoke it in case:

– the decision is based on incorrect information for which one of the undertakings is responsible or where it has been obtained by deceit; or
– the undertakings concerned commit a breach of an obligation attached to the decision.[760]

2. Second Phase

644. In case the Commission opens the second phase, it has to take a decision within ninety working days of the date on which the proceedings are initiated. This period will be increased to 105 working days in case the undertakings concerned offer commitments after the fifty-fifth working day. Moreover, a twenty working days' extension can be obtained by the parties (if they request this no longer than fifteen days after the initiation of the Phase II investigation) or by the Commission (at any point in case the parties agree).

This period can be suspended in case the Commission has to request information by decision or order an investigation by decision.[761]

The Commission can adopt two types of decisions:

(1) clear the concentration and declare it compatible with the common market. In this case, this decision will cover also all ancillary restrictions. Here as well, the Commission can attach conditions and obligations to its decision in order to ensure that the undertakings concerned comply with the commitments they proposed to the Commission with a view to rendering the concentration compatible with the common market;[762]
(2) prohibit the concentration by declaring it incompatible with the common market,[763] where it significantly impedes competition, in particular as a result of the creation or strengthening of a dominant position.

In case the Commission does not take a decision within the time limits mentioned above, the concentration will be deemed to have been declared compatible with the common market.[764]

The Commission may revoke its decision on the same grounds as the ones mentioned for phase 1.[765]

---

760. Article 6(3) EUMR.
761. Article 10(4) EUMR.
762. Article 8(2) EUMR.
763. Article 8(3) EUMR.
764. Article 10(3) and (6) EUMR.
765. *See* Arts 6(3) and 8(6) EUMR.

B. Simplified Procedure

645. In some cases, where a concentration does not raise any substantive doubts, this concentration will be able to benefit from a simplified procedure.[766] The Commission Notice on a simplified procedure sets out the conditions for a special short-form decision, in which case the amount of time normally needed to complete the notification will be reduced. In case all conditions of the Notice are met and there are no special circumstances, then the Commission will adopt a decision within twenty-five working days from the date of notification.

C. Commitments

646. Articles 6(2) and 8(2) EUMR expressly provide that the Commission may decide to declare a concentration compatible with the internal market following modification by the parties, both before and after the initiation of proceedings. Such modifications are more commonly described as 'remedies' since their object is to eliminate the competition concerns identified by the Commission.

There are two different kinds of commitments: structural and behavioural ones. Behavioural commitments are commitments by one or more undertakings to behave or not to behave in a certain way on the market. Examples of this kind of commitments include an agreement by the new entity resulting from the concentration not to use a trade mark or to granting access to essential facilities on non-discriminatory terms. Structural commitments tend to be more permanent as they affect market structure. Examples of structural commitments include for example the divestiture of certain specific assets.

Whilst commitments have to be offered by the parties, the Commission may ensure the enforceability of commitments by making its authorization subject to compliance with them.

647. The Commission Notice on remedies provides some guidance on the general principles, the types of remedies, situations where remedies might be difficult, requirements for the submission of remedies and the practical implementation of remedies.[767]

---

766. Commission Notice on a simplified procedure for treatment of certain concentrations under Council Regulation (EC) No 139/2004Text with EEA relevance, *OJ* 2005, C 56/32.
767. Commission Notice on remedies acceptable under Council Regulation (EC) No 139/2004 and under Commission Regulation (EC) No 802/2004, *OJ* 2008, C 267/1.

D. Fines

648. In case of procedural infringements (such as supplying incorrect, misleading or incomplete information) or substantive infringements (such as failing to comply with a condition or obligation), the Commission may by decision impose fines up to 10% of the aggregate turnover of the undertaking concerned.[768]

E. Judicial Review

649. The parties to the concentration and third parties who demonstrate standing can lodge an appeal against a decision of the Commission before the GC pursuant to Article 263 TFEU. Judgments of the GC can be appealed, on points of law only, before the CJEU.

The Court of Justice has unlimited jurisdiction to review decisions whereby the Commission has imposed a fine or a periodic penalty payment. It can cancel or reduce or increase the fine or periodic penalty payment.[769]

F. Statistics, Publications and Future Reforms

650. DG COMP maintains up-to-date statistics regarding the number of notifications and the resulting decision adopted. It is interesting to note that the number of concentrations referred to the European Commission always increased from the 1990s until 2007 at the beginning of the economic and financial crisis where it peaked at 402 notified concentrations and then fell. This number is increasing again and reached 362 notified concentrations in 2016.

In the majority of cases the Commission approves notified concentration, although to an increasing extent subject to commitments by the parties. Since 1990 until the end of 2018 7,219 mergers have been notified and 157 have been examined by the Commission on request of Member States. A total of 6,378 mergers have been cleared in the first phase (of which 308 with commitments) and in 265 cases the second phase has been opened (with eventually 27 prohibitions and 128 approvals with commitments). The most recent prohibition of a merger by the Commission is Siemens' proposed acquisition of Alstom. The merger would have harmed competition in markets for railway signalling systems and very high-speed trains.[770]

Reports, studies and other publications reflecting on the functioning on various aspects of concentration control are often made available to the public on the website of DG COMP.

651. As to future reforms, the European Commission held a public consultation and published a White Paper in 2014 exploring ways to make merger control more

---

768. *See* Arts 14 and 15 EUMR.
769. Article 16 EUMR.
770. Commission press release of 6 February 2019.

effective including the possibility to have jurisdiction over the acquisition of non-controlling minority shareholdings. The Commission takes the view that the acquisition of a non-controlling minority shareholding may harm competition, and thus consumers, in similar ways i.e., horizontal, non-coordinated and vertical effects, as acquisitions of control falling in the scope of the EUMR. In order to fill this enforcement gap, the Commission has outlined three options consisting in: (i) a notification system, which would extend the current system of *ex ante* merger control to acquisitions of non-controlling minority shareholdings under certain conditions, (ii) a transparency system, which would require parties to submit an information notice informing the Commission of acquisitions of non-controlling minority shareholdings, and (iii) a self-assessment system, which would not require parties to notify acquisitions of non-controlling minority shareholdings in advance of completion. Under option (iii), the Commission could, however, initiate an investigation of potentially problematic minority shareholding acquisitions on the basis of its own market intelligence or complaints.

Time will tell if this ongoing reflection shall be implemented in a future modification of the EUMR.

§11. STATE AID

I. Introduction

652. The basic rules on EU State aid rules[771] are Articles 107 and 108 TFEU. The objective of State aid control is to prevent a detrimental subsidy race between Member States by prohibiting aid funded by public resources which distorts or threatens to distort competition by favouring certain undertakings or the production of certain goods insofar as it affects competition and trade between Member States in a harmful way.

Article 107(1) TFEU provides that any State aid that distorts competition and affects trade between Member States is incompatible with the internal market.[772]

653. Pursuant to Article 108 TFEU, the European Commission is entrusted with the task to control the grant of State aid. Article 108(3) TFEU contains a notification requirement: where a Member State (its government, local authorities or other public bodies) plans to grant new and/or to alter existing aid, the Member State must: (i) notify their plans to the Commission for prior approval (notification requirement), and (ii) they have to refrain from putting the proposed measures into effect until the Commission has taken a decision (standstill requirement).

---

771. For more detailed information on this subject, *see inter alia* L. Hancher, T. Ottervanger & P. Slot, *EC State Aids* (5th ed., Sweet & Maxwell 2016); C. Quigley & A. Collins, *EU State Aid Law and Policy* (3rd ed., Hart Publishing 2015); and the website of DG Competition.
772. State aid may be granted under the form of an individual aid or under the form of an aid scheme. For this § the use of words 'aid' or 'State aid' refers to both individual and aid scheme unless provided otherwise.

II. The Notion of State Aid

654. Articles 107 and 108 TFEU apply to state aid to 'undertakings', a notion that the same as for the application of Articles 101 and 102 TFEU and the merger rules. In *Scuola Elemenare Maria Montessori*[773]the (grand chamber of the) Court of justice found, with regard to educational activities, that courses provided by educational establishments financed essentially by private funds that do not come from the provider itself constitute services offered in the market and hence qualify these establishments as undertakings.

655. The Treaty does not define 'State aid'. State aid is a very similar concept to subsidy.[774] However, the concept of 'aid' emphasizes the purpose and seems especially devised for an objective which cannot normally be achieved without outside help. The concept of aid is thus wider than that of a grant of money because it embraces not only positive benefits, such as direct payments, but also interventions which, in various forms, mitigate the charges which are normally included in the budget of an undertaking and which, without, therefore being subsidies in the strict meaning of the word, are similar in character and have the same effect.[775]

656. In 2003, in the *Altmark* case,[776] examining whether compensation granted to undertakings in consideration for *public service obligations* imposed on them constituted State aid, the CJEU confirmed (*see* already Article 107(1) TFEU, discussed in paragraph 667) that to establish the existence of an aid 'First, there must be an intervention by the State or through State resources. Second, the intervention must be liable to affect trade between Member States. Third, it must confer an advantage on the recipient. Fourth, it must distort or threaten to distort competition.'[777]

657. In 2016, in the framework of the State Aid Modernisation programme, the Commission published a Communication on the notion of aid (the 'NOA Communication') which provides guidance to public administrations, undertakings and other stakeholders in order to identify whether a given measure constitutes State aid.[778] It carries the views of the Commission on a selected number of – sometimes novel – issues arising in the identification of State aid following overall the case law of the European Court.

---

773. Judgment of 6 November 2018, *Scuola Elementare Maria Montessori*, C-622/16 P to C-624/16 P, EU: C:2018:873.
774. The concept of 'subsidy' *senso strictu* is however limited to measures which fall within WTO rules.
775. Judgment of 23 February 1961, *De Gezamenlijke Steenkolenmijnen in Limburg v. High Authority of the European Coal and Steel Community*, C-30/59, EU:C:1961:2; Judgment of 7 March 2002, *Italian Republic v. Commission of the European Communities*, C-310/99, EU:C:2002:143, para. 51.
776. Judgment of 24 July 2003, *Altmark Trans*, C-280/00, ECLI:EU:C:2003:415.
777. *Ibid.*, *Altmark Trans*, para. 75.
778. Commission Notice on the notion of State aid as referred to in Art. 107(1) of the Treaty on the Functioning of the European Union, *OJ* 2016, C 262/1.

A. Conditions

658. Article 107(1) TFEU provides that a measure benefitting to an undertaking constitutes State Aid if the following cumulative conditions are fulfilled;[779]

a) the measure provides the undertaking(s) with an economic advantage it would not have received under the normal commercial conditions;
b) the measure is granted by an intervention of the State **and** through State resources;
c) the advantage is selective, i.e., it favours only certain undertaking(s) or certain productions ;
d) the advantage distorts or threatens to distort competition and it affects trade between Member States.

1. Existence of an Advantage

659. A measures will constitute aid if it mitigates the charges normally included in the budget of an undertaking. In case a public authority intervenes on the market as a guarantor, a shareholder, a lender or in another capacity in relationship with an undertaking, its action will only be likely to generate State aid if the conditions of State interventions do not mirror market conditions. In other words there is aid where the undertaking concerned receives an economic advantage which it would not have received under normal market circumstances.[780] This is often referred as the Market Economy Investor Principle or MEIP developed by the Court of Justice[781] and which is also applicable mutatis mutandis to the State acting as a creditor, a guarantor, etc., more recently called generically Market Economy Operator Principle (MEOP).

In *Commission v. FIH Holding*,[782] the Court of Justice clarified, in an appeal judgment, the MEOP concerning a measure taken by Denmark in 2009 to the benefit of a Danish bank that had suffered from the financial crisis.

---

779. *See also* the *Altmark* case mentioned above.
780. *See inter alia* Judgment of 10 July 1986, *Belgium v. Commission*, 40/85, ECLI:EU:C:1986:305, paras 13 et al.
781. Judgment of 2 February 1988, *Kwekerij Gebroeders van der Kooy BV v. Commission*, C-67/85, EU:C:1988:38.
782. Judgment of 6 March 2018 (Grand Chamber), *Commission v. FIH Holding*, C-579/16P, EU:C:2018:159.

2.   State Intervention

660. The concept of 'State' within the meaning of Article 107 TFEU is very broad. It does not only comprise the central authority but also regional or local government bodies, private undertakings dominated by the government, public undertakings, or an institution over which a decentralized government or a public undertaking has – directly or indirectly – a dominating influence.

3.   Transfer of State Resources

661. This condition implies that the measure must create a burden on public financial resources.

In the *Pearle* case,[783] the CJEU held that funds paid to a public body did not amount to State aid in the circumstances of the case which were the following. At the request of a private opticians' association, the Nederlandse Unie van Opticiens ('NUVO'), of which Pearle was a member, the Hoofdbedrijfschap Ambachten (Central Industry Board for Skilled Trades; 'the HBA'), a trade association governed by public law, imposed on its members a 'compulsory earmarked levy' to finance a collective advertising campaign for the undertakings in the sector.

Pearle and others brought an action against the HBA seeking annulment of the by-laws introducing the levies and reimbursement of the amounts paid. According to them, the services provided by means of the advertising campaigns constituted State aid, so that the by-laws which provided for their financing ought to have been notified to the Commission. The CJEU held that where a compulsory levy was paid to a public body at the initiative of a private association (NUVO) to cover the cost of a general advertising campaign, this did not constitute State aid since that public body (HBA) never had the power to use the resources (levies) freely.

That being said even in cases where the State does not make direct out of the pocket expenses with the tax payer's money, advantages received by undertakings with the involvement of a State body should always be carefully scrutinized with a view to determining whether there is no indirect aid granted by the State, i.e., where a body vested with public authority decides on allocation of money that originates from the treasury of the State. Indeed, the State can act through a great variety of instruments, such a public holding companies, funds, public private partnerships and so on.

4.   Selectivity

662. According to settled case law of the Court of Justice, the assessment of the selectivity condition requires a determination whether, under a particular legal regime, a national measure is such as to favour 'certain undertakings or the production of certain goods' over other undertakings which, in the light of the objective

---

783. Judgment of 15 July 2004, *Pearle*, C-345/02, ECLI:EU:C:2004:448.

pursued by that regime, are in a comparable factual and legal situation and who accordingly suffer different treatment that can, in essence, be classified as discriminatory.[784]

In principle, general measures which apply to all undertakings in the common market will not constitute State aid.

In situations where the measure at issue is conceived as an aid scheme and not as individual aid, the selectivity criterion is fulfilled where that measure, although it confers an advantage of general application, confers the benefit of that advantage exclusively on certain undertakings or certain sectors of activity.[785]

The Court of Justice has developed a specific three-step analysis in cases involving fiscal State aid.[786] First, the normal/ordinary tax regime (the reference framework) in the Member States concerned must be identified, in order to serve as a benchmark for establishing whether the measure under scrutiny is selective. Second, once the reference framework is identified, it is necessary to assess whether the measure constitutes a prima facie derogation by differentiating between economic operators that are in a comparable factual and legal situation in light of the objective assigned to the tax system of the Member State concerned.[787] Third, assuming this is the case, it is still possible to escape from the qualification of State aid where the derogation is justified by the nature and general scheme of the reference framework, i.e., whether the 'measure results directly from the basis or guiding principle of its tax system'[788] and '[ensures] that those [measures] are consistent with the principle of proportionality and do not go beyond what is necessary, in that the legitimate objective being pursued could not be attained by less farreaching measures'.[789]

A recent example where selectivity was deemed to be absent is the *A-Brauerei* case.[790]

The Grand Chamber of the Court held:

> (44) It should, however, be borne in mind, in the second place, that, according to the settled case-law of the Court, the concept of 'State aid' does not cover measures that differentiate between undertakings which, in the light of the objective pursued by the legal regime concerned, are in a comparable factual and legal situation, and are, therefore, a priori selective, where the Member

---

784. Judgments of 21 December 2016, *Commission v. World Duty Free Group SA, Banco Santander SA, Santusa Holding SL*, C-20/15 P et C21/15 P, EU:C:2016:981, para. 54 and cited case law.

785. Judgments of 21 December 2016, *Commission v. World Duty Free Group SA, Banco Santander SA, Santusa Holding SL*, C-20/15 P et C21/15 P, EU:C:2016:981, para. 55 and cited case law.

786. Judgment of 2 July 1974, *Italy v. Commission*, C-173/73, EU:C:1974:71, para. 15.

787. Judgment of 8 September 2011, *Paint Graphos and Others*, C-78/08, EU:C:2011:550, para. 49 and cited case law.

788. Judgment of 8 November 2001, *Adria-Wien Pipeline and Wietersdorfer & Peggauer Zementwerke*, C-143/11, EU:C:2001:598, para. 42.

789. Judgment in *Paint Graphos and others*, above, paras 73–75. *See* for reference purposes only the Commission Notice on the application of the State aid rules to measures relating to direct business taxation, *OJ* 1998, C 384/3, para. 12, now replaced by the Commission Notice on the notion of State aid as referred to in Art. 107(1) of the Treaty on the Functioning of the European Union (*OJ* 2016, C 262/1) and especially section 5.4., pp. 34–40.

790. Judgment of 19 December 2018, *A-Brauerei*, C-347/17, EU:C:2018:1024.

State concerned is able to demonstrate that that differentiation is justified since it flows from the nature or general structure of the system of which the measures form part (see judgment of 21 December 2016, Commission v World Duty Free Group and Others, C-20/15 P and C-21/15 P, EU:C:2016:981, paragraph 58 and the case-law cited).

The Court concluded, after an analysis of the German tax measure in question, that the tax advantage, which consists in exempting from real property transfer tax the transfer of ownership of a property which occurred because of a restructuring procedure involving only companies of the same group, linked by a shareholding of at least 95% during a minimum, uninterrupted period of five years prior to that procedure and of five years thereafter, does not fulfil the condition relating to the selectivity of the advantage concerned, laid down in Article 107(1) TFEU.

5. Distortion of Competition and Effect on Trade

663. To constitute State aid, a measure shall distort or threaten to distort competition and affect trade between Member States. The European Commission and the European Courts give a broad interpretation to the distortion of the market. The Court of Justice has acknowledged that it is only required to demonstrate that the aid in question is likely to distort competition without the need to undertake a full analysis of the market, and that trade must be affected by an aid if it strengthens the position of an undertaking compared to other competitors in the EU.[791] In other words, the threshold is quite low. But, on the other hand, the Commission has to show that it had examined those conditions in its analysis.[792]

B. De Minimis Measures

664. The *de minimis* Block Exemption regulation[793] provides that *de minimis* aid being aid granted to a single undertaking over a given period of time that does not exceed a certain fixed amount, is deemed not to meet all the criteria laid down in Article 107(1) TFEU and is therefore not subject to the notification procedure. The current *de minimis* block exemption regulation sets that, in principle, the total amount of *de minimis* aid granted per Member State to a single undertaking shall not exceed EUR 200,000 over any period of three fiscal years. This principle is subject to certain sectoral limitations and a specific threshold is provided for services of general economic interest.

---

791. Judgement of 30 April 2009, *Commission of the European Communities v. Italian Republic and Wam SpA.*, C-494/06 P, EU:C:2009:272, paras 50–51.
792. Judgment of 24 October 1996, *Federal Republic of Germany, Hanseatische Industrie-Beteiligungen GmbH and Bremer Vulkan Verbund AG v. Commission of the European Communities*, joined cases C-329/93, C-62/95 and C-63/95, EU:C:1996:394.
793. Commission Regulation (EU) No 1407/2013 of 18 December 2013 on the application of Arts 107 and 108 of the Treaty on the Functioning of the European Union to de minimis aid, *OJ* 2013, L 352/1.

C. Services of General Economic Interest

665. In 2003, in *Altmark*,[794] the CJEU had to rule on the question whether compensation granted to undertakings in consideration for public service obligations imposed on them constitutes State aid. According to the Court of Justice, such compensation does not constitute State aid in case four cumulative conditions are satisfied: (i) the recipient undertaking is actually required to discharge clearly defined public service obligations, (ii) the parameters for the calculation of the compensation must be established in advance in an objective and transparent manner, (iii) the compensation does not exceed what is necessary to cover all or part of the costs incurred in discharging the public service obligations, considering the relevant receipts and a reasonable profit for discharging these obligations, (iv) the undertaking which is to discharge public service obligations has to be either chosen in a public procurement procedure, or – when this is not the case – the level of compensation needed has to be determined on the basis of an analysis of the costs which a typical undertaking, well run so as to be able to meet the necessary public service requirements, would have incurred in discharging those obligations, taking into account the relevant receipts and a reasonable profit for discharging the obligations.

Following the *Altmark* case, the Commission adopted successive packages in order to define the conditions under which State aid in the form of public service compensation can be considered compatible with the EU rules.

The current package includes a *de minimis* Regulation[795] setting that *de minimis* aid granted to any one undertaking providing services of general economic interest below a threshold of EUR 500,000 over any period of three fiscal years, is deemed not to be aid and is exempt from the notification requirement. The package also contains a decision[796] and a framework[797] specifying the conditions under which State aid in the form of public service compensation is compatible with the internal market and a communication clarifying key concepts related to State aid for SGEIs.[798]

---

794. Judgment of 24 July 2003, *Altmark Trans*, C-280/00, ECLI:EU:C:2003:415.
795. Commission Regulation on the application of Arts 107 and 108 of the Treaty on the Functioning of the European Union to *de minimis* aid granted to undertakings providing services of general economic interest, *OJ* 2012, L 114/8.
796. Commission Decision of 20 December on the application of Art. 106(2) of the Treaty on the Functioning of the European Union to State aid in the form of public service compensation granted to certain undertakings entrusted with the operation of services of general economic interest, *OJ* L 7, 11.1.2012, pp. 3–10.
797. Communication from the Commission, European Union framework for State aid in the form of public service compensation (2011), *OJ* 2012, C8/15.
798. Communication from the Commission on the application of the European Union State aid rules to compensation granted for the provision of services of general economic interest *OJ* 2012, C8/4.

III. Exemptions

666. In case an aid is incompatible with Article 107(1) TFEU, it may nevertheless benefit from an exemption under Article 107(2) or (3) TFEU or obtain an individual exemption under Article 108 TFEU. All exceptions must be interpreted narrowly since they are derogations from the general principle of the prohibition of the grant of State aid.

A. *The Automatic Exemptions under Article 107(2) TFEU*

667. Notification of State aid to the Commission (*see* hereafter) is required even if the State aid later benefits from one of the exemptions of Article 107(2) TFEU. However, once the Commission considers that the aid falls into one of the three categories of Article 107(2) TFEU, exemption will be automatic. The three categories are the following:

(1) Article 107(2)(a) TFEU: aid of a social character granted to individual consumers and not resulting in an indirect benefit for undertakings.

This category includes aid with a social purpose. It must target a specific group of individuals of the population of a Member State.[799] This exemption shall not be used either to favour national production of goods or services via a financial support a certain group of individuals in the purchase of certain products or services.[800]

(2) Article 107(2)(b): aid to make good damage caused by natural disasters or exceptional occurrences.

This category includes aid designed to alleviate the negative impact of natural disasters (hurricanes, tornadoes, forest fires, seismic activity such as earthquakes and volcanic eruption, natural diseases affecting natural life forms such as BSE crises, etc.) as well as cases of force majeure (war, serious internal disturbances and tensions, terrorist attacks such as 9/11 events, nuclear and radiation incidents, etc.) To be exempted under this category, an aid must display a direct link with the damage caused by the natural disaster or case of force majeure and it must be limited to what is necessary to compensate the harm suffered by the beneficiaries of the aid.[801]

(3) Article 107(2)(c): aid for certain areas of the Federal Republic of Germany.

Article 107(2)(c) TFEU considered 'aid granted to the economy of certain areas of the Federal Republic of Germany affected by the division of Germany, in so far as such aid is required to compensate for the economic disadvantages caused by that division' to be compatible with the internal market and thus

---

799. Judgment of 4 March 2009, *Associazione italiana del risparmio gestito and Fineco Asset Management SpA v. Commission of the European Communities*, T-445/05, EU:T:2009:50.

800. Regarding aid of a social character regarding the transport of residents of remote regions, *see* Art. 51 of Commission Regulation 651/2014 (the 'Block Exemption Regulation' or 'GBER').

801. Judgment of 25 June 2008, *Olympiaki Aeroporia Ypiresies AE v. Commission of the European Communities*, T-268/06, EU:T:2008:222. The current Block Exemption Regulation 651/2014 provides detailed conditions of exemption including eligible costs for this category of aid under Art. 50.

regarded as an exemption. This provision was designed to be inherently applicable during a limited period. In *Germany v. Commission*,[802] the Court of Justice confirmed that this exception shall be restrictively construed and limited to make good the economic disadvantages caused by the isolation of certain regions and not to compensate for their economic backwardness compared to the whole of West Germany, due to the different political and economic systems of the two German States between 1949 and 1990.

In practice, the Commission indicates that the bulk of the aid was granted between 1960 and the time of German unification under the German 'Berlin promotion law' and the 'Border area promotion law' schemes, in favour of West Berlin and the border areas of West Germany, to Czechoslovakia and the German Democratic Republic (GDR). After the reunification, aid was actually granted on the basis of Article 107(2)(c) in only two cases: in West Berlin (Daimler-Benz, Potsdamer Platz) in 1992 and in Bavaria (Tettauer Winkel) in 1994.

B.   The Available Exemptions under Article 107(3) TFEU

668.   The categories of aid provided in Article 107(3) TFEU *may be* compatible with the internal market if the Commission, upon notification of these measures, approves them. There are four categories of possible exemption in Article 107(3) TFEU:

(1) Article 107(3)(a) TFEU: aid to certain regions where the standard of living is abnormally low or where there is serious underdevelopment.
     This category includes regional aid which aim at improving the economic situation (e.g., reduction of unemployment) of regions which display a clear disadvantage compared to the whole EU, e.g., less than the threshold of 75% of the average Gross domestic product (GDP) in the EU as used in the Regional Guidelines.[803]
(2) Article 107(3)(b) TFEU: aid to promote an important project of common European interest or to remedy a serious disturbance in the economy of a Member State.
     This category includes on the one hand an exemption that is limited to aid supporting projects which by their nature and description are of common European interest and are included in a transnational European programme supported by several Member States to address common issues. The eligibility conditions are described in Communication of the Commission.[804]

---

802. Judgment of 19 September 2000, *Federal Republic of Germany v. Commission of the European Communities*, Case C-156/98, EU:C:2000:46, para. 52.
803. *See* para. 150 of the Guidelines on regional State aid for 2014–2020, *OJ* 2014, 198/30.
804. Communication from the Commission – Criteria for the analysis of the compatibility with the internal market of State aid to promote the execution of important projects of common European interest, *OJ* 2014, C 188/4.

On the other hand, this category encompasses aid which is designed to remedy a serious disturbance in the economy of a Member State. The use of this category was quite marginal until the 2007 economic and financial crisis during which it constituted the basis of most State aid intervention in favour of the banking and financial sectors.

(3) Article 107(3)(c) TFEU: aid to facilitate the development of certain economic activities or of certain economic areas.

This category includes all forms of regional aid and is larger in scope than the exemption available under Article 107(3)(a) TFEU because the benchmarks against which the economic situation of a region is assessed is the national average.[805] The Commission considers that the purpose of regional State aid is to support economic development and employment. To meet these objectives, the Commission has clarified the eligibility conditions in successive versions of the regional aid guidelines to help Member States support investments in new production facilities in the less advantaged regions of Europe or modernize existing facilities. The guidelines are also based on regional aid maps drawn up by Member States delineating the geographical areas where companies can receive regional State aid, and at which intensities.[806]

(4) Article 107(3)(d) TFEU: aid to promote culture and heritage conservation.

This exemption includes aid related to the objectives pursued by Article 167 TFEU, including the flowering of the cultures of the Member States, while respecting their national and regional diversity and at the same time bringing the common cultural heritage to the fore in the areas of improvement of the knowledge and dissemination of the culture and history of the European peoples, conservation and safeguarding of cultural heritage of European significance, non-commercial cultural exchanges and artistic and literary creation, including in the audiovisual sector. The eligibility conditions are outlined in Article 52 of the General Block Exemption Regulation 651/2014.

(5) Article 107(3)(e) TFEU: other categories of aid specified by the Council.

This exemption constitutes an example of power that the Council was retained in order to be able to exempt certain aid measures at its discretion. This was notably the case for aid measure to facilitate the close of uncompetitive coal mines.[807] It should be noted that pursuant to Article 107(3)(e) TFE, this power of the Council is subject to the submission of a proposal from the Commission.

C. Article 109 TFEU: Block Exemptions

669. In a concern to modernize and simplify State aid control, the Council authorized the Commission to adopt so-called Block Exemption Regulations for

---

805. Judgment of 14 October 1987, *Federal Republic of Germany v. Commission of the European Communities*, C-284/84, EU:C:1987:437.
806. *See* for example the overview of regional maps for the period 1 January 2018 – 31 December 2020 available at http://ec.europa.eu/competition/state_aid/regional_aid/regional_aid_2018_2020.pdf, last accessed on 5 January 2017.
807. *See* notably the German Coal mine closure plan N708/2007, *OJ* C 284, 20.9.2012.

State aid.[808] With these regulations, the Commission can declare specific categories of State aid compatible with the internal market if they fulfil certain conditions, thus exempting Members States from the requirement of prior notification and Commission approval.[809] Limited reporting obligations remain in order to ensure transparency to the public of the grant of State aid by Member States and to facilitate the monitoring by the Commission.[810]

670. The Commission has adopted several Block Exemption Regulations on the basis of that delegation. Today there is a General Block Exemption Regulation covering aid to SMEs and their financing, aid for research & development, aid for training, aid for disadvantaged workers and for workers with disabilities, aid for environmental protection, aid to make good the damage caused by certain natural disasters, social aid for transport for residents of remote regions, aid for broadband infrastructures, aid for culture and heritage conservation, aid for sport and multifunctional recreational infrastructures, aid for local infrastructures;[811] a block exemption regulation for the agricultural and forestry sectors and in rural areas,[812] etc.

D. Additional Guidance Provided by the European Commission

671. In addition to indications provided in block exemption regulations, the Commission has issued numerous communications and notices to provide guidance to stakeholders to assess whether a measure constitutes State aid and, if so whether it may be compatible with the internal market. These soft law instruments are only binding on the Commission but they constitute an important source of information for stakeholders to help them decide whether a measure shall be subject to the notification requirement and, for Member States and public administrations, how measures shall ideally be designed to be declared compatible with the internal market.

---

808. Council Regulation (EC) No 1588/2015 of 13 July 2015 on the application of Arts 107 and 108 of the Treaty on the Functioning of the European Union to certain categories of horizontal State aid, *OJ* 2015, L 248/1. This regulation replaced as of 14 October 2015 Council Regulation (EC) No 994/98 of 7 May 1998 on the application of Arts 92 and 93 (now 87 and 88 respectively) of the Treaty establishing the European Community to certain categories of horizontal State aid, *OJ* 1998, L 142/ 1, as amended.
809. Regulation (EC) No 994/98 of 7 May 1998.
810. Pursuant to Arts 10–12 of Regulation No 651/2014 (*see* further in the text), Member States have the obligation to comply with the transparency provisions of GBER 651/14. In practical terms this means that Member State have to publish information on their national or regional transparency website on individual aid awards above EUR 500,000 that were awarded after 1 July 2016 and that they have to send an information sheet to the Commission including the full text of the aid.
811. Commission Regulation (EU) No 651/2014 of 17 June 2014 declaring certain categories of aid compatible with the internal market in application of Arts 107 and 108 of the Treaty, *OJ* 2014, L 187/7.
812. Commission Regulation (EU) No 702/2014 of 25 June 2014 declaring certain categories of aid in the agricultural and forestry sectors and in rural areas compatible with the internal market in application of Arts 107 and 108 of the Treaty on the Functioning of the European Union, *OJ* 2014, L 193/75.

672. Current communications and notices include guidance on the identification of aid,[813] temporary rules established in response to the economic and financial crisis,[814] important projects of common European interests,[815] aid to disadvantages and disabled workers,[816] training aid,[817] regional aid,[818] research and development and innovation,[819] environmental aid,[820] risk capital,[821] rescue and restructuring aid,[822] sector-specific rules for agriculture,[823] audiovisual production,[824] broadcasting,[825]

---

813. Commission Notice on the notion of State aid as referred to in Art. 107(1) of the Treaty on the Functioning of the European Union, *OJ* 2016, C 262/50.

814. Since the beginning of the financial crisis, the Commission adopted six 'Crisis Communications' adopted on the basis of Art. 107(3)(b) of the Treaty, which exceptionally allowed for aid to remedy a serious disturbance in the economy of a Member State. They which have provided provide a comprehensive framework for coordinated action in support of the financial sector so as to ensure financial stability while minimizing distortions of competition between banks and across Member States in the single market. It replaces from 1 August 2013, previous rules to support measures in favour of banks in the context of the financial crisis, (*OJ* 2013, C 216/1), now sets out the necessary adaptations to the parameters for the compatibility of crisis-related State aid to banks as from 1 August 2013. In particular, this Communication: (a) replaces the 2008 Banking Communication, and provides guidance on the compatibility criteria for liquidity support; (b) adapts and complements the Recapitalisation and Impaired Assets Communications; (c) supplements the Restructuring Communication by providing more detailed guidance on burden sharing by shareholders and subordinated creditors; (d) establishes the principle that no recapitalization or asset protection measure can be granted without prior authorization of a restructuring plan, and proposes a procedure for the permanent authorization of such measures; (e) provides guidance on the compatibility requirements for liquidation aid.

815. Communication from the Commission – Criteria for the analysis of the compatibility with the internal market of State aid to promote the execution of important projects of common European interest, *OJ* 2014, C 188/4.

816. Communication from the Commission – Criteria for the compatibility analysis of State aid to disadvantaged and disabled workers subject to individual notification, *OJ* 2009, C 188/6.

817. Communication from the Commission – Criteria for the compatibility analysis of training State aid cases subject to individual notification, *OJ* 2009, C 188/1.

818. Guidelines on regional State aid for 2014–2020 and Communication from the Commission amending Annex I to the Guidelines on regional aid for 2014–2020, *OJ* 2016, C231/1.

819. Framework for State aid for research and development and innovation *OJ* 2014, C 198/1.

820. Guidelines on State aid for environmental protection and energy 2014–2020, *OJ* 2014, C 200/1.

821. Guidelines on risk finance aid for 2014–2020, *OJ* 2014, C19/4.

822. Guidelines on State aid for rescuing and restructuring non-financial undertakings in difficulty, *OJ* 2014, C 249/1.

823. European Union Guidelines for State aid in the agricultural and forestry sectors and in rural areas 2014 to 2020, *OJ* 2014, C 204/1.

824. Guidelines for the application of State aid rules in relation to the rapid deployment of broadband networks, *OJ* 2013, C25/1.

825. Communication from the Commission on the application of State aid rules to public service broadcasting, *OJ* 2009, C 257/1.

electricity,[826] postal service,[827] shipbuilding,[828] steel,[829] transport; State guarantees,[830] export-credit insurance,[831] services of general Economic interest.[832]

IV. Procedure Before the European Commission

A. Obligation to Notify

673. Article 108(3) TFEU provides that Member States are in principle (i) obliged to notify their intended State aid measures to the Commission and (ii) not to implement them before the Commission takes a final decision. The prohibition to implement an aid also applies in case the aid was not notified.

The applicable rules for a notification are included in Procedural Regulation 2015/1589[833] and the forms and practical instructions are included in Implementing Regulation 2015/2282.[834]

In practice, the notification must be transmitted to the Commission (addressed to the Secretary General) by the Permanent Representative of the Member State concerned. Since 1 January 2006 notifications must be transmitted electronically to the Commission, unless otherwise agreed by the Commission and the notifying Member State. All correspondence in connection with a notification submitted after 1 January 2006 also has to be transmitted electronically.

The notification contains detailed questions about the aid such as the objectives of the aid, the beneficiaries, the amount of the aid or the annual expenditure, etc.

However, as mentioned above, there is an exception to this principle: Member States are relieved from the notification obligation when aid measure may be exempted under a block exemption regulation.

The consequences of the failure to comply with the notification requirement pursuant to Article 108(3) TFEU are described in section D.

---

826. Commission Communication relating to the methodology for analysing State aid linked to stranded costs, Commission letter SG (2001) D/290869 of 6 August 2001.
827. Notice from the Commission on the application of the competition rules to the postal sector and on the assessment of certain State measures relating to postal services, *OJ* 1998, C 39/2.
828. Framework on State aid for shipbuilding, *OJ* 2001, C 364/9.
829. *See* the list available on the website of DG COMP at http://ec.europa.eu/competition/state_aid/le gislation/specific_rules.html, last accessed on 6 January 2017.
830. Commission Notice on the application of Arts 87 and 88 of the EC Treaty to State aid in the form of guarantees, *OJ* 2008, C 155/10.
831. Communication from the Commission amending the Annex to the Communication to the Member States on the application of Arts 107 and 108 of the Treaty on the Functioning of the European Union to short-term export-credit insurance, *OJ* 2016, C244/1.
832. *See* paras 549 et seq on SGEI.
833. Council Regulation (EU) 2015/1589 of 13 July 2015 laying down detailed rules for the application of Art. 108 of the Treaty on the Functioning of the European Union, *OJ* 2015, L 248/9 (which replaces as of 14 October 2015 Council Regulation No 659/1999 of 22 March 1999 laying down detailed rules for the application of Art. 108 of the Treaty on the Functioning of the European Union, *OJ* 1999, L 83/1, as amended).
834. Commission Regulation (EU) 2015/2282 of 27 November 2015 amending Regulation (EC) No 794/2004 as regards the notification forms and information sheets, *OJ* 2015, L 325/180.

B. Decisions of the Commission

674. Once the Commission has received the notification of the intended aid measure, it will conduct a preliminary examination within a period of two months and at the end of which, it must take one of the following decisions:[835]

– decision that the notified measure does not constitute aid;
– decision not to raise objections (clearance decision); or
– decision to initiate the formal investigation procedure.

These decisions are published in the Official Journal.

Where the Commission has not taken a decision within two months, the aid will be deemed to have been authorized by the Commission.[836]

In case of a decision to initiate the formal investigation procedure, this decision will contain a summary of the relevant issues of fact and law and the Commission's doubt as to the compatibility of the measure with the State aid rules. The decision will invite the Member State and interested parties (e.g., the recipient firm) to submit comments within a prescribed period which will normally not exceed a month.

There are no strict time limits for the Commission to adopt a final decision though the Procedural Regulation provides that the Commission will as far as possible endeavour to adopt a decision within a period of eighteen months from the opening of the procedure.[837]

At the end of the formal procedure, the final decision of the Commission may be a clearance decision, a decision to prohibit the measure or a decision to clear the measure subject to conditions and obligations.[838]

C. Complaint to the European Commission

675. The Commission takes the view that complaints constitute an essential source of information for detecting infringement to State aid rules. Pursuant to Article 108(2) TFEU and of Article 1(h) of Procedural Regulation 2015/1589, interested parties, i.e., any Member State and any person, undertaking or association of undertakings whose interests might be affected by the granting of aid, in particular the beneficiary of the aid, competing undertakings and trade associations may submit complaints containing a required number of information via an online portal[839] or a form to fill[840] regarding unlawful aid and set in motion an investigation of the Commission.

---

835. Article 4 of Procedural Regulation 2015/1589.
836. Article 4(6) Procedural Regulation.
837. Article 7(6) of Procedural Regulation 2015/1589.
838. Article 9 of Procedural Regulation 2015/1589.
839. *See* http://ec.europa.eu/competition/forms/sa_complaint_en.html, last on accessed 1 January 2017.
840. *See* http://ec.europa.eu/competition/forms/download_en.html, last on accessed 1 January 2017.

D. Recovery of Aid

676. In case the Member States do not notify the aid or in case they grant aid before the Commission has taken a decision, the aid will be 'unlawful'. In most cases, the Commission will have knowledge of 'unlawful' aid through complaints[841] or via publicly available information.

The Commission may order suspension or recovery of an unlawful aid by an injunction,[842]

The Commission will review unlawful aid under the formal procedure to assess whether they may be exempted. The Commission indicated in a communication that it shall always assess the compatibility of unlawful State aid with the internal market in accordance with the substantive criteria set out in any instrument in force at the time when the aid was granted.[843]

Where unlawful aid cannot be exempted, the Commission will issue a negative decision ordering recovery of the aid to the Member State. The CJEU underlined that the recovery of unlawful and incompatible aid is not a penalty, but the logical consequence of the finding that it is unlawful.[844]

To improve the effectiveness of recovery of aid at national level, the Commission issued a communication summarizing the principles applicable to recovery.[845] It provides guidance notably regarding the identification of beneficiaries from which the aid shall be recovered, the specific issue of insolvent beneficiaries and the determination of the amount subject to recovery.

677. The principles applicable to recovery include: (i) that recovery is not required by the Commission if it would be contrary to a general principle of Union law, (ii) recovery decisions impose an obligation on the Member State to take all necessary measures to recover the aid from the beneficiary, (iii) in addition to the amount of the aid, an interest shall be paid from the date on which the unlawful aid was at the disposal of the beneficiary until the date of its recovery.

The Procedural Regulation provides that recovery shall be effected without delay and in accordance with the procedures under the national law of the Member State concerned, if they allow the immediate and effective execution of the Commission's decision.[846]

---

841. *See* section C above.

842. Pursuant to Art. 13 of Procedural Regulation 2015/1589, the Commission may, after giving the Member State concerned the opportunity to submit its comments, adopt a decision requiring the Member State to suspend any unlawful aid until the Commission has taken a decision on the compatibility of the aid with the internal market. Alternatively, the Commission may order recovery if the following criteria are met: (i) according to an established practice there are no doubts about the aid character of the measure concerned, (ii) there is an urgency to act, (iii) there is a serious risk of substantial and irreparable damage to a competitor.

843. Commission notice on the determination of the applicable rules for the assessment of unlawful State aid (notified under document number C (2002) 458), *OJ* 2002, C 119/22.

844. Judgment of 10 June 1993, *Commission v. Greece*, Case C-183/91, EU:C:1993:233, para. 16.

845. Notice from the Commission – Towards an effective implementation of Commission decisions ordering Member States to recover unlawful and incompatible State aid, *OJ* 2007, C 272/4.

846. Article 16(3) of Procedural Regulation 2015/1589.

To guarantee legal certainty, the Procedural Regulation provides for a period of limitation of ten years with regard to unlawful aid, after the expiry of which no recovery can be ordered by the Commission and any aid with regard to which the limitation period has expired shall be deemed to be existing aid.[847] This limitation period begins on the day on which the unlawful aid is awarded to the beneficiary either as individual aid or as aid under an aid scheme. It is worth noting that any action taken by the Commission or by a Member State, acting at the request of the Commission, about the unlawful aid shall interrupt the limitation period. Each interruption shall start time running afresh. In addition, the limitation period shall be suspended for as long as the decision of the Commission is the subject of proceedings pending before the CJEU.

Finally, it is important to note that challenging a negative decision of the Commission ordering recovery before the GC pursuant to Article 263 TFEU does not have automatically a suspensive effect, unless the suspension is asked for.

E. Procedure Before National Courts

678. In its 2005 State Aid Action Plan, the European Commission highlighted the importance of the role of national courts in the framework of the private enforcement of State aid rules at national level.[848] A 2006 study commissioned by the European Commission revealed that the number of legal challenges, notably initiated by competitors, aimed at enforcing compliance with the State aid rules was relatively small.[849] In order to boost private enforcement, the Commission issued a communication to help national courts enforce State aid rules.[850]

First, national courts have a role to play to enforce the standstill obligation contained in Article 108(3) TFEU in cases where an undertaking challenges the grant of State support which it considers to amount to State aid to a competing beneficiary. Remedies available before national courts include: (i) preventing the payment of unlawful aid; (ii) recovery of unlawful aid (regardless of compatibility); (iii) recovery of illegality interest; (iv) damages for competitors and other third parties; and (v) interim measures against unlawful aid.

Those powers of national courts exist until the Commission adopts a final decision. Indeed, an investigation before the Commission may run at the same time, e.g., based on a complaint submitted by the same competitor. In practice, to avoid potentially conflicting decisions, national courts will usually wait for the outcome of the review of the Commission but adopt interim measures to protect the interests of all

---

847. Article 17 of Procedural Regulation 2015/1589.
848. State Aid Action Plan: Less and better targeted State aid: a roadmap for State aid reform 2005–2009, COM(2005) 107 final.
849. Available at http://ec.europa.eu/comm/competition/state_aid/studies_reports/studies_reports.cfm The 2006 study only covered EU-15 and was updated in 2009 notably to cover EU-27, *see* http://ec.europa.eu/competition/state_aid/studies_reports/enforcement_study_2009.pdf, last accessed on 6 January 2017.
850. Commission notice on the enforcement of State aid law by national courts, *OJ* 2009, C 85/1.

parties in the meantime. In '*CELF*', the CJEU clarified that the national court's obligation to order full recovery of unlawful State aid ceases if, by the time the national court renders its judgment, the Commission has already decided that the aid is compatible with the common market.[851]

Second, national courts also play an important role to enforce recovery decisions adopted by the Commission under the Procedural regulation, where the Commission's assessment concludes that unlawful aid is incompatible with the internal market and enjoins the Member State concerned to recover it from the beneficiary. National courts are also involved by beneficiaries which usually lodge actions for review of the legality of the repayment request issued by national authorities.[852]

F. Procedure Before the Court of Justice

679. In principle, under Article 263 TFEU all decisions and procedural conducts of the Commission in application of State aid rules are subject to review by the GC (full review) and ultimately by the ECJ on grounds of law only.

Appeals before the GC[853] and before the Court of Justice[854] are subject to standing requirements and shall comply with the respective rules on procedures.

The Court of Justice also supplements State aid rules through numerous rulings issued in response to references for preliminary rulings made in the framework of proceedings before national courts under Article 267 TFEU.

---

851. Judgment of 12 February 2008, *CELF and Ministre de la Culture et de la Communication*, Case C-199/06, EU:C:2008:79, paras 45, 46 and 55.
852. Commission notice on the enforcement of State aid law by national courts, *OJ* C 85, 9.4.2009, para. 21.
853. Rules of Procedure of the General Court of 4 March 2015 (*OJ* 2015, L105/1), amended on 13 July 2016 (*OJ* 2016, L 217/1).
854. Rules of Procedure of the Court of Justice of 25 September 2012 (*OJ* 2012, L 265), as amended on 18 June 2013 (*OJ* 2013, L 173/65) and on 19 July 2016 (*OJ* 2016, L 217/69).

Chapter 2. The Economic and Monetary Union

680. Provisions on the progressive establishment of an EMU were inserted in the EC Treaty in 1993 by the Treaty of Maastricht. A timetable and criteria were set for accession to the monetary union. The most notable aspect of the EMU is the introduction of a single currency, the EURO. Not all Member States could or wanted to adopt the EURO. Today only seventeen of the twenty-eight Member States of the EU are member of the monetary union. A notable non-member is the UK, which, much later, in a referendum in 2016, decided to leave the EU altogether (according to a timetable that had not yet been set at the moment that this monograph went to press). The definitive phase of the EMU started on 1 January 1999, with the launch of the EURO and the creation of the ECB (in Frankfort). A cornerstone for the EMU was the full liberalization of capital markets (for all EU Member States) by the Treaty of Maastricht (as explained above capital markets had already been largely liberalized on the basis of a Directive of 1991). Since the financial crisis of 2008 and the ensuing Euro crisis that started in 2009, the future of the EURO is constantly challenged by financial markets and politicians.

681. Article 119 TFEU contains the basic principles of the EMU:

(1) For the purposes set out in Article 3 of the TEU, the activities of the Member States and the Union shall include, as provided in the Treaties, the adoption of an economic policy which is based on the close coordination of Member States' economic policies, on the internal market and on the definition of common objectives, and conducted in accordance with the principle of an open market economy with free competition.

(2) Concurrently with the foregoing, and as provided in the Treaties and in accordance with the procedures set out therein, these activities shall include a single currency, the euro, and the definition and conduct of a single monetary policy and exchange-rate policy the primary objective of both of which shall be to maintain price stability and, without prejudice to this objective, to support the general economic policies in the Union, in accordance with the principle of an open market economy with free competition.

(3) These activities of the Member States and the Union shall entail compliance with the following guiding principles: stable prices, sound public finances and monetary conditions and a sustainable balance of payments. As to the Economic policy, Article 120 TFEU provides that Member States shall conduct their economic policies with a view to contributing to the achievement of the objectives of the Union, as defined in Article 3 of the TEU, and in the context of the broad guidelines referred to in Article 121(2). The Member States and the Union shall act in accordance with the principle of an open market economy with free competition, favouring an efficient allocation of resources. Pursuant to Article 121(1) TFEU, Member States shall regard their economic policies as a matter of common concern and shall coordinate them within the Council, in accordance with the provisions of Article 120. Article 121(2) continues that the Council shall, on a recommendation from the Commission, formulate a draft for the *broad guidelines* of the economic policies of the Member

States and of the Union, and shall report its findings to the European Council which then adopts the broad guidelines. *See* presently Council Recommendation 2010/410/EU of 13 July 2010 on broad guidelines for the economic policies of the Member States and of the Union.[855]

682. There are six broad guidelines, of which only the essence is given here:

(1) *Ensuring the quality and the sustainability of public finances*: obligation to implement budgetary consolidation strategies under the Stability and Growth Pact (SGP) and, in particular, recommendations addressed to Member States under the excessive deficit procedure, and/or in memoranda of understanding, in the case of balance-of-payments support.

(2) *Addressing macroeconomic imbalances:* Member States should avoid unsustainable macroeconomic imbalances, arising notably from developments in current accounts, asset markets and the balance sheets of the household and corporate sectors (including adequate wage setting, in the context of which the social partners have an important role to play).

(3) *Reducing imbalances within the euro area*: Member States whose currency is the euro should regard large and persistent divergences in current account positions and other macroeconomic imbalances as a matter of common concern and take urgent action to reduce the imbalances where necessary. Macroeconomic imbalances should be closely monitored within the Eurogroup, which should propose remedial actions when needed.

(4) *Optimizing support for R & D and innovation, strengthening the knowledge triangle and unleashing the potential of the digital economy:* the EU headline target, on the basis of which Member States will set their national targets, is to improve the conditions for research and development, in particular with the aim of bringing combined public and private investment levels in this sector to 3% of GDP by 2020. The Commission will elaborate an indicator reflecting R & D and innovation intensity.

(5) *Improving resource efficiency and reducing greenhouse gases*: the EU headline target, on the basis of which Member States will set their national targets, is to reduce by 2020 greenhouse gas emissions by 20% compared to 1990 levels; to increase the share of renewable energy sources in our final energy consumption to 20%; and moving towards a 20% increase in energy efficiency; the Union is committed to take a decision to move to a 30% reduction by 2020 compared to 1990 levels as its conditional offer with a view to a global and comprehensive agreement for the period beyond 2012, provided that other developed countries commit themselves to comparable emission reductions and developing countries contribute adequately according to their responsibilities and respective capabilities.

(6) *Improving the business and consumer environment, and modernizing and developing the industrial base in order to ensure the full functioning of the internal market:* Member States should ensure that markets work for citizens,

---

855. *OJ* 2010, L 191/28.

consumers and businesses. The external dimension of the internal market should be further developed with the aim of enhanced trade and investment.

683. The Treaty also provides for a sanctions in case a Member State does not respect the broad guidelines. Where it is established, that the economic policies of a Member State are not consistent with the broad guidelines or that they risk jeopardizing the proper functioning of EMU, the Commission may address a warning to the Member State concerned. The Council, on a recommendation from the Commission, may address the necessary recommendations to the Member State concerned. The Council may, on a proposal from the Commission, decide to make its recommendations public. The Council, on a proposal from the Commission, may decide, in a spirit of solidarity between Member States, upon the measures appropriate to the economic situation, in particular if severe difficulties arise in the supply of certain products, notably in the area of energy. Where a Member State is in difficulties or is seriously threatened with severe difficulties caused by natural disasters or exceptional occurrences beyond its control, the Council, on a proposal from the Commission, may grant, under certain conditions, Union financial assistance to the Member State concerned. The President of the Council shall inform the EP of the decision taken (*see* Article 122).

684. Article 126 TFEU relates to excessive government deficits, which the Member States shall avoid. The Commission shall monitor the development of the budgetary situation and of the stock of government debt in the Member States with a view to identifying gross errors. In particular, it shall examine compliance with budgetary discipline on the basis of the following two criteria:

(1) whether the ratio of the planned or actual government deficit to gross domestic product exceeds a reference value, unless:
  – either the ratio has declined substantially and continuously and reached a level that comes close to the reference value;
  – or, alternatively, the excess over the reference value is only exceptional and temporary and the ratio remains close to the reference value.
(2) whether the ratio of government debt to gross domestic product exceeds a reference value, unless the ratio is sufficiently diminishing and approaching the reference value at a satisfactory pace.

The reference values are specified in the Protocol on the excessive deficit procedure annexed to the Treaties.

685. If a Member State does not fulfil the requirements under one or both of these criteria, the Commission shall prepare a report. The Economic and Financial Committee shall formulate an opinion on the report of the Commission. If the Commission considers that an excessive deficit in a Member State exists or may occur, it shall address an opinion to the Member State concerned and shall inform the Council accordingly. The Council decides. Where the Council decides that an excessive deficit exists, it shall adopt, without undue delay, on a recommendation from the Commission, recommendations addressed to the Member State concerned with

a view to bringing that situation to an end within a given period. Where it establishes that there has been no effective action in response to its recommendations
within the period laid down, the Council may make its recommendations public. If
a Member State persists in failing to put into practice the recommendations of the
Council, the Council may decide to give notice to the Member State to take, within
a specified time limit, measures for the deficit reduction which is judged necessary
by the Council in order to remedy the situation. As long as a Member State fails to
comply with a decision taken, the Council may decide to apply or, as the case may
be, intensify one or more of the following measures:

– to require the Member State concerned to publish additional information, to be
  specified by the Council, before issuing bonds and securities;
– to invite the European Investment Bank to reconsider its lending policy towards
  the Member State concerned;
– to require the Member State concerned to make a non-interest-bearing deposit of
  an appropriate size with the Union until the excessive deficit has, in the view of
  the Council, been corrected;
– to impose fines of an appropriate size.

For the nineteen Member States that adopted the euro, the ECB is the central bank
(in Frankfort). The ECB's general mission is to safeguard the value of the euro and
maintain price stability.

The ECB's primary task is the monetary policy for the countries of the euro area,
but it is also responsible for the prudential supervision of banks located in the euro
area. Large banks are supervised by the ECB.

In addition in 2014, the Single resolution Board[856] was established to respond to
the EURO area crisis. It is one of the pillars of the European Banking Union, and
its task is to avoid bail-out and worst-case scenarios in the banking sector.

---

856. Regulation (EU) No 806/2014, *OJ* 2014, L 225/1.

Chapter 3. The External Action of the Union

§1. Treaty Provisions on External Relations: Express External Powers and 'Implied Powers'

686. Pursuant to Article 3(1)(e) TFEU, the Union has exclusive competence in the field of the CCP. Paragraph 2 adds that the Union shall also have exclusive competence for the conclusion of an international agreement when its conclusion is provided for in a legislative act of the Union or is necessary to enable the Union to exercise its internal competence, or insofar as its conclusion may affect common rules or alter their scope.

The exclusivity of the Union's competence in the field of the CCP had already been recognized before the Lisbon Treaty.[857]

Where an international agreement contains aspects that belong to the competence of the Member States, the latter shall be co-signatories of the international agreement concluded by the Union.[858]

687. The TFEU contains a certain number of express provisions relating to external powers. First and foremost, as already mentioned, the Union has an exclusive competence in the field of the CCP (Articles 3(1)(e) and 207 TFEU[859]). Since the Lisbon Treaty, the CCP includes services (before it only related to goods).

688. Union shall also foster cooperation with third countries and international organizations in the fields of education (Article 165(3) TFEU), vocational training (Article 166(3) TFEU), culture (Article 167(3) TFEU), public health (Article 168(3), social policy (Article 153 TFEU). A similar or comparable provision does not appear in the title (XV part III) on consumer protection. With regard to social policy, the EU is competent to conclude international agreements although the EU's internal competence in this field is limited. *See* (ILO) *Opinion 2/91.*[860]

689. It may happen that a shared competence becomes an exclusive Union competence through pre-emption as a result of the adoption of EU action (Opinion Lugano Convention),[861] while others remains shared, such as development cooperation, humanitarian aid, technological development, *see* Article 4(3) and (4). Express external powers in relation to the internal market only exist with regard to

---

857. Opinion of 11 November 1975, No 1/75, EU:C:1975:145; for mixed agreements (including other aspects than pure trade aspects) likewise: Opinion of 4 October 1979, No 1/78, EU:C:1979:224.
858. *See* Opinion of 15 November 1994, 1/94, EU:C:1994:284, on the GATS (General Agreement on Trade in Services) and TRIPS (Trade Related Aspects of Intellectual Property Rights) agreements, Marrakesh 1994; 'Open Skies' judgments of 5 November 2002, *inter alia* Judgment in *Commission v. Germany,* C-476/98, EU:C:2002:631.
859. *See* in more detail, hereafter § 2.
860. Advocate General Tesauro in Opinion in case 2/91, EU:C:1993:106.
861. Opinion of the Court 1/03 of 7 February 2006, ECLI:EU:C:2006:81.

the free movement of capital and the CU (Articles 64(3), 65(4) and 31 TFE). *A contrario* it would seem that for the other internal market freedoms, external powers can only be construed on the basis of 'implied powers' or Article 352 (*see* hereafter).

690. Pursuant to Article 217 TFEU, the Union may conclude an *association agreement* with one or more third countries or international organizations in order to establish an association involving reciprocal rights and obligations, common actions and special procedures. Association agreements, especially those preparing for accession, very often contain provisions on consumer protection. In *Demirel,*[862] the CJEU said that the Union has the power to 'guarantee commitments towards non-member countries in all the fields covered by the Treaties'.[863] In view of the large number of countries with which the Union has association agreements, the discussion on implied powers (*see* the next section) has become less important.

691. In the past, *implied powers* played an important role in external relations of the EU (then the EC). The notion of implied powers has been developed by the Court of Justice. Where the Treaty has not conferred express powers on the Union, in particular as regards its external action, the Court has recognized, under certain conditions, that a Union power, especially to conclude an international agreement, could be derived from an existing power e.g., an internal power relating to the subject matter.

692. Article 216(1) TFEU now provides that:

> The Union may conclude an agreement with one or more third countries or international organisations where the Treaties so provide or where the conclusion of an agreement is necessary in order to achieve, within the framework of the Union's policies, one of the objectives referred to in the Treaties, or is provided for in a legally binding Union act or is likely to affect common rules or alter their scope (see Art. 3(2): this competence is an exclusive EU competence.

693. The implied powers referred to in this article seem to cover the following situations where the Court of Justice has recognized the existence of such powers:

– An external power can flow from internal measures where external power is necessary to ensure the effectiveness of the internal measures (Opinion 2/91 (ILO)), in particular where the international agreement could affect the internal rules or alter their scope.[864]
– An implied external power also exists where the conclusion of an agreement is necessary in order to achieve, within the framework of the Union's policies, one of the objectives referred to in the Treaties, An example can be found with regard

---

862. Judgment of 30 September 1987, *Demirel,* C-12/86:EU:C:1987:400, point 10.
863. *See* K. Lenaerts & P. Van Nuffel, *European Union Law* 979 (3rd ed., 2011).
864. *See* Judgment of 31 March 1971, *Commission v. Council (AETR/ERTA),* 22/70, EU:C:1971:32.

to the freedom of establishment: ownership and control clauses in bilateral agreements with third countries affecting freedom of establishment within the EU.[865]
– Finally where an internal power cannot be effectively exercised without involving third countries, the Union is entitled *ipso facto* to act externally, even if the first use made of the power is to conclude an international agreement.[866] Pursuant to Article 216(1) TFEU the existence of internal power can thus possibly be the basis for an external power of the Union. This question has been tested in 2006 in *EP & Council v. Commission.*[867] In this Grand Chamber, the Court of Justice annulled Council Decision 2004/496/EC of 17 May 2004 on the conclusion of an Agreement between the EC and the United States of America on the processing and transfer of PNR data by Air Carriers to the United States Department of Homeland Security, Bureau of Customs and Border Protection and Commission Decision 2004/535/EC of 14 May 2004 on the adequate protection of personal data contained in the Passenger Name Record of air passengers transferred to the United States Bureau of Customs and Border Protection. The directive on the protection of personal data was not a sufficient internal basis for the agreement with the US because the transfer of PNR data to CBP constitutes processing operations concerning public security and the activities of the State in areas of criminal law and not in the area of the free provision of services.

694. Finally Article 351 TFEU provides for a residual power (not confined to the external action of the Union). If action by the Union should prove necessary, within the framework of the policies defined in the Treaties, to attain one of the objectives set out in the Treaties, and the Treaties have not provide the necessary powers, the Council acting unanimously on a proposal from the Commission and after obtaining the consent of the EP, shall adopt the appropriate measures. In view of the increased number of Union competences and the requirement of unanimity within the Council by that article, the significance of the residuary legal basis is now considerably reduced.

§2. THE COMMON COMMERCIAL POLICY

I. The Treaty Provision

695. The Nice Treaty extended the scope of the CCP – for which the Union has an exclusive competence (*see* above) – to services and trade-related aspects of IP. The Lisbon Treaty extended it to foreign direct investments. Under the original EC

---

865. Judgments of 5 November 2002, *Commission v. United Kingdom, Denmark, Sweden, Finland, Belgium, Luxembourg, Austria, Germany,* C-466/98, C-467/98, C-468/98, C-469/98, C-471/98, C-472/98, C-475/98 and C-476/98EU:C:2002:624 et seq.
866. *See* Opinion of 26 April 1977, Opinion 1/76, EU:C:1977:63 and Opinion of 15 November 1994, No 1/94, ECLI:EU:C:1994:384.
867. Judgment of 30 May 2006, *EP & Council v. Commission,* C-317/04 and C-318/04, EU:C:2006:346.

Treaty, the CCP only related to trade in the strict sense, i.e., trade in goods (including aspects of IPR relating to the trade in goods). Article 207 still contains some procedural peculiarities with regard to trade in services and transport in particular.

696. Article 207 TFEU now reads:

1. The common commercial policy shall be based on uniform principles, particularly with regard to changes in tariff rates, the conclusion of tariff and trade agreements relating to trade in goods and services, and the commercial aspects of intellectual property, foreign direct investment, the achievement of uniformity in measures of liberalisation, export policy and measures to protect trade such as those to be taken in the event of dumping or subsidies. The common commercial policy shall be conducted in the context of the principles and objectives of the Union's external action.

2. The European Parliament and the Council, acting by means of regulations in accordance with the ordinary legislative procedure, shall adopt the measures defining the framework for implementing the common commercial policy.

3. Where agreements with one or more third countries or international organisations need to be negotiated and concluded, Article 218 shall apply,[868] subject to the special provisions of this Article.

    The Commission shall make recommendations to the Council, which shall authorise it to open the necessary negotiations. The Council and the Commission shall be responsible for ensuring that the agreements negotiated are compatible with internal Union policies and rules.

    The Commission shall conduct these negotiations in consultation with a special committee appointed by the Council to assist the Commission in this task and within the framework of such directives as the Council may issue to it. The Commission shall report regularly to the special committee and to the European Parliament on the progress of negotiations.

4. For the negotiation and conclusion of the agreements referred to in paragraph 3, the Council shall act by a qualified majority.

    For the negotiation and conclusion of agreements in the fields of trade in services and the commercial aspects of intellectual property, as well as foreign direct investment, the Council shall act unanimously where such agreements include provisions for which unanimity is required for the adoption of internal rules.

    The Council shall also act unanimously for the negotiation and conclusion of agreements:

    (a) in the field of trade in cultural and audiovisual services, where these agreements risk prejudicing the Union's cultural and linguistic diversity;

---

868. The Council shall authorize the opening of negotiations, while the Commission shall conduct the negotiations. The Council shall adopt a decision to conclude the agreement by a qualified majority (for some matters unanimity is required, *see* the text of Art. 217).

(b) in the field of trade in social, education and health services, where these agreements risk seriously disturbing the national organisation of such services and prejudicing the responsibility of Member States to deliver them.

5. The negotiation and conclusion of international agreements in the field of transport shall be subject to Title VI of Part Three and to Article 218.

6. The exercise of the competences conferred by this Article in the field of the common commercial policy shall not affect the delimitation of competences between the Union and the Member States, and shall not lead to harmonisation of legislative or regulatory provisions of the Member States in so far as the Treaties exclude such harmonisation.

697. It follows from Article 207 that the Union can adopt unilateral measures (which can be based on international agreements) and conclude agreements with other countries or international organizations. The following sections contain examples of both.

II. The Customs Union

698. The EU is based on a CU. Hence the Union has a CCT. Pursuant to Article 31 TFEU, duties shall be fixed by the Council on a proposal from the Commission.

Article 206 TFEU (ex Article 131 TEC) reads: By establishing a CU in accordance with Articles 28–32, the Union shall contribute, in the common interest, to the harmonious development of world trade, the progressive abolition of restrictions on international trade and on foreign direct investment, and the lowering of customs and other barriers.

The European Commission[869] defines the CCT as follows. The tariff is common to all EU members, but the rates of duty differ from one kind of import to another depending on what they are and where they come from. The rates depend on the economic sensitivity of products. The tariff is therefore the name given to the combination of the nomenclature (or classification of goods) and the duty rates which apply to each class of goods. In addition the tariff contains all other Community legislation that has an effect on the level of customs duty payable on a particular import, for example country of origin.

The tariff is a concept, a collection of laws as opposed to a single codified law in itself. There is however a kind of working tariff, called TARIC, which is not actually a piece of legislation.

Through the tariff, the Community applies the principle that domestic producers should be able to compete fairly and equally on the internal market with manufacturers exporting from other countries.

699. An important customs matter is the fight against counterfeit which is now governed by Regulation 608/2013 concerning customs enforcement of IPR[870]

---

869. *See* website European Commission.
870. *OJ* 2013, L181/15.

replacing Council Regulation (EC) No 1383/2003. Pursuant to its Article 1(1) the Regulation sets out the conditions and procedures for action by the customs authorities where goods suspected of infringing an IPR are, or should have been, subject to customs supervision or customs control within the customs territory of the Union in accordance with Council Regulation (EEC) No 2913/92 of 12 October 1992 establishing the Community Customs Code,[871] particularly goods in the following situations:

(a) when declared for release for free circulation, export or re-export;
(b) when entering or leaving the customs territory of the Union;
(c) when placed under a suspensive procedure or in a free zone or free warehouse.

The concept of IPRs in the Regulation is very broad and encompasses: trade marks, designs, geographical indications, copyright and relate rights, patents and SPC for medicinal products, plant variety rights, chips, utility models and trade names.

The regulation provides for actions, including sanctions, by the national customs authorities.

III. Trade in Goods: General Provisions

700. Regulation 260/2009[872] lays down common rules on imports. Importation is free, subject to safeguard measures provided for under WTO law. In 2015 a codified version was published: Regulation (EU) 2015/478 of 11 March 2015 on common rules for imports.

701. Regulation 1061/2009[873] establishes common rules on exports. In 2015 a codified version was published: Regulation (EU) 2015/479 on common rules for exports. Exportation is free as a matter of principle (Article 1). The Regulation however does not apply to oil (*see* the Annex for a description of the products concerned). Furthermore, in order to prevent a critical situation from arising on account of a shortage of essential products, or to remedy such a situation, and where Union interests call for immediate intervention, the Commission, acting at the request of a Member State or on its own initiative, and taking account of the nature of the products and of the other particular features of the transactions in question, may make the export of a product subject to the production of an export authorization, the granting of which shall be governed by such provisions and subject to such limits as the Commission shall lay down pending subsequent action by the Council (Article 6).

---

871. *OJ* 1992, L 302/1 (*see* consolidated version on 'eurlex')
872. *OJ* 2009, L 84/1.
873. *OJ* 2009, L 291/1.

IV. Trade Defence Instruments

702. While imports are generally free, the Union has adopted, over the years, instruments of defence against unfair competition from third countries and their companies. These instruments include anti-dumping and protection against subsidized imports from third countries. The most important one in practice is anti-dumping. It will be discussed hereafter.

A. Anti-dumping: General

703. Presently the rules on *anti-dumping* are laid down in Council Regulation (EU) 2016/1036 on protection against dumped imports from countries not members of the EU (consolidated version).[874] There is dumping when goods originating in a third country are sold in the EU below their normal value, i.e., the price normally charged in the exporting country.[875]

An anti-dumping duty may be imposed where three conditions are fulfilled: (i) there shall be dumping, (ii) there is an injury to the Union industry, and (iii) there is a need to act in the interest of the Union (Article 1).

Pursuant to Article 1(2) a product is to be considered as being dumped if its export price to the Union is less than a comparable price for the like product, in the ordinary course of trade, as established for the exporting country. The normal value shall normally be based on the prices paid or payable, in the ordinary course of trade, by independent customers in the exporting country. However, where the exporter in the exporting country does not produce or does not sell the like product, the normal value may be established on the basis of prices of other sellers or producers (Article 2(1)). In case of imports from non-market economy countries, normal value shall be determined on the basis of the price or constructed value in a market economy third country, or the price from such a third country to other countries, including the Union (Article 2(7)).

Pursuant to Article 4 the term 'Union industry' shall normally be interpreted as referring to the Union producers as a whole of the like products or to those of them whose collective output of the products constitutes a major proportion of the total Union production of those products.[876]

Upon complaint the Commission examines within forty-five days whether there is sufficient evidence to justify initiating a proceeding. If so it initiates proceedings and publishes a notice in the *Official Journal of the European Union* (Article 5(9)).

The Commission can impose provisional anti-dumping duties as well as definitive anti-dumping duties (before 2014 the imposition of definitive anti-dumping duties was a competence of the Council). But the Commission is subject to control by the Member States.[877] Interested parties enjoy certain procedural rights (*see*

---

874. *OJ* 2016, L 176/21.
875. *See* further rules to determine whether there is dumping in Art. 2 of the Regulation.
876. But *see* the special circumstances mentioned in that article.
877. Regulation 182/2011 laying down the rules and general principles concerning mechanisms for control by Member States of the Commission's exercise of implementing powers, *OJ* 2011, L 55/13,

Article 6 of the basic Regulation). Commission decisions can be challenged before the GC (with an appeal possibility before the Court of Justice). Since the calculations leading to the establishment that there is dumping requires an appraisal of complex economic situations, the Union Courts have conferred a wide margin of discretion on the Commission (and the Council when it was still competent to impose anti-dumping duties) in that regard. In recent judgments, the Union Courts have turned to a more intrusive examination of anti-dumping decisions, notably by ruling that the powers given to the EU in the Anti-dumping Regulation have to be interpreted in the light of the WTO Anti-dumping Agreement.[878]

704. The Regulation requires the existence of dumping and an 'injury'. Pursuant to Article 3, the term 'injury' shall, unless otherwise specified, be taken to mean material injury to the Union industry, threat of material injury to the Union industry or material retardation of the establishment of such an industry and shall be interpreted in accordance with the provisions of this Article. A determination of injury shall be based on positive evidence and shall involve an objective examination of both: (a) the volume of the dumped imports and the effect of the dumped imports on prices in the Union, and (b) the consequent impact of those imports on the Union industry. Determination as to whether the Union interest calls for intervention shall be based on an appreciation of all the various interests taken as a whole, including the interests of the domestic industry and users and consumers, and a determination pursuant to this Article shall only be made where all parties have been given the opportunity to make their views known pursuant to paragraph. In such an examination, the need to eliminate the trade distorting effects of injurious dumping and to restore effective competition shall be given special consideration. Measures, as determined on the basis of the dumping and injury found, may not be applied where the authorities, on the basis of all the information submitted, can clearly conclude that it is not in the Union interest to apply such measures (Article 21(1) and (2)).

B. Anti-dumping Procedure

705. An anti-dumping procedure is opened, as a matter of principle, by the lodging of a complaint (Article 6(1). In special circumstances, the Commission can open the procedure of its own motion (Article 5(6)). A written complaint shall be lodged by any natural or legal person, or any association not having legal personality, acting on behalf of the Union industry. An investigation shall not be initiated unless it has been determined, on the basis of an examination as to the degree of support for, or opposition to, the complaint expressed by Union producers of the like product, that the complaint has been made by or on behalf of the Union industry. The complaint shall be considered to have been made by or on behalf of the Union industry if it is supported by those Union producers whose collective output constitutes more than 50% of the total production of the like product produced by that portion of the

---

as amended by Regulation 37/2014 amending certain regulations relating to the common commercial policy as regards the procedures for the adoption of certain measures, *OJ* 2014, L 18/1.
878. *See.* P. Koutrakos, *EU International Relations Law* 370–371 (Hart 2015).

Union industry expressing either support for or opposition to the complaint. However, no investigation shall be initiated when Union producers expressly supporting the complaint account for less than 25% of total production of the like product produced by the Union industry.

706. Article 6 describes the investigation by the Commission. The Commission, acting in cooperation with the Member States, shall commence an investigation at Union level. Such investigation shall cover both dumping and injury and these shall be investigated simultaneously. For the purpose of a representative finding, an investigation period shall be selected which, in the case of dumping shall, normally, cover a period of no less than six months immediately prior to the initiation of the proceeding. Parties receiving questionnaires used in an anti-dumping investigation shall be given at least thirty days to reply. The Commission may request Member States to supply information. The Commission may also request Member States to carry out all necessary checks and inspections and to carry out investigations in third countries. The interested parties which have made themselves known in accordance with Article 5(10) shall be heard if they have, within the period prescribed in the notice published in the *Official Journal of the European Union*, made a written request for a hearing showing that they are an interested party likely to be affected by the result of the proceeding and that there are particular reasons why they should be heard. The Regulation organizes their right of being heard and to receive information.

C. Anti-dumping Decisions

707. The Commission can take provisional measures pursuant to Article 7. The amount of the *provisional anti-dumping duty* shall not exceed the margin of dumping as provisionally established, but it should be less than the margin if such lesser duty would be adequate to remove the injury to the Union industry. Provisional duties shall be secured by a guarantee, and the release of the products concerned for free circulation in the Union shall be conditional upon the provision of such guarantee.

Upon condition that a provisional affirmative determination of dumping and injury has been made, the Commission may accept satisfactory *voluntary undertaking offers* submitted by any exporter to revise its prices or to cease exports at dumped prices, if, after specific consultation of the Advisory Committee, it is satisfied that the injurious effect of the dumping is thereby eliminated (Article 8).

The procedure may be terminated where the complaint is withdrawn, unless such termination would not be in the Community interest. Where, after consultation, protective measures are unnecessary and there is no objection raised within the Advisory Committee, the investigation or proceeding shall be terminated. (Article 9).

708. Where the facts as finally established show that there is dumping and injury caused thereby, and the Union interest calls for intervention, a *definitive anti-dumping duty* shall be imposed by the Commission, on an examination procedure

(an advisory committee),[879] in the appropriate amounts in each case, on a non-discriminatory basis, on imports of a product from all sources, found to be dumped and causing injury, except for imports from those sources from which undertakings have been accepted (Article 9(5).

V. Trade Agreements/the EU and the WTO

709. The law of external relations of the Union in the economic sphere does not only rest on unilateral acts, forming its autonomous trade policy (e.g., the anti-dumping Regulation, discussed here above), but also on international agreements with other countries and international organizations. Examples are the EEA and Association agreements (Article 217 TFEU).

710. The most important part of the EU's conventional trade policy is its participation in the WTO created by the Treaty of Marrakesh in 1994, which replaced the General Agreement on Tariffs and Trade (GATT) of 1947. The WTO Treaties relate to trade in goods (the new GATT), services (General Agreement on Trade in Services (GATS)) and commercial aspects of intellectual property rights (TRIPS). WTO law is based in the principles of the most favourite nation clause (and advantage granted by a country to another country applies to all WTO-members). The WTO influences various EU policies and rules, *inter alia* its customs law, the CAP, public procurement and IPR.

---

879. *See* Art. 5 Regulation 182/2011 (Comitology), *OJ* 2011, L 55/1.

Chapter 4. The Common Agricultural Policy

§1. Introduction

711. When the EEC was established (in 1957) Agriculture and fisheries were heavily regulated at the national level of the Member States and were often protective of national markets. In order to create an internal market for these products a common policy (the CAP) at the EU level became necessary. The CAP was originally focused on market intervention, in particular by supporting prices, guaranteeing a minimum income to the agricultural population. Later structural measures and direct subsidies gained more importance. More recently other policy objectives of the EU were integrated in the CAP: protection of the environment, public health, energy policy, protection of the marine environment (etc.).

§2. Treaty Provisions

712. Article 38 TFEU contains general provisions:

(1) The Union shall define and implement a common agriculture and fisheries policy. The internal market shall extend to agriculture, fisheries and trade in agricultural products.
(2) 'Agricultural products' means the products of the soil, of stockfarming and of fisheries and products of first-stage processing directly related to these products. References to the CAP or to agriculture, and the use of the term 'agricultural', shall be understood as also referring to fisheries, having regard to the specific characteristics of this sector. Annex I to the Treaty contains a list.
(3) Save as otherwise provided in Articles 39–44, the rules laid down for the establishment and functioning of the internal market shall apply to agricultural products.
(4) The operation and development of the internal market for agricultural products must be accompanied by the establishment of a CAP.

713. Article 39(1) defines the objectives of the CAP:

(a) to increase agricultural productivity by promoting technical progress and by ensuring the rational development of agricultural production and the optimum utilization of the factors of production, in particular labour;
(b) thus to ensure a fair standard of living for the agricultural community, in particular by increasing the individual earnings of persons engaged in agriculture;
(c) to stabilize markets;
(d) to assure the availability of supplies;
(e) to ensure that supplies reach consumers at reasonable prices.

Article 39(2) adds that in working out the CAP and the special methods for its application, account shall be taken of:

(a) the particular nature of agricultural activity, which results from the social structure of agriculture and from structural and natural disparities between the various agricultural regions;
(b) the need to effect the appropriate adjustments by degrees;

the fact that in the Member States agriculture constitutes a sector closely linked with the economy as a whole.

714. Article 40(1) provides for the way in which the objectives of Article 39 shall be achieved, i.e., by establishing a common organization of agricultural markets (CMO Regulation).
This organization shall take one of the following forms, depending on the product concerned:

(a) common rules on competition;
(b) compulsory coordination of the various national market organizations;
(c) a European market organization.

In practice, the Union has opted for European market organizations which existed for the various agricultural products (e.g., wine, sugar, pig meat, milk, butter etc.). Council Regulation (EC) No 1234/2007 of 22 October 2007 has established one single common organization of agricultural markets and contained specific provisions for certain agricultural products (Single CMO Regulation).[880] It has been replaced by Regulation 1308/2013.[881]

715. Pursuant to Article 40(2), the common organization established in accordance with paragraph 1 may include all measures required to attain the objectives set out in Article 39, in particular regulation of prices, aids for the production and marketing of the various products, storage and carryover arrangements and common machinery for stabilizing imports or exports. The common organization shall be limited in pursuit of the objectives set out in Article 39 and shall exclude any discrimination between producers or consumers within the Union.
Article 40(3) provides for the possibility of establishing one or more agricultural guidance and guarantee funds.[882]

716. Article 41 refers to structural measures. To enable the objectives set out in Article 39 to be attained, provision may be made within the framework of the CAP for measures such as:

(a) an effective coordination of efforts in the spheres of vocational training, of research and of the dissemination of agricultural knowledge; this may include joint financing of projects or institutions;

---

880. *OJ* 2007 L 299/1.
881. *See* hereafter para. 732.
882. Presently, there are the European Agricultural Guarantee Fund (EAGF) and the European Agricultural Fund for Rural Development (EAFRD).

(b) joint measures to promote consumption of certain products.

717. Pursuant to Article 42, the Treaty competition rules shall apply to agricultural products only to the extent determined by the EP and the Council within the framework of Article 43(2), account being taken of the objectives set out in Article 39.

718. Article 43 grants extensive powers to the EU to act in the field of agriculture. The ordinary legislative procedure applies. In constant case law, the Court of Justice has recognized the discretionary character of these powers.[883]

(1) The Commission shall submit proposals for working out and implementing the CAP, including the replacement of the national organizations by one of the forms of common organization provided for in Article 40(1), and for implementing the measures specified in this Title.

   These proposals shall take account of the interdependence of the agricultural matters mentioned in this Title.

(2) The EP and the Council, acting in accordance with the ordinary legislative procedure and after consulting the Economic and Social Committee, shall establish the CMO Regulation provided for in Article 40(1) and the other provisions necessary for the pursuit of the objectives of the CAP and the CFP (common fisheries policy).

(3) The Council, on a proposal from the Commission, shall adopt measures on fixing prices, levies, aid and quantitative limitations and on the fixing and allocation of fishing opportunities.

(4) In accordance with paragraph 2, the national market organizations may be replaced by the common organization provided for in Article 40(1) if:

   (a) the common organization offers Member States which are opposed to this measure and which have an organization of their own for the production in question equivalent safeguards for the employment and standard of living of the producers concerned, account being taken of the adjustments that will be possible and the specialization that will be needed with the passage of time;

   (b) such an organization ensures conditions for trade within the Union similar to those existing in a national market.

(5) If a common organization for certain raw materials is established before a common organization exists for the corresponding processed products, such raw materials as are used for processed products intended for export to third countries may be imported from outside the Union.

---

883. Judgment of 21 February 1990, *Wuidart*, C-267/88, EU:C:1990:79, point 14; Judgment of 5 October 1994, *Crispoltoni*, C-133/93, point 43); Judgment of 12 July 2001, *Jippes*, C-189/01, EU:C:2001:420, point 84.

§3. History of the CAP

719. In the 1960s twenty-three common market organizations were set up for the most important agricultural products (cereals, poultry, pig meat, beef, milk, dairy products, sugar, wine).[884] The central instrument was a guaranteed price for the producers. Where market prices decreased below a certain level price supporting mechanisms were put in place, such as: purchase of surpluses by national intervention office and several forms of subsidies for production, trade, transformation etc. Cheaper agricultural products imported from third countries were subject to import duties, and exportation to third countries was encouraged by export subsidies (restitutions). These measures led to structural surpluses and accounted for the major part of the Union budget (up to two-thirds in the mid-1980s). They also led to conflicts with other agricultural powers in the world, notably the US and Australia. In the 1990s, the policy was geared to a better focus on structural measures and income guarantees for producers were replaced by direct income subsidies (although the possibility of market interventions has not disappeared).

§4. The Single CMO Regulation

720. Regulation 1234/2007 of 22 October 2007 replaced the then existing twenty-three common market organizations for various products by one single common organization of agricultural markets ('Single CMO Regulation').[885] Regulation 1234/2007 has been replaced by Regulation 1308/2013.[886] The new Regulation contains some specific provisions for certain agricultural products. The Regulation contains a general framework for market interventions, subsidies, quality standards, the role of private organizations in the management of markets, trade with third countries (import licences and import duties and levies, export licences and export licences, export refunds, designations of origin and sectoral rules, such as for milk, sugar and wine).

§5. The Common Fisheries Policy

721. Regulation 1380/2013[887] sets out the economic, environmental and social basis of the CFP, the objective of which is to guarantee sustainable exploitation of living aquatic resources. The measures adopted under this Regulation are based on applying the precautionary principle and sound scientific advice. They concern the conservation and protection of fish stocks and marine ecosystems, access to waters and resources, the fleet, control of activities, decision-making and the involvement of stakeholders at all stages of the policy.

---

884. *See* R. Barents & L.J. Brinkhorst, *Grondlijnen van Europees recht* 763 et seq (13th ed., Kluwer 2012).
885. *OJ* 2007, L 299/1.
886. *OJ* 2013, L 347/671.
887. *OJ* 2013, L 354/22.

Chapter 5. The Common Transport Policy

§1. General Introduction

722. With the CAP, the common transport policy, is the only sector-specific common policy with a Treaty basis, as from the original EEC Treaty. The reasons for the existence of specific provisions on a common transport policy are to a certain extent comparable to those that led the fathers of the Treaty to provide for a specific regime, with extensive regulatory powers at the EU (then EEC) level for agriculture: the existence of heavy State intervention at the time of the conclusion of the EEC Treaty and the resulting difficulties in establishing an internal market for these goods and services (agricultural products, respectively transport services) without specific action, i.e., regulation at the EU level. For transportation the existing national limitations (such as licences) and bilateral agreements between some Member States needed to be replaced by common rules. The Treaty chapter on transport merely contained and contains some general principles and the legal basis for action by the Union.

723. Whereas the chapter on transportation in the original Treaty, which remained largely unchanged, was basically confined to liberalization (to be organized by EU legislation), *inter alia* granting access to the transport market of Member States to transporters from other Member States, a prohibition of discrimination, one on tariffs and some provisions on competition (State aid, but not essentially different from the general provisions on State aid in the Treaty), today the EU's transport policy is characterized by a much greater variety of objectives. The Treaty itself also refers incidentally to safety measures, which of course today are an important aspect of transport policy. In the early years also social measures saw the light, in order to create a level playing field. More recently the following policy objectives have been added: building integrated transport networks, which draw together different means of transport or modes, creating multimodal hubs, improving infrastructure in new Member States, emphasizing research, innovation, investing in transport for the future without dependence on oil.[888] In addition in its transport policy, the EU takes heavily into account the improvement of the environment and the protection of passengers (with specific regulations to that effect). Finally, where the Treaty recognizes the importance of services of general economic interest (*see* Article 106 TFEU), EU legislation for the different modes of transport contain specific rules in that regard.

724. The central provisions of the Treaty, that have not changed (apart from the reference to the ordinary legislative procedure according to the Lisbon Treaty) are Articles 90 and 91 and 100 TFEU:

Article 90 TFEU reads:

---

888. Roadmap to a single European Transport Area, White Paper, COM (2011) 144 def.

The objectives of the Treaties shall, in matters governed by this Title, be pursued within the framework of a common transport policy.

Article 91:

For the purpose of implementing Article 90, and taking into account the distinctive features of transport, the European Parliament and the Council shall, acting in accordance with the ordinary legislative procedure and after consulting the Economic and Social Committee and the Committee of the Regions, lay down:

a. common rules applicable to international transport to or from the territory of a Member State or passing across the territory of one or more Member States;
b. the conditions under which non-resident carriers may operate transport services within a Member State;
c. measures to improve transport safety;
d. any other appropriate provisions.

2. When the measures referred to in paragraph 1 are adopted, account shall be taken of cases where their application might seriously affect the standard of living and level of employment in certain regions, and the operation of transport facilities.

Article 100

1. The provisions of this Title shall apply to transport by rail, road and inland waterway.
2. The European Parliament and the Council, acting in accordance with the ordinary legislative procedure, may lay down appropriate provisions for sea and air transport. They shall act after consulting the Economic and Social Committee and the Committee of the Regions.

These articles only contain the legal basis of EU transport policy, leaving it to the Union legislature to take appropriate liberalization measures and other measures with respect to transport. For transport by rail, road and inland waterway, the Union shall act (*see* Article 91(1)), whereas for sea and air transport this is not an obligation, but only a power ('may lay down'). This difference explains the difference in pace of development of legislation in both fields (*see* next section).

§2. HISTORY OF EU TRANSPORT LAW

725. In the field of road since 1974 transport directives have recognized the freedom of establishment.[889] Note that the freedom of establishment in the Treaty (now Article 49 TFEU) has always applied directly to transport. Transport is only

---

889. *See* L. Dubois & C. Bluman, *Droit matériel de l'Union européenne* 466 (6th ed. Montchrestien 2012).

excluded from the direct application of Article 56 on the freedom to provide services (*see* Article 58(1)). With respect to the freedom to provide services the Council (at that time sole responsible to adopt legislative measures) failed to adopt proposals from the Commission. In 1985, in a landmark judgment, the Court of Justice found, at the request of the EP, that in breach of the Treaty the Council had failed to ensure freedom to provide services in the sphere of international transport and to lay down the conditions under which non-resident carriers may operate transport services in a Member State.[890] This was the starting point for the Council to act, in particular with regard to road transport, and later with regard to inland and rail transport.

726. The history of legislation in the field of sea and air transport is different because, as said above, for these modes of transport the Treaty does not require the Union legislature to act, but rather gives it the power to do so. An impetus to do so came from the express recognition by the Court of Justice that the general Treaty provisions, such as the competition rules, and indeed also the freedom of establishment, nevertheless apply to transport, including sea and air transport.[891]

727. In a first judgment, known as 'French Seamen', the Court acknowledged that since transport is basically a service, it has been found necessary to provide a special system for it, taking into account the special aspects of this branch of activity. With this object, a special exemption has been provided by Article 61(1) (now Article 58(1) TFEU) under which freedom to provide services in the field of transport 'shall be governed by the provisions of the Title relating to transport',[892] thus confirming that the general rules of the Treaty must be applied insofar as they are not excluded. In that case, the Court therefore ruled that maintaining provisions of labour law applicable to seamen that were not in conformity with the free movement of workers (Article 48 EEC, now Article 45 TFEU) France had failed to fulfil its obligations under that Treaty provision and Article 4 of Regulation No 1612/68 of the Council of 15 October 1968.

728. In a second case known as 'Nouvelles Frontières',[893] the Court also referred to Article 61 of the Treaty (now Article 58 TFEU) according to which freedom to provide services in the field of transport is governed not by the provisions of the chapter on services but by the provisions of the title relating to the common transport policy. Therefore, the objective laid down in Article 59 of the Treaty (now Article 56 TFEU) of abolishing during the transitional period restrictions on freedom to provide services should have been attained in the framework of the common policy provided for in Articles 74 and 75 (now Articles 90 and 91 TFEU). However, the Court continued, no other provision in the Treaty makes its application to the transport sector subject to the realization of a common transport policy.

---

890. Judgment of 22 May 1985, *European Parliament v. Council*, 13/83, EU:C:1985:220.
891. Judgment of 30 April 1986, *Asjes e.a.*, C-209/84, EU:C:1986:188.
892. Likewise, Directive 2006/123 on Services in the Internal Market excludes services in the field of transport from its scope of application.
893. *See* above *Asjes*.

As regards the competition rules in particular, the Court referred to Article 77 (now Article 97 TFEU) according to which aids are compatible with the Treaty if they meet the needs of coordination of transport or if they represent reimbursement for the discharge of certain obligations inherent in the concept of a public service. Such a provision clearly presupposes that the Treaty competition rules of which the provisions on State aids are part, are applicable to the transport sector whether or not a common transport policy has been established. As regards transport, there is no provision in the Treaty which, like Article 42 (agriculture) excludes the application of the competition rules or makes it subject to a decision by the Council. Hence the rules in the Treaty on competition, in particular Articles 85–90 (now Articles 101–106 TFEU) are applicable to transport. As regards air transport in particular, the Court considered that, as is clear from the actual wording of Article 84 (Article 100 TFEU) and its position in the Treaty, that article is intended merely to define the scope of Articles 74 et seq. (now Articles 90 et seq. TFEU) as regards different modes of transport, by distinguishing between transport by rail, road and inland waterway, covered by paragraph 1, and sea and air transport covered by paragraph 2.

'Nouvelles Frontières' led, some years later, to the adoption of a first legislative package in the field of air transport, including rules on the freedom to provide services and competition law.

§3. ROAD TRANSPORT

729. Today road transport of goods and persons (touring cars and busses) is totally liberalized through a system of EU licences delivered for five years by the Member State of establishment on condition that the qualitative requirements for the exercise of the activity are fulfilled.[894] There are also common rules on social protection, costs of infrastructure and safety.[895]

§4. RAIL TRANSPORT

730. The first so-called railway package dates from 2001.[896] One of the well-known features of this package is the separation between infrastructure and the transportation services. The physical integration of national railway systems is the object of the second package. To that effect, the European Railway Agency was created in 2005. The third railway package adopted in October 2007 introduced open access rights for international rail passenger services including cabotage by 2010. Operators may pick up and set down passengers at any station on an international route, including at stations located in the same Member State. Furthermore, the third

---

894. Regulation 1072/2009, *OJ* 2009, L300/72 (goods) and Regulation 1073/2009, *OJ* 2009 L300/88 (persons).
895. *See* references in R. Barents & L.J. Brinkhorst, *Grondlijnen van Europees Recht* 79 (13rd ed., Kluwer 2012).
896. *See* Directive 2001/12 on infrastructure; Directive 2001/13 on licences and Directive 2001/14 on capacity, *OJ* 2001, L 1, 26 and 46.

railway package introduced a European driver licence allowing train drivers to circulate on the entire European network (the certification of cross-border drivers is foreseen as from 2009 and of all other drivers as from 2011). The drivers will have to meet basic requirements concerning their educational level, age, physical and mental health, specific knowledge and practical training of driving skills. Last but not least, the third railway package strengthened the rail passengers' rights. While long-distance travellers will enjoy a wider range of rights, minimum quality standards (non-discrimination of handicapped travellers or persons with reduced mobility, liability in case of accidents, availability of train tickets and personal security of passengers in stations) will have to be guaranteed to all passengers on all lines.[897] In 2013, the Commission proposed its fourth package to remove remaining obstacles to a Single Railway Area.[898]

§5. Air Transport

731. After 'Nouvelles Frontières', the Commission proposed a first air transport package to the Council, including rules on free movement and competition. The package was adopted in 1992. Nowadays the rules are consolidated in one Regulation 1008/2008 on common rules for the operation of air services in the Community (Recast).[899] The general rules on competition (such as Regulation 1/2003) now apply to all forms of transport, including air transport.

Regulation 1008/2008 contains rules on operating licences for Union carriers (a single licence for the EU), access to routes (free provision of services, general principles for public service obligations, environmental measures, emergency measures), pricing and information and non-discrimination (of passengers)(Article 3).

One should also mention Regulation 549/2004 laying down the framework for the creation of the single European sky (the framework Regulation) and three accompanying regulations.[900] The regulation concerns air safety. The European Agency for Air Safety (EASA, Cologne) has *inter alia* as its task the certification of compliance with the safety standards.

§6. Maritime Transport

732. The basic act is Regulation 4055/86 applying the principle of freedom to provide services to maritime transport between Member States and between Member States and third countries.[901] The Regulation gives Member State nationals (and non-Union shipping companies using ships registered in a Member State and controlled by Member State nationals) the right to carry passengers or goods by sea

---

897. On the 3rd package, *see* European Commission, website Transport and Mobility.
898. Communication from the Commission on 'The Fourth Railway Package – Completing the Single European Railway Area to foster European competitiveness and growth', COM(2013) 025 final.
899. *OJ* 2008, L 293/3.
900. *OJ* 2004, L 96/1 et seq.
901. *OJ* 1986, L 378/1.

between any port of a Member State and any port or off-shore installation of another Member State or of a non-Union country.

Union legislation in the field of maritime transport also includes rules on the protection of the environment[902] and safety (for which a separate agency was created, the European Maritime Safety Agency in Lisbon).[903]

§7. Passenger Rights

733. In the air transport sector Article 23 of Regulation 1008/2008 provides that passengers have certain rights to information and it is stipulated that the final price to be paid shall at all times be indicated and shall include the applicable air fare or air rate as well as all applicable taxes, and charges, surcharges and fees which are unavoidable and foreseeable at the time of publication. Optional price supplements shall be communicated in a clear, transparent and unambiguous way at the start of any booking process and their acceptance by the customer shall be on an 'opt-in' basis. In its *ebookers judgment*,[904] the Court of Justice explained that the concept of 'optional price supplements', referred to in the last sentence of Article 23(1) of Regulation No 1008/2008, must be interpreted as meaning that it covers costs, connected with the air travel, arising from services, such as the flight cancellation insurance at issue in the main proceedings, supplied by a party other than the air carrier and charged to the customer by the person selling that travel, together with the air fare, as part of a total price.

734. Passengers also have rights of assistance, and sometimes of compensation, in case of denied boarding, cancellation and delay. First these rights were conferred on air passengers only, now by Regulation 261/2004,[905] later on rail passengers by Regulation 1371/2007,[906] bus and coach passengers by Regulation 181/2011[907] and on sea and inland waterway passengers by Regulation 1127/2010. Regulation 261/2004 (air passengers) has given rise to a lot of case law that will not be discussed here. The Court of Justice decided *inter alia* in *Wallentin-Hermann*[908] that a technical problem in an aircraft which leads to the cancellation or delay of a flight is not covered by the concept of 'extraordinary circumstances' that exclude the passenger's right to compensation unless that problem stems from events which, by their

---

902. *See*, e.g., directive 2009/123 on ship-source pollution and on the introduction of penalties for infringements, *OJ* 2009, L 280/52.
903. Regulation 1406/2002, *OJ* 2002, L 208/1.
904. Judgment of 19 July 2012, *ebookers,* C-112/11, EU:C:2012:487.
905. Regulation 261/2004 establishing common rules on compensation and assistance to passengers in the event of denied boarding and of cancellation or long delay of flights, *OJ* 2004 L 46/1, presently under review.
906. Regulation 1371/2007 on rail passengers' rights and obligations, *OJ* 2004, L 315 14.
907. Regulation concerning the rights of passengers in bus and coach transport, *OJ* 2011, L 55/1.
908. Judgment of 22 December 2008, *Wallentin-Hermann,* C-549/07: EU:C:2008:71; *see also* Judgment of 19 November 2009, *Sturgeon,* C-402/07, EU:C:2009:716.

nature or origin, are not inherent in the normal exercise of the activity of the air carrier concerned and are beyond its actual control.[909] In contrast to Pešková,[910] the Court held that a collision between an aircraft and a bird (a 'bird strike') is an extraordinary circumstance which may exempt the air carrier from its obligation to pay compensation in case of delay. However, where an authorized expert finds after the collision that the aircraft concerned is airworthy, the carrier cannot justify the delay by invoking the need to carry out a second check.

In *Krüsemann*,[911] the Court of Justice ruled that the spontaneous absence of a significant part of the flight crew staff ('wildcat strikes'), which stems from the surprise announcement by an operating air carrier of a restructuring of the undertaking, following a call echoed not by the staff representatives of the company but spontaneously by the workers themselves who placed themselves on sick leave, is not covered by the concept of 'extraordinary circumstances' within the meaning of the Regulation.

In *Claudia Wegener*,[912] the CJEU held that the air passenger rights Regulation applies to a passenger transport effected under a single booking and comprising, between its departure from an airport situated in the territory of a Member State and its arrival at an airport situated in the territory of a third State, a scheduled stopover outside the EU with a change of aircraft.

Finally, In *Dirk Harms*,[913] the Court decided that that the price of the ticket to be taken into consideration for the purposes of determining the reimbursement owed by the air carrier to a passenger in the event of cancellation of a flight includes the difference between the amount paid by that passenger and the amount received by the air carrier, which corresponds to a commission collected by a person acting as an intermediary between those two parties, unless that commission was set without the knowledge of the air carrier, which it is for the referring court to ascertain.

---

909. Judgment in *Sturgeon*.
910. Judgment of 4 May 2017, *Pešková*, C-315/15, EU:C:2017:342.
911. Judgment of 17 April 2018, *Krüsemann*, C-195/17 et seq., EU:C:2018:258.
912. Judgment of 31 May 2018, *Claudia Wegener*, C-537/17, EU:C:2018:361.
913. Judgment of 12 September 2018, *Dirk Harms*, C-601/17, EU:C:2018:702.

Selected Bibliography

Barents, R. & L.J. Brinkhorst. *Grondlijnen van Europees recht*, 13th edn. Alphen aan den Rijn: Wolters Kluwer, 2012.

Bluman, C. & L. Dubois, *Droit matériel de l'Union européenne*, 7th edn. L.G.D.J., 2015.

Barnard, C. *The Substantive Law of the EU, The Four Freedoms*, 5th edn. Oxford: Oxford University Press, 2016.

Chalmers, D., G. Davies & G. Monti. *European Union Law*, 3rd edn. Cambridge: Cambridge University Press, 2014.

Craig, P. & G. de Búrca. *EU Law. Text, Cases and Materials*. 6th edn. Oxford: Oxford University Press, 2015.

Hartley, T.C. *The Foundations of European Union Law*. 8th edn. Oxford: Oxford University Press, 2014.

Kapteyn, P.D., P. Verloren van Themaat & L. Gormley. *Introduction to the Law of the European Communities*, 4th edn. Deventer: Kluwer, 1987.

Lenaerts, K., et al. *European Union Law*, 3rd edn. London: Sweet & Maxwell, 2011.

Reich, N., H.-W. Micklitz & P. Rott, *Understanding EU Law*. Antwerpen-Oxford: Intersentia, 2009.

Soulard-Brunessen, C., et al. Introduction au marché intérieur. Libre circulation des marchandises, Commentaire J. Mégret, Editions de l'Université Libre de Bruxelles, Brussels, 2015.

Whish, R. & D. Bailey. *Competition Law*, 9th edn. Oxford: Oxford University Press, 2018.

Selected Bibliography

Index

The numbers here refer to paragraph numbers.

Index